Socializing Care

feminist constructions

Series Editors: Hilde Lindemann, Sara Ruddick, and Margaret Urban Walker

Feminist Constructions publishes accessible books that send feminist ethics in promising new directions. Feminist ethics has excelled at critique, identifying masculinist bias in social practice and in the moral theory that is used to justify that practice. The series continues the work of critique, but its emphasis falls on construction. Moving beyond critique, the series aims to build a positive body of theory that extends feminist moral understandings.

Socializing Care

Feminist Ethics and Public Issues

Edited by
Maurice Hamington and
Dorothy C. Miller

ROWMAN & LITTLEFIELD PUBLISHERS, INC.
Lanham • Boulder • New York • Toronto • Oxford

ROWMAN & LITTLEFIELD PUBLISHERS, INC.

Published in the United States of America
by Rowman & Littlefield Publishers, Inc.
A wholly owned subsidiary of The Rowman & Littlefield Publishing Group, Inc.
4501 Forbes Boulevard, Suite 200, Lanham, Maryland 20706
www.rowmanlittlefield.com

PO Box 317
Oxford
OX2 9RU, UK

British Library Cataloguing in Publication Information Available

Library of Congress Cataloging-in-Publication Data

Socializing care : feminist ethics and public issues / edited by Maurice Hamington and
Dorothy C. Miller.
    p. cm. — (Feminist constructions)
ISBN-13: 978-0-7425-5034-1 (cloth : alk. paper)
ISBN-10: 0-7425-5039-7 (cloth : alk. paper)
ISBN-13: 978-0-7425-5040-7 (pbk. : alk. paper)
ISBN-10: 0-7425-5040-0 (pbk. : alk. paper)
  1. Feminist ethics. 2. Caring. 3. Ethics. I. Hamington, Maurice. II. Miller, Dorothy C.
III. Series.

  BJ1395.S63 2005
  170'.82—dc22   2005024516

Printed in the United States of America

∞™ The paper used in this publication meets the minimum requirements of American
National Standard for Information Sciences—Permanence of Paper for Printed Library
Materials, ANSI/NISO Z39.48-1992.

For Valda, Stephanie, and Rosemary, whose care makes our intellectual collaborations possible.

Contents

Acknowledgments

The publication of an anthology is an incredibly time-consuming project involving many people. We would like to acknowledge several crucial contributions. We would like to thank Joan Tronto for her insightful and pioneering work that weaves its way throughout this anthology. Special thanks also go to Hilde Lindemann Nelson and Margaret Urban Walker, whose input helped us shape the final character of the book. Most of all we express our appreciation to all the contributors who gave their time to this project. Unfortunately, anthologies are markers of inclusion and exclusion. We would also like to acknowledge all those who submitted papers that were not included in the final collection. We had a very difficult task and were forced to turn away some fine scholarship. Finally, we have had the good fortune of developing our ideas about socializing care over the course of four panel presentations at the National Women's Studies Association annual meetings from 2002 through 2005. The NWSA Annual Meetings are wonderful opportunities for interactions between feminist scholars and activists and provide an appropriate forum for ideas about socializing care to flourish. We are grateful to NWSA for the opportunities it provides.

Dorothy C. Miller and Maurice Hamington

Introduction: A Modern Moral Imperative

Maurice Hamington and Dorothy C. Miller

> I find care the most basic moral value. Without the actual practice of care,
> there cannot be human life at all, because human beings require it to survive.
>
> —Virginia Held

There was a minor revolution in the study of ethics during the 1980s. The constellation of the moral universe in Western culture was enlarged by the introduction of "care ethics." It wasn't so much a sudden breakthrough as it was the coalescence of longstanding themes that were finally specifically identified. In 1982, Carol Gilligan's landmark book, *In A Different Voice: Psychological Theory and Woman's Development*, was published, followed by Nel Noddings's *Caring: A Feminine Approach to Ethics and Moral Education* in 1984. A new approach to ethics was introduced that emphasized relationships, empathy, and compassion over formulations of principles. Early work on care ethics was fraught with theoretical concerns that critics were quick to address. There was a certain amount of ambiguity regarding the moral essentialism of men and women. There was a questionable gulf between principled morality and relational morality. There were concerns about the political implications of an ethic of care for women. There was also a lack of clear definitions for what care ethics constituted. These issues were serious and some are still being worked out. Nevertheless, the concerns paled in comparison to the momentum garnered for a new way of thinking about morality. Both Gilligan and Noddings had identified an overlooked aspect of moral consideration: care.

Care is such a simple word. Its usage is so vast and diffuse that, like "love," care seems to have lost its precision through its widespread application. It is also so pervasive to human existence that care is an easy concept to overlook as morally significant. Care ethicists have crafted a specialized understanding for the term. In many ways care ethics constitutes a shift in the moral framework rather than a competing moral theory. Care refocuses ethical content away from adjudication to consider the process, context, and affects of behavior. Care describes a relational approach to morality born out of the notion that human beings are not simply independent rational agents. Care ethicists begin with the premise that humans are fundamentally social beings enmeshed in a web of relationships. Any action of moral significance takes place in a particular context that includes and impacts many other beings. Accordingly, care ethics favors concrete considerations over abstract ones. Understanding the real people and implications involved in any situation regarding choice is crucial to care. The moral agent is not simply an ambiguous other but a flesh and blood human being to which we have a connection despite significant differences of culture, class, or gender. Empathy and compassion are valued over hypothetical applications of moral reasoning. Appropriately, care ethicists often find themselves reconsidering the place of emotions in morality. Feelings are a natural outgrowth of beings who imaginatively consider the position of other beings in relation to themselves. This is not to assume that one can "own" someone else's experiences, but that despite vast differences there is always room for some degree of understanding. Knowledge is viewed not as simply an amalgamation of facts and propositions but as potentially disruptive to the routines of our lives. Understanding one another leads to sympathetic connections that have the potential to draw us to act on behalf of others. Care ethics, then, addresses both the nature of ethics and the nature of knowledge.

What Gilligan labeled the "ethics of justice," the time-honored formulation of morality in terms of rules and rights, is much more certain and easier to grasp than care ethics. If one has a hierarchy of rules or rights, than one can adjudicate a moral dilemma by building rational arguments over the superior rule or right to apply. Care ethicists do not deny the significance of rules, rights, or consequences, but they claim that such formulations do not exhaust our moral resources.

Subsequent to the publication of Gilligan's and Noddings's original works on care, a number of fascinating responses occurred. Gilligan developed and refined her ideas over the course of a number of books and articles. Some critics focused on the issue of whether gender differences in morality were adequately established. These concerns, although worthwhile, missed the broader point about the significance of the new moral voice identified. For example, Gilligan came to view the moral voices of justice and care as existing in a dynamic and potentially harmonic relationship. Such harmony has been harmed by the suppression of the voice of care, but the reclaiming of this voice could produce a healthy balance. To most of the casual observers of Gilligan's work, her subsequent trajectories of inquiry were of little consequence. In an age that fetishizes gender differences, many commentators and texts became fixated on Gilligan's original work as the harbinger of a "woman's morality" and failed to recognize the larger significance of care ethics as an important reframing of moral considerations.

From the mid-1980s through the present, the number of publications on care ethics has been impressive.[1] Although often misrepresented or marginalized, care ethics is now mentioned in virtually every ethics textbook. Theorists began to push care ethics in new and interesting directions. One of the early concerns about care ethics is that while it may represent a serviceable personal morality, it has little application to social or political spheres. Joan Tronto, in her 1993 book, *Moral Boundaries: A Political Argument for an Ethic of Care*, was one of the first theorists to suggest that care might have important social and political implications. Tronto describes a traditional boundary between morality and politics. The central concern of politics is "a struggle for power and the control of resources, territory, etc." while the central concern of morality is value and action.[2] Tronto was unconvinced that thus far care had been effectively demonstrated to be a viable political ethic: "those who have written eloquently about care as a virtue, whether a social virtue as in [Charlotte Perkins] Gilman or a private virtue as in Noddings, have been unable to show a convincing way of turning these virtues into a realistic approach to the kinds of problems that caring will confront in the real world."[3] Fortunately, scholars have begun taking on this task.

In many ways, *Socializing Care* is an extension of the last chapter of Tronto's book where she describes the need for altering political theory to accommodate a different moral voice. Tronto does not posit care as superior or a substitute for existing moral concerns but instead claims that "the practice of care describes the qualities necessary for democratic citizens to live together well in a pluralistic society, and that only in a just, pluralistic, democratic society can care flourish."[4] Our social and political morality has continually failed oppressed members of society. Notions of rights and rules have not been sufficiently formulated, for example, to overcome narratives of free market liberalism to argue for the alleviation of homelessness. Care may not fare any better, but it starts with a concern for others and self that is less susceptible to being hijacked by abstract formulations. Many of the authors in *Socializing Care* pay homage to Tronto's groundbreaking analysis and vision.

DEFINITION OF SOCIALIZING CARE

We define the concept of socializing care as the theoretical understanding and application of care ethics in public life. At the intersection of care ethics and social concerns, the socialization of care assumes that the thoughtful application of care ethics can forge reconstructed notions of institutions, politics, and social dynamics. It represents a paradigm shift that helps to deconstruct the permeable boundary between the domains of home and community.

Although many theorists have shown that a bifurcated social landscape is a false dichotomy, depicting an erroneous description of social and political life, cultural and social institutions continue to assume the existence of such a boundary in the formation of public policy. New policy analysis and formulations by care ethicists are severing these boundary assumptions with grounded theoretical applications of care ethics in the public realm. This volume represents some of the best expressions of this innovative work.

RELEVANCE OF SOCIALIZING CARE

Socializing care has the potential of infusing care values into political decisions and accepted ideas that underlie social values. Although the United States has numerous public programs explicitly related to care and policies targeted to provide benefits to individuals and families, such provisions have been unambiguously created as an inferior substitute for private, family care. Most programs, from welfare to disaster relief, are residual in nature, designed to make up for the unanticipated loss of the individual's or family's capacity to provide care. Even the most institutionalized program, Social Security benefits for the retired, survivors, disabled, and blind, was conceptualized as the most efficient way to provide for the loss of income by an individual worker and his/her family due to an unforeseen happenstance. The fundamental responsibility for self and family care remained undisturbed and indeed strengthened by the assumptions built into the program. Increased political and social emphasis on individualism in American life has over time even further curtailed programs that were established to provide a narrowly defined public infrastructure of care policies.

Over the past thirty years, basic income maintenance payments to childless adults have been reduced or eliminated by the states. Welfare payments to families with children have decreased in value. Recently, the encoded right to sustenance payments to eligible families has been purged. Ironically, the very program, Social Security, that championed social provision in response to the stock market debacle that precipitated the Great Depression, may be changed to allow individuals to make market choices with some of their taxes.

Public policies not specifically related to normative notions of care also are remarkably devoid of the influence of care ethics. Thus, a uniform "three strikes and you're out" policy in criminal justice adheres to a principled notion of fairness in justice ethics. The rule betrays both particularity of individual circumstances and an ethic of care that might take into account methods of criminal restitution and/or rehabilitation. Environmental and other civic issues, such as pollution laws that allow companies to emit more poison if they "trade" with others, incorporate rules that preclude attention to the welfare of specific surrounding communities.

Western morality is staunchly grounded in individualistic constructs such as consequences, rights, and principles. It shapes what we mean when we define citizenship and what we expect of each other and our government. It defines our narratives of good and bad. Heroes, not collective action, are acclaimed for moral victories, such as the abolition of slavery or the achievement of women's suffrage. Although domestic violence and sexual assault among acquaintances are rampant in society, common narratives depict the perpetrators as crazed individual strangers. Likewise, the prevailing notion of family poverty blames individual single mothers, the existence of other categories of poor families notwithstanding. The application of care ethics into public policy analysis would ask how efforts to change social and cultural norms for the social benefit of all might alleviate these problems.

Embedded in a social ethic of care is a positive human ecology that favors the structuring of human intercourse for mutual benefit. Such an ecology acknowledges the existence of interdependence and mutuality in life. It embraces the particularity of human beings, at the same time honoring the obligation to uphold that particularity in a social context of rights and fairness. There is enormous social potential in shifting the theoretical discourse to care ethics in public life. This discourse is relevant to every concern that affects the human family, from the stress of high-powered Western executives attempting to juggle work and family to the continuing crisis of global hunger. In this volume, we present some of this discourse.

SOCIALIZING CARE: ARTICLES IN THIS VOLUME

Socializing Care brings together scholars from a variety of fields who believe that care has something to offer public concepts of morality. *Ultimately, this collection responds to the question of how society might be different if care ethics were taken seriously in terms of policy and practice.* Consistent with the concrete nature of care ethics, all the articles in this collection include considerations of both theory and practice. In fact, seldom are anthologies published with the theoretical consistency and integration found among the authors as is found in *Socializing Care*. Virtually every article makes mention of the groundbreaking work of Tronto and Noddings, who have also offered original work for this volume. Furthermore, the authors included have such impressive publication records in regard to care ethics that many of them make extensive references to one another's previous work. What emerges is a sense that the field of care ethics has matured and considerations of its social dimension have begun to coalesce and energize a number of feminist theorists. As Noddings quipped, "Even theories, like children, can grow up and move into the public world."[5]

The first section of articles, "Care, Society, and the State," includes essays that tend to emphasize care theory and its implications for the state, but this emphasis is not at the expense of providing significant examples. One theme that runs through a number of the articles in the first section is a redefinition of citizenship. Accordingly, the demands of citizenship are thought to be reshaped if care is a serious consideration. The second section of articles, "Care in Social Action and Context," focuses more on examples of how institutions can integrate care into their policies and practices. These articles take as a starting point some very specific issues or practices, but they do not ignore theoretical considerations.

Given that Joan Tronto was one of the early theorists to write extensively about the political dimensions of care, it is only appropriate that we begin *Socializing Care* with her article, "Vicious Circles of Privatized Caring." Tronto reinforces her claim that care has an important untapped social dimension, but she takes the critics of care seriously. Tronto cautions that "unless we are willing to reconceptualize care fundamentally, the ability to move the care debate forward will remain caught in a vicious circle in which care reinforces social and economic inequality." Tronto is concerned that what has been overlooked in much of the care literature is the relative imbalance in individual capacity to care. One's context, including social location and relative power, will greatly impact one's ability to care. Furthermore, most of the attention in developing care theory has been placed upon caregivers rather than on the cared-for, but this belies the reality that as humans, we all require care. Tronto suggests that "to accept this weakness of always being among the cared-for, provides us with the strength to recognize common cause in making certain that everyone is well cared for." Tronto seeks to make care a public value that citizens embrace as part of their identity.

Although her writings were seminal in the development of care theory, Nel Noddings's early work received much criticism, including from Tronto, regarding, among other issues, its alleged failure to include an institutional dimension. In 2002, Nel Noddings published *Starting at Home: Caring and Social Policy*, which took the basic ideas developed in her landmark 1984 book, *Caring*, and expanded them to address how caring values found in the private sphere might be extended to the public sphere in a process that reverses the traditional ways that philosophers looked at morality. In "Caring and Social Policy," Noddings continues to suggest that the morality established in good homes has a great deal to offer public practice. Noddings provides a commonsense model of caring: "There are no recipes. Care demands listening, discussing, and responding." As simple as that appears, Noddings notes that social trends are moving in ever more noncaring trajectories. For example, Noddings is quite concerned with the institution of rigid social rules with labels such as "zero tolerance" and "uniform penalties." Instead, Noddings contends that the basic caring attitude, "'I am here,' should be encouraged by flexible guidelines and backed by peer support." In her article, Noddings applies a responsive approach to public policy addressing some of the vexing issues of our day, including health care, abortion, capital punishment, and education.

In "Care and Order: The Feminization of Liberalism," Eloise A. Buker invokes recent economic history to argue that the modern industrial state must provide care previously assumed to be supplied by women not engaged in paid labor. Buker finds care ethics providing a corollary/corrective to a state governed by law and order. The long-standing jurisprudence model, particularly in the United States, has been a "liberal model of law, just punishment and order, under the belief that law will produce order." A law and order approach operates under the hidden assumption that care is being provided by a large resource of women who stayed in the private sphere. As women increasingly entered the workforce, those care resources were stretched thin. Buker suggests that the state must step in to provide balance: "I am arguing that one way to reframe care as a public matter is to give it parallel status with the role of law enforcement and punishment, so that the public will come to understand that the primary mechanism for sustaining political order depends on both law and care." Ultimately, Buker wishes to raise the political value of care in the public imagination.

The destabilization of the state can provide a unique opportunity for the reassessment of national commitments and values. In "South African Social Welfare Policy: An Analysis through the Ethic of Care," Selma Sevenhuijsen, Vivienne Bozalek, Amanda Gouws, and Mare Minnaar-Mcdonald contend that an ethic of care should be thought of as an aspect of citizenship in a just society. In *Citizenship and the Ethics of Care: Feminist Considerations on Justice, Morality, and Politics*, Sevenhuijsen argued for the central role of care in a robust democratic theory. Here, the authors further explicate socializing care through an analysis of the development of welfare policy in South Africa. After the breakdown of apartheid and the emergence of a new government, national discussions took place over the nature and future of social welfare policies. While the authors praise the public dialogue over the state's role in providing care, they are concerned with the family-centered language regarding caregiving: "the policy of indicating the family as the preferred social location for care is ridden with complexities." The authors are worried that making the family the primary locus of care will unfairly burden women and puts forth a rigid and regressive understanding of family.

Dorothy Miller also addresses rigid formulations of the family. In "The Potential of Same-Sex Marriage for Restructuring Care and Citizenship" she employs a combination of empirical data and feminist analyses to suggest that the legalization of same-sex marriage has important implications for socializing care both within the institution of marriage and beyond. Legitimated gay marriages have the potential for destabilizing existing patterns of care historically established among heterosexual couples: "Although most married persons 'care about' each other, it is evident that women do most of the 'caring for' in traditional heterosexual families." Although economics have led to shifting resources of care as women have engaged increasingly in paid labor, studies repeatedly indicate an asymmetrical care-labor burden within the heterosexual family. The lack of gendered markers in a same-sex marriage will mean that asymmetrical care burdens will have to be justified according to other rationales, if at all. Consistent with Tronto's claims, Miller wants to push care into the public sphere. If "the gendered divisions become problematized, de-normalized, then perhaps care will no longer be 'extra' and perhaps no longer private." Accordingly, same-sex marriage becomes a significant marker of socializing care.

Much of the analysis regarding socializing care in this volume addresses present or future institutional practices and policies. In "An Inverted Home: Socializing Care at Hull-House," Maurice Hamington looks to the past for a model of socializing care that integrates aspects of Noddings's mining of domestic morality with Tronto's desire to transform the nature of citizenship. Hull-House was the most renowned endeavor of the settlement movement, and its leader and resident public philosopher was Jane Addams. The women-centered environment that was Hull-House included a community of residents who were at a crossroads of public and private space. The largely college-educated women were looking for an outlet for positively impacting society at a time when such avenues were mostly closed to women. The community-based settlement house gave women an opportunity to radiate care, usually reserved for the home, to their neighborhood. The work done by the women of Hull-House has been sometimes pejoratively described as "social housekeeping," but it also included extending an alternative voice of morality: "Addams and her colleagues did engage in public projects that were familiar to women in homemaking—caring for children and cleaning up the neighborhood—but they also applied moral dispositions from idealized homes to these social problems: listening, responding, and caring." Hamington describes a unique historical example of socializing care with widespread impact and implications.

While Hamington describes a positive example of socializing care from the past, Deborah L. Little provides a timely look at a negative example of socializing care in the present. In "From 'Giving Care' to 'Taking Care': Negotiating Care Work at Welfare's End," Little identifies a dangerous trend in welfare reform that runs contrary to Tronto's vision of infusing care into the social and political arena. The reformation of welfare began in a vacuum of listening and responding: "A discussion of care was absent from the national legislative debates as most policy makers consider the problem resolved with the provision of some monies for paid child care." Little traces the various phases of welfare philosophy leading up to the present day which she describes as the "workfare regime" characterized by an emphasis on training and paid labor over caregiving to children: "During the workfare regime fulltime mothering, as identity and activity, was no longer a valid choice within the welfare system." Little utilizes the example of a particular welfare agency, New York's Community Education Center (CEC), to demonstrate the shift in welfare ethos from giving care to taking care. Under the new state-supported definition, wage work is considered caring for the family rather than traditional notions of direct caring. This shift has some intriguing implications for the gendered division of care labor, but Little is more concerned that caring is becoming no one's responsibility: "the meaning of caregiving can be manipulated to reduce demands on the state." The danger is in making socializing care into a zero-sum game rather than a widespread commitment.

The second section of articles, "Care in Social Action and Context," which focuses on a variety of caring practices, begins with Margaret Urban Walker's "The Curious Case of Care and Restorative Justice in the U.S. Context." In *Moral Understanding: A Feminist Study in Ethics* and later *Moral Contexts*, Walker has effectively demonstrated a much-overlooked concrete aspect to morality. She is concerned that traditional works of ethics ignore the role of race, class, gender, and history in formulating theories of universal morality. In this article, Walker identifies a worldwide, albeit nascent, movement toward care in jurisprudence: restorative justice. In restorative justice programs the guilt of the offender is presupposed and the focus of collective deliberation turns to comprehensive considerations of healing and restoring all the constituents involved. Although Walker recognizes restorative justice as a minority effort at this point, she suggests that "the case of restorative justice shows that the values and points of focus of care ethics can in fact become a legitimate and legitimating discourse in a significant area of public policy in the United States." Walker speculates at length as to why care language has not been further integrated into similar policy actions. One of her conclusions is that socializing care is ultimately threatening to existing institutions and beliefs: "The language of care in its most characteristic applications reminds people of a largely uncontrollable vulnerability." Traditional ethical approaches do not demand nearly as much affective responsibility on the part of moral agents as does care ethics and therefore elicits far less discomfort.

While Walker is concerned with the marginalization of care in U.S. public policy, Fiona Robinson addresses the dilatory impact of international globalization led by the United States in "Ethical Globalization?: States, Corporations, and the Ethics of Care." Robinson, the author of *Globalizing Care: Ethics, Feminist Theory, and International Relations*, claims that "a normative framework of care ethics can contribute toward imagining, articulating, and implementing real alternatives to neoliberalism." Robinson's sweeping article integrates the theoretical work of Sevenhuijsen, Tronto, and Walker while addressing the potential for care among nation-states as well as multinational corporations. For Robinson, globalization represents a realignment and destabilization of relationships. Neoliberalism lacks the adequate resources to restore relational equilibrium. Consequentially, socializing care is a necessary corrective to the fractionation currently underway worldwide. "Because the ethics of care is neither explicitly nor historically tied to orthodox, liberal understandings of the relationship between state and citizens, it provides a potential basis for rethinking the 'social bond' which, it has been argued, is becoming unraveled by the trends associated with economic globalization."

Some feminists have been accused of discriminatory approaches to women who choose to forgo paid labor in favor of tending to children in their home. Similarly, some feminist theorists have attempted to distance themselves from maternal language in describing care ethics so as not to marginalize care as a strictly private sphere concern and thus reinforcing patriarchal gender roles. In "Care as a Cause: Framing the Twenty-First-Century Mother's Movement," Judith Stadtman Tucker challenges both approaches by suggesting that socializing care is not just about getting the state to take on care previously provided by women; socializing care also means valuing care enough to give women and men the legitimate choice to undertake unpaid care labor. She foresees (and is helping to develop) a new mothers' movement. Stadtman Tucker, who is the founder and editor of the Mothers' Movement Online, suggests "a feminist ethic of care . . . might be the best approach to satisfy the diverse and sometimes paradoxical demands of the new mothers' movement while advancing the status of women." She views liberal feminism as lacking the theoretical resources to strike the balance she is suggesting because it derives so much of its impetus from post-Enlightenment individualism. According to Stadtman Tucker, care ethics—particularly as Tronto has characterized it—provides a framework for valuing care labor without reinforcing traditional gender roles.

Socializing Care concludes with Cheryl Brandsen's article, "A Public Ethic of Care: Implications for Long-Term Care." Brandsen reminds the reader that socializing care is not merely a euphemism for shifting more of the country's welfare requirements to the private sector in the form of voluntary labor. She warns that socializing care should not be co-opted by the "family values" movement. "Conservative 'family value' ideology is, in fact, antithetical to a public ethic of care" because such values stress families taking care of their own, which privatizes care and is based on certain class assumptions. Brandsen uses the issue of long-term care for frail elders as an important benchmark for the communal will to socialize care. As our society ages, will it find the collective moral impetus to fund the programs necessary to properly take care of its elderly? According to Brandsen, "Caring practices are essential and valuable to a well-functioning society; subsequently, collective responsibility for such is required."

Brandsen implicitly poses the question that underlies the articles in this volume. We all have the resources to care as individuals, but can we find the collective ability to care?

NOTES

1. Some of the significant publications on care ethics include: Seyla Benhabib, *Situating the Self: Gender, Community and Postmodernism in Contemporary Ethics* (New York: Routledge, 1997); Peta Bowden, *Caring: Gender-Sensitive Ethics* (London: Routledge, 1997); Claudia Card, ed., *Feminist Ethics* (Lawrence, Kans.: University Press of Kansas, 1991); Grace Clement, *Care, Autonomy and Justice: Feminism and the Ethic of Care* (Boulder: Westview Press, 1996); Peggy DesAutels and Joanne Waugh, eds., *Feminists Doing Ethics* (Lanham, Md.: Rowman and Littlefield, 2001); Carol Gilligan, *In a Different Voice: Psychological Theory and Women's Development* (Cambridge: Harvard University Press, 1982); Carol Gilligan, ed., *Mapping the Moral Domain* (Cambridge: Harvard University Press, 1988); Carol Gilligan, *Making Connections: The Relational Worlds of Adolescent Girls at Emma Willard School* (Cambridge: Harvard University Press, 1990); Joram G. Haber and Mark S. Halfon, eds., *Norms and Values: Essays on the Work of Virginia Held* (Lanham, Md.: Rowman and Littlefield, 1998); Maurice Hamington, *Embodied Care: Jane Addams, Maurice Merleau-Ponty and Feminist Ethics* (Urbana, Ill.: University of Illinois Press, 2004); Susan Hekman, *Moral Voices, Moral Selves: Carol Gilligan and Feminist Moral Theory* (Philadelphia:

Pennsylvania State University Press, 1995); Eve Feeder Kitty and Diana T. Meters, eds., *Women and Moral Theory* (Lanham, Md.: Rowman and Littlefield, 1987); Virginia Held, *Feminist Morality: Transforming Culture, Society and Politics* (Chicago: University of Chicago Press, 1993); Mary Jeanne Larrabee, ed., *An Ethic of Care: Feminist and Interdisciplinary Perspectives* (New York: Routledge, 1993); Rita Manning, *Speaking from the Heart: A Feminist Perspective on Ethics* (Lanham, Md.: Rowman and Littlefield, 1992); Nel Noddings, *Caring: A Feminine Approach to Ethics and Moral Education* (Berkeley: University of California Press, 1984); Nel Noddings, *Starting at Home: Caring and Social Policy* (Berkeley: University of California Press, 2002); Fiona Robinson, *Globalizing Care: Ethics, Feminist Theory, and International Relations* (Boulder: Westview Press, 1999); Sara Ruddick, *Maternal Thinking: Toward a Politics of Peace* (Boston: Beacon Press, 1989); Selma Sevenhuijsen, *Citizenship and the Ethics of Care: Feminist Considerations on Justice, Morality and Politics* (London: Routledge, 1998); Joan Tronto, *Moral Boundaries: A Political Argument for an Ethic of Care* (New York: Routledge, 1993); Margaret Urban Walker, *Moral Understandings: A Feminist Study in Ethics* (New York: Routledge, 1998); Margaret Urban Walker, *Moral Contexts* (Lanham. Md.: Rowman and Littlefield, 2003).

2. Tronto, *Moral Boundaries,* 8.
3. Tronto, *Moral Boundaries,* 161.
4. Tronto, *Moral Boundaries,* 161–2.
5. Noddings, *Starting at Home,* 2.

Part I

CARE, SOCIETY, AND THE STATE

Chapter One

Vicious Circles of Privatized Caring

Joan Tronto

Bernard de Mandeville, in *The Fable of the Bees* (1714), described how the pursuit of private vices could produce the public good of greater social wealth. This argument bears a close family resemblance to the contemporary neoliberal ideology. Neoliberals believe that encouraging the private pursuit of wealth, and limiting the public intrusion in this process, is the surest way to achieve collective happiness. In this essay, I shall argue a converse position: out of admirable personal conduct a public harm can arise. When unequal citizens only care privately, they deepen the vast inequalities and the exclusion of some from the real prospect of being full citizens.

This essay tells a cautionary tale. Many powerful individuals and organizations in the world tout the organization of social and political life in the United States as a model of how a modern society can provide a fine way of life for its citizens. American military, political, and economic power also spread this neoliberal ideological message around the globe. Indeed, Americans live surrounded by material wealth and express satisfaction with their lives. At the same time, however, a widening gap between rich and poor makes it doubtful whether the equal standing of all citizens, a starting point for democracy, will long describe the United States. Of course, citizens are never fully equal, but in civil rights we assume some equality. I shall argue in this essay, however, two propositions. The first, established by Eva Kittay (1999), is that as long as care continues to shape the capacities of citizens to be citizens differently, there can be no genuine equality among citizens. The second is that as long as neoliberals continue to insist that the separation of public and private life accurately describes the limits of government's power, they provide an ideological justification for the deepening circles of unequal care.

The justification of deepening circles of unequal care rises out of two questions about citizens: Who are citizens and what do citizens do?

3

Who are citizens? In the historical tradition in Western societies, citizens presented themselves to the political order (the polis, the king, the state) as ready to serve, and their ability to serve qualified them as citizens. Thus, for some ancient Greek city-states, a citizen was one who could equip himself with the requisite tools for military combat; in post–World War II Western societies, a citizen is one who can present himself ready to work unencumbered by household responsibilities.[1] Throughout much of the history of Western societies women have been barred from those activities that qualified men as citizens: excluded from military service, from political participation, some parts of the workforce, and so forth. Thus, women have only been included as citizens in a different way. Citizens, after all, have to be born, and immediately, women are involved in the creation of citizens. Women's citizenship has usually been mediated by women's connection to the political order through men: husbands, fathers, sons.[2] What women have done for male citizens is to take care of them. Women's status within the formal ranks of citizens remained partial and defined by their caring roles.

If we recognize the separation of life into public and private spheres, we can now make the further observation that citizenship is bestowed upon people for their public, not for their private, capacities. What this juridical fiction ignores, of course, is that any person's public existence floats upon the enormous amount of care work and reproductive labor that has come before and transformed a human infant into a capable citizen. Thus care, the disposition and work of maintaining ourselves, is the deep and ignored background to citizenship.

In the last generations, it has become more difficult to maintain the fictional separations of public and private life. As those formal barriers to women's public participation have dropped, it has become clear how intertwined public and private life are. Nevertheless, in constructing models of citizenship, we cannot take the structure of "care" for granted. If we do, we will miss seeing an important way in which exclusions and inequalities continue to exist and miss the central challenge of how we must change them to make a truly inclusive form of citizenship.

If we ask the second question, what do citizens do? then we recognize once again that traditionally, care has been outside of the realm of citizenship. The preparation of citizens for work and for public service is itself largely conceived to be outside of the public realm and prior to what citizens do. Nonetheless, if we take seriously that one of the roles of democratic citizens is to make judgments about public life, then we must think about the consequences of an inaccurate portrait of the separation of public and private life and of the place of care in our lives. The inaccuracy of the usual description of the separation of life into public and private realms makes it possible for vicious circles of unequal care to perpetuate themselves.

Care has not been conceived as a part of the work of citizens, nor as an important part of what citizens should spend their collective energy thinking about. In this essay I shall argue, however, that if unequal opportunity poses a threat to democratic society, then democratic citizens have to take seriously a collective commitment to care. In the end, I will suggest some ways that we might conceive of care as a public value.[3]

DEFINING CARE

Before beginning, the question of how to define care needs to be addressed. Scholars define care in a number of ways, but for most scholars, care is the "labor of love" in which private or intimate activity is performed in a particular emotional state. For example, Francesca Cancian follows the pioneering British sociologists, Janet Finch and Dulcie Groves (1983), in offering this account:

> My working definition of care is: a combination of feelings of affection and responsibility, with actions that provide for an individual's personal needs or well-being in a face-to-face interaction. (Cancian 2000)

Such a definition has both strengths and weaknesses. One of its strengths is that it combines care as a disposition and an action. Nevertheless, there are also a number of problems with such a definition. It presumes that care is only the activity of individuals directed toward other individuals. Not only does this exclude care for the self, but it also excludes the possibility that institutions or groups of individuals can care, or that people can care from a distance. These possibilities are included in our everyday use of the language of care, and there are good reasons to include them.

Such a definition of care also excludes "bad care" from being care at all. Imagine a nursing home attendant who hates the patients and only performs her work in the most desultory fashion in order to avoid being fired and to collect her pay. Surely such a person is "caring," though not well. Thus building in affection and responsibility prejudge the quality of care.

The contrasting broad definition of care I shall use and defend was worked out by Berenice Fisher and me in 1990:

> a species activity that includes everything that we do to maintain, continue, and repair our "world" so that we can live in it as well as possible. That world includes our bodies, our selves, and our environment, all of which we seek to interweave in a complex, life-sustaining web. (Fisher and Tronto 1990)

Fisher and I then determined that there are four phases of care: caring about, caring for, caregiving, and care receiving. Caring about involves recognizing the need for care in the first place. Caring for involves assumption of responsibility for the caring work that needs to be done. Caregiving is the actual work of care, and care receiving is the response of the thing or person cared for. We also noted that care can be provided in the household, in social institutions, and through market mechanisms.

This definition confounds many ways that social scientists divide their disciplines and perspectives; care for the self seems a psychological category, care for others a sociological category, care for the "world" economic and political categories. Further, this definition seems to combine normative standards ("as well as possible") with non-normative concerns, though it still allows us to adjudge some "caring" as bad care; it is not excluded by definition. This definition points to the advantages of a holistic over an analytical approach; for example, while "responsibility" is a part of the entire process of care, it is possible to imagine it absent from a particular care act (a nurse's aide only provides the medications because she was handed a cup of pills and told to dispense them).[4]

I do want to insist, however, that the more typical definition of care, cited above in Francesca Cancian's account, contains two main problems that obscure other possible ways to conceptualize care. These two conceptual problems are: 1) looking at care always from the perspective of *caregivers*, not care *receivers*, and 2) lacking a way to distinguish among types of care to reflect adequately the power relationships in care. These two problems will be fully explored at the end of this essay, but it is important to realize that if we resolve these problems, we also sidestep many of the serious objections that feminists have raised to care as a way to think about forwarding a feminist agenda.

That discourses of care can lead to the greater oppression of women is not a new critique of feminist advocates of an ethic of care. Scholars have frequently demurred about care, presuming that it fits too neatly into older discourses of "separate spheres" for women, that it extols women's sacrifices (Hoagland 1988), that it functions discursively to convince women to support unjust practices such as colonialism (Narayan 1995). Scholars writing about care in a favorable light have faced a different and yet related problem. Having observed the ways in which ascription of care roles to women and "lower status" people in society reinforce and reproduce social inequality, the proposals for transforming these inequalities have failed to capture public imagination and to lead to social change. In this paper I shall argue that unless we are willing to reconceptualize care fundamentally, the ability to move the care debate forward will remain caught in a vicious circle in which care reinforces social and economic inequality.

VICIOUS CIRCLES OF UNEQUAL CARE:
MEASURABLE, MATERIAL IMBALANCES IN CARE EXIST

We should first recognize that there are measurable, material imbalances in the amount of care that various people receive and in the amount of resources that people have to accomplish their caring work. These imbalances closely mirror the configurations of social class and status (primarily racial status) in the United States.

Let us begin with children. Even at the beginning of one's life, the care one has received helps to determine one's future. Children born underweight have more significant risks of developing health problems later on; such children are more likely to be born to poorer mothers. In a cross-nation comparison, children who have a parent present during the first year of life seem to thrive better than children who do not, and children whose parents have more generous parental leave benefits do better (Ruhm 2000); (white) children whose mothers work during their first year in the United States develop cognitive skills more slowly (Han, Waldfogel, and Brooks-Gunn 2001). Parents who are better off economically are more likely to have good "wellness" care for their children (Ronsaville and Hakim 2000). Children who have adequate food do better in school. Success in school[5] and pursuit of postsecondary education still correlates most completely with parents' income and education (Postsecondary participation 2002). Jody Heymann has exhaustively demonstrated that working class parents are less likely to have such resources as "personal days" at their disposal, and working class children's poorer school attendance performance correlates with such lack of resources (Heymann 2000).

Poorly cared-for children never make up the care deficit that they have suffered, and so we should not be surprised to learn that children who have been poorly educated and received inadequate health care become adults with fewer resources to draw upon and less success in the world. Globally, "poverty and ill-health are intertwined" (Wagstaff 2002) and this is so in the United States as well (Shi, Macinko, Politzer, and Xu 2005). Mental health correlates also with income, education, and race in the United States (Ostrove, Feldman, and Adler 1999). Although Christopher Jencks has questioned whether it is proper still to say that mortality varies with economic inequality, race still correlates with a shortened life span (Jencks 2002), and others still argue that poverty decreases the life span (Duncan et al. 2002).

In every category of caring for oneself and one's family that we might mention, the more affluent have greater resources for caring and better take advantage of these resources than those who are less well off. Nursing home care provided for the more affluent is more pleasant than the care provided for public assistance recipients. The more affluent are more likely to have access to better food and eat more nutritiously, are more likely to engage in exercise as a form of leisure activity, are more likely to seek help from doctors and mental health practitioners. The more affluent are more likely to have access to resources that provide the "infrastructure" of care as well: for example, better access to transportation, more, better, and safer housing. There is no doubt that people who are more affluent have the opportunity to receive better care.

Those who receive better care, however, are also somewhat less burdened by the demands to care for others. In the formal economy, care work is among the least well-paid work in our society. Those who do caring work are disproportionately women, people of color, immigrants, and working class people. Furthermore, much care work occurs in informal and unpaid sectors of the economy, so that care workers are likely to be the least well protected and organized and to receive the fewest benefits (Heymann 2000) in order to care for their own families.

Structurally, several aspects of care practices contribute to such inequities. First, in terms of the allocation of resources, care work is both undervalued and ascribed to women and lower class and lower status people. They are the result of long-standing discrimination in the workforce, and of structural differences in the ways that we think about paying for care work (Nelson 1999). Second, in terms of the allocation of power, since needs for care are overwhelmingly ascribed to "vulnerable" people, such as children, the elderly, the infirm, and others who are dependent, *control* for meeting these needs is placed in the hands of those who are deemed competent and independent. Thus, it is difficult to generate a public discourse in which are heard the voice and views of the vulnerable.

Among others, Charles Tilly (1998) has argued that small initial advantages of one group over another embed themselves into large-scale patterns of oppression by using ascriptive differences to structure social institutions and practices. The ways in which care is provided, and for whom, seem to illustrate this point. The more wealthy you are in the United States, then, the chances are, the better you are cared for and the less likely that you work doing care work for others. This is the initial pattern, then, that is reinforced in a vicious circle of uncaring for others.

THE SOCIAL PSYCHOLOGY OF UNEQUAL CARE

We might expect that such inequalities of care and access to care resources would generate some concern in American society and among political leaders. After all, among children, there is an obvious importance of the quality of care someone receives as an indicator of her or his capacity to develop into the most productive citizen. If Americans are serious about equality of opportunity, then they should be quite serious about the adequate provision of care at an early age (cf. Harrington 1999; Heymann 2000). President Bush's labeling of his educational reform as "No Child Left Behind" may be merely rhetoric, but it captures a commitment to equality of opportunity. And for the elderly, viewed as senior citizens, there is a greater level of support for making their lives easier than for other social groups. Similarly, the infirm receive public benefits through the Social Security system, and their care seems to be partly a public concern. The problem is, however, that these commitments do not translate into any real commitment to equality of care. Indeed, I shall argue that the opposite happens, for a variety of reasons.

In the first place, since Americans generally conceptualize care as a private concern, the language and framework of market choices guide how we describe and think about care options. The effect of this framework is to make care primarily outside of public concern. One way to understand care inequalities is to see them as the outcomes of "choices" that competing actors make in the marketplace. Through monetary and temporal resources, both in the market and outside, one way to understand care imbalances is to see them as the result of long chains of individual choices. For example, if parents choose to spend their time, their money, etc., in ways that do not benefit their children, while that choice may be deplorable, it is their own individual choice and not a social responsibility. The language of the market and of choice here diminishes our abilities to see the ways in which economic inequalities contribute to social incapacities. Because care seems to be about intimate life, it makes sense to think of the "unit of analysis" or "level of analysis" at which to think about care as the individual actor or family. Each family or person wishes to care for its/her/his/their charges as well as possible. The consequences of assuming that all actors are intimate caregiving actors is to see all care activities as the result of actions by particular individuals, a kind of methodological individualism. In thinking about how others act, the market becomes a leading way to describe all such behavior, and thus the market serves as a powerful way to describe how care distributions operate in capitalist societies (Slater and Tonkiss 2001).

This worldview obscures how people make judgments about others' choices, and for that matter, how individuals make choices for themselves. There are a variety of sociopsychological mechanisms that seem to be at work in justifying inequality of the amount of care available to different individuals. Consider these three:

Competitive Caring

This argument for equality of care presumes that care can be distributed within liberal frameworks of justice. Yet there are limits to starting from liberal principles of justice and expecting care simply to fit within that framework. To illustrate this point, let me use Jody Heymann's (2000) argument, that equality of opportunity demands that family time for caring should be equalized. Heymann argues that if time were organized more rationally around care, then more children would have chances to succeed in school, more elderly relatives would receive adequate care, work and productivity would improve, and society would be better.[6]

There is a basic flaw in this argument: as long as caring remains a subordinate activity and value within the framework of a competitive, "winner-take-all" society, caring well within one's family will make one not a friend but an enemy of equal opportunity. Heymann follows our usual assumption of care with the intimate and personal, and translates care into the preexisting models of family care. When people care, then, almost by definition they do not think of society; they think of intimates and their concrete and particular needs. In a competitive society, what it means to care well for one's own children is to make sure that they have a competitive edge against other children. On the most concrete level, while parents may endorse a principle of equality of opportunity in the abstract, their daily activities are most visibly "caring" when they gain special privileges and advantages for their children. Arguments about the value of public education, etc., lose their force when they affect the possibility of *one's own* children's future. This example demonstrates that when care is embedded in another framework of values, it does not necessarily lead in a progressive direction.

Idealized middle class family care in the United States thus requires, structures, and perpetuates some of the very inequities of care that Heymann describes. A "career person" (Walker 1999) only wants what is best for his or her family. This leads to the assumption that such people care for themselves, and that "care" is only a concern for the dependent and infirm; that is, the young, the unhealthy, and the old. In fact, the model of the self-caring person is a deception: while working adults may not require the *necessary care* of others (that is, the expertise of professional caregivers), they may use a great deal of other people's *care services* (that is, routine caring work; cf. Waerness 1990) to keep their busy lives on keel. In American society, the more elite one becomes, the more dependent one becomes upon others' meeting one's basic caring needs: providing edible food, clean clothing, attractive shelter. Thus, the parents who have flexible work schedules, whose children succeed at school, are probably using a vast array of care services. Such labor is among the poorest paid and least well organized in our society. Heymann's widening gap is thus also a caring gap, though the ideology of "caring" covers up its roots and makes it more intractable.

Unsympathetic Disregard

A second sociopsychological mechanism that might explain why people are not willing to assume the responsibilities to care for others in a public manner arises when people make judgments about whether other citizens deserve their support. I shall call such an argument unsympathetic disregard.[7]

In his recent writings on why inequality persists in the United States, Ian Shapiro (2002) describes several elements of social psychology: individuals tend to identify with those who are better off than they, but not with those who are less well off than they (an "empathy gap").[8] Further, geographical segregation in the United States makes empathy more difficult.

Another important element that Shapiro could have mentioned, but did not, is the way in which, as long as care is individualized and privatized, it is possible to praise oneself for one's caring and decry the ways in which others care. Such praise and blame will likely follow lines of race, class, ethnicity, region, and religion. Such praise and blame will likely make it more difficult to see inequalities as a result of lack of choice and to see them more as the result of deliberate bad actions, decisions, and ways of life of others. As a result, people are likely not to be very sympathetic to such lapses on the part of others.

One of the reasons that this element is especially important is that when we ask people to make public judgments, they are often wise enough not simply to generalize from their own experience. What they are likely to do, however, is use available generalizations about "others" to make judgments.

An illustration of this tendency is found in Martin Gilens's account of why Americans hate welfare. Since most Americans presume that most recipients of welfare are African American, are only willing to support welfare if they believe recipients work hard, and believe most African Americans are lazy, they are then unwilling to support welfare (Gilens 1999). People are not evaluating their own beliefs and actions, but those of others that come up short.

Although this is a subject for empirical research, it would be interesting to discover to what extent such thinking influences how people think about care. Everyone believes that they do the best that they can for their charges. But when other people fail to act in the same way, regardless of the reason, they can be dismissed—"they simply don't care."

If we recall the ways in which absence of resources prevent less well-off individuals from caring for their own families, we can see how care becomes a vicious ideological circle. Parents who see that the other parents do not show up for school plays, etc., might conclude that those parents "don't care," not that they work in jobs where they cannot get time off from work to attend. Thus, in addition to the lack of material resources that unequal care presents, it also may create the conditions for diminished sympathy.

Privileged Irresponsibility

"Privileged irresponsibility" refers to the ways in which the division of labor and existing social values allow some individuals to excuse themselves from basic caring responsibilities because they have other and more important work to perform (Tronto 1993). To use the conceptual distinction of Kari Waerness, privileged irresponsibility is a special kind of personal service in which the recipient of others' caring work simply presumes an entitlement to such care. Furthermore, the existence of such an entitlement permits it to "run in the background," that is, not to be noticed, discussed, or much remarked upon. Consider, as an example, the ideological version of the traditional division of household labor. A breadwinning husband "took care" of his family by earning a living; in return, he expected his wife to convert these earnings into comfortable shelter, edible food, clean clothing, a social life, management of the household, and so forth. Nor did the breadwinner husband think it was a part of his responsibility to know very much about the complexities of food preparation, household management, etc. Such men rarely learned how to "take care of themselves." Care work, invisibly and efficiently performed, was a privilege of his role. As to the caring needs he had and had met by the labor of those around him on "the other side of the paycheck" (Bridges 1979), he felt no sense of responsibility. Hence, privileged irresponsibility.

Peggy McIntosh (1988) and others (Hobgood 2000 and Johnson 2001) who write extensively about "privilege" assume that when people learn that they are privileged by ascription, they will go through a process of "consciousness raising" and surrender their privilege, since it is unjust. Privileged irresponsibility operates under a somewhat different logic.

Like the "privilege" described above, privileged irresponsibility is rarely visible. One of the great benefits or privileges that come from being in a position of superiority in a hierarchical system is that one need not consider one's role or responsibility in maintaining that system. Thus, such systems come to rely upon the peculiar ignorance of the beneficiaries of the system. Such privileged irresponsibility usually takes the form of complete ignorance of a problem, but it may also involve misinterpretation or unclear perception of a problem (Mills 1997).

Nevertheless, when privileged irresponsibility does become visible, privileged people need not only be transformed by their new consciousness, but need only to remind themselves about the nature of their responsibilities. Unless basic questions about the nature of social responsibility are rethought, there is no reason to expect that noting this privilege will cause any discomfort. It may be the case (to use the same example) that the husband recognizes that he is getting a good deal, but he is likely to think that his wife is also getting a good deal. Especially in a culture that emphasizes how much each of us is only responsible for our own lives, and ignores the caring that supports such lives, such privilege is very difficult to unseat.

Let's carry this analysis one step deeper, and think about personal service and necessary care in terms of the power relationships that they reflect. In necessary care, the caregiver is relatively powerful, because the caregiver is essential to the well-being of the care receiver. In personal service, the caregiver is not essential to the well-being of the care receiver, and the care receiver could thus dispense with the caregiver's role. The result is that care receivers have more power in personal service than they do in necessary care.

Because caring is complex, and psychologically, we might only think that we are caring when we engage in necessary care activities, people may come to believe that they fulfill their necessary caring obligations at the same time that they demand very high levels of personal service from others. What they fail to recognize in doing so is that they are taking advantage of those from whom they are demanding personal service. Privileged irresponsibility always concerns personal service and not necessary care. Yet this distinction is not usually made or present in our thinking. The situation becomes more complex still. Usually, the privileged also expect that others will provide the personal service that they require on terms that are agreeable to them.[9] The idea that this situation reflects a proper division of labor in society, however, prevents any reconsideration of responsibility. Thus, by using personal service to fulfill their own necessary care roles, those who can afford to hire others to do their personal service work for them think of themselves as accomplished in caring while they are able to ignore the ways in which their own caring activities continue to perpetuate inequality (see, inter alia, Tronto 2002).

The privatization of reproductive care that has accompanied the growing public nature of productive work reflects as well the relative social power of different groups to make their contributions more highly prized and recognized. Relatively more powerful people in society have a lot at stake in seeing that their caring needs are met under conditions that are beneficial to them, even if this means that the caring needs of those who provide them with services go unmet. More powerful people can fob the work of care on to others: men to women, upper to lower class, free men to slaves. Care work itself is often demanding and inflexible. People who do such work recognize its intrinsic value, but it does not fit well in a society that values innovation and accumulation of wealth.

Regardless of what assumptions we make about humans, then, whether they are greedy or benevolent, once there is inequality in care, thinking about how others take care of themselves and their charges is likely to make people feel less inclined to take their care problems seriously. Ideologically as well as materially, then, inequality in care creates a vicious circle.

GENDER, CLASS, AND THE ECOLOGY OF CARE

If there are sociopsychological factors that obscure people's abilities to understand the "caring choices" that others make, there is still more trouble ahead. It is also the case that what constitutes "good care" varies along some ascriptive characteristics as well. For example, Annette Lareau (2002) has explored the differences between middle class and working class parents' attitudes about the kind of care that their children need. For middle class parents, children's talents and opportunities require constant cultivation. That cultivation often requires the intervention of professional service providers (piano teachers, tennis coaches, etc.) and require that the parent negotiate the interactions of children with others (for example, in learning how not to be too deferential to doctors but to ask questions). For working class parents, on the other hand, children will develop naturally and according to their different natures if left to their own devices. Once children are adequately protected from danger, letting nature take its course will result in their growth in the ways that are naturally intended (Lareau 2002). Note that the cultivating, intensive form of child care that characterizes middle class upbringing requires more extensive reliance upon the professional and skilled services of others. It requires, obviously, resources of time and money to pay for such services.[10]

Although this discussion has focused on class, we could make a similar argument about ethnic and racial differences in attitudes toward child rearing (Omolade 1994). These differences do not apply only to children. Ethnic and racial differences dictate different treatment of elders, of disabled members of the community, and of infirm members of the family and community.

Gender differences also dictate that girls and women are presumed to be the "default" givers of care when a situation arises. On a global level, scholars have demonstrated the serious consequences of such assumptions for girls and women who are expected to eat last, be less educated, receive less health care attention, and so forth (Sen 1992). Women may demand care appropriate for their station, but they still remain the caregivers in their own homes, either by directly providing care or by being responsible for organizing such services.

To point to these differences is not simply to make an argument that some people care one way and others care another way, though this point is also true. The differences are not simply about preferences, but about a structure of inequality that is deeply embedded in other structures in society.

A VICIOUS CIRCLE

This account of unequal care began with the view that, since people may choose to offer different views of what constitutes decent caring, they may make different choices in the market. For a variety of complex reasons (a set of psychosocial mechanisms and class, racial, ethnic, and gender differences), people are not likely to recognize the care imbalance as a result of unequal power, economic and social inequality, and patterns of discrimination. Thus, they are unlikely to see that the care imbalance requires social responsibility and a collective response.

Short of a social change in attitudes of responsibility, this vicious circle seems intractable.

Reconceptualizing Care as a Public Value

When care as a concept has to be accommodated to a world in which (according to starting assumptions) autonomous actors pursue rational goals, care will necessarily appear shadowy. Given the realities of human fragility and dependence, the assumption that actors are autonomous presumes an immense background of sociological, psychological, economic, and political processes and events that have made them into such actors. When such basic aspects of life are pushed into the background, the result is an account of social life that is incomplete. Part of the social logic of care, then, is *not* to think about care.

There is a related and serious problem. The division of "autonomous" actor and "dependent" recipient operate intellectually to transform the care receiver into "the other" (Beauvoir 1968). As Simone de Beauvoir and others have demonstrated, this process of making someone into an "other" interferes with an ability to analyze the "other's" situation, to make judgments, and to see what is going on for them.

Autonomous actors, who think of themselves primarily as caregivers rather than as care receivers, are thus apt to misunderstand the nature of their own situation and to project their loathing about dependency onto care receivers. The result is both to misconstrue care and to misconstrue care's place in society.

"Care Receivers, All!"

Almost all discussions of care start from the perspective of the caregiver, not the care receiver. It is perhaps a necessary intellectual trend in a society in which the lives of autonomous actors are taken as the norm for human action that care will be discounted as an aspect of human life.

Michel Foucault's important late work on "care for the self" was an important break in the understanding of care as simply an act of passivity. Foucault's earlier work emphasized the ways in which social practices and capillary-like modes of power literally constitute individuals (indeed, the very notion of an "individual" or "subject"). In writing about the care of the self as an ethical category, Foucault sought to challenge the view that being cared for is necessarily a kind of passive activity (Foucault 1997).[11] The capacity to see oneself as vulnerable is not highly valued in our culture. Until we recognize that we

Joan Tronto

are "care receivers, all" there can be no change in the ways that we think about care and no basic change in how care is undervalued.

Two effects follow once all actors are willing to view themselves as recipients of care. First, care, the view of the self as recipient of care becomes normalized. This change may seem small, but it undermines completely the presumption that people are only rational actors able to compete in a marketplace, and forces us to recognize the limits of market life as the metaphor for all human actions. Second, care recipients cease to be viewed as "others." Once people can begin to make judgments about these "others" as if they were themselves, a different social psychological process of more genuine empathy will be necessary. That people can exercise such empathy is well established, though its scope is limited. Changing our understanding of care allows the scope of empathy to be expanded.

Ignoring the ways in which we are interdependent upon others for care allows us to continue to follow ideologies of competitive caring and unsympathetic disregard for others. Recognizing our own vulnerability undercuts these processes.

CARE VERSUS SERVICE

An attentive reader must find my argument somewhat contradictory. If it is correct that everyone needs care so completely, then how is it possible that this fact is suppressed?[12] How can such knowledge be missing? The answer to this question is simple: not all care is seen as care. Here, the important distinction is the one between *care* and *service*.

Kari Waerness (1990) actually identified three forms of care: spontaneous care, necessary care, and personal service. Spontaneous care is a kind of good Samaritan act in which no ongoing relationship of care is established. Necessary care is care that the recipient could not provide for him or herself. As an example, doctors provide necessary care to patients. Not all necessary care is highly skilled; young children cannot change their own diapers, but the skill required is not very exalted. "Personal service," Waerness's third category, is the care that one could provide to oneself but someone else provides it instead. One could wash one's own car, but one takes it to the car wash; one could do one's own manicure but prefers to go to the nail parlor. Waerness's example is husbands who expect their wives to clean up the house receive personal service (Waerness 1990). I shall use Waerness's distinction slightly more broadly than she does, but the basic difference between care and service remains the same.

Notice that the difference between care and service is *not* the act performed, nor the intimacy of the relationship of the work, nor the nature of the relationship established by the care work. What is different is that in "service," the more powerful, or active, actors command the care work which is provided by care workers; in "care," the more powerful, active, actors provide the care work for recipients. The care workers in both cases might have expertise, or they might be performing care work that is more routine and doable by everyone. The difference is in who appears to be in command.

Thus, service is a way to receive care without surrendering one's sense of command or autonomy. If one thinks of the child care worker as providing a useful service, rather than as primarily providing necessary care, then it is easier to persist in paying the child care worker low wages. The language of service preserves the illusion of independence and obscures dependence. It permits those who are relatively autonomous and able to act with discretion about how to fulfill their caring needs to rationalize the way in which they depend upon others. It permits the myth of market choice to replace the reality of deep interdependency, and it obscures the social and political dimension of our collective need for care. Further, it allows people to continue to avoid recognizing their responsibility for such collective care through a kind of privileged irresponsibility.

Thinking of the care that people receive as "service" obscures the reality of the ways in which people are all dependent upon others for their care. Every able-bodied, independent adult who goes off to work each day still requires care. It is surely the case that more of this care is now obtained through market mechanisms than it used to be, which makes it appear to be "service" purchased on the market rather than to be care. The presumption that only the vulnerable need care, however, belies our common human fate of depending upon others.

One reason to use the language of care broadly is to create the possibility for seeing this point. While there are useful results to gain from distinguishing, for example, paid from unpaid care work, care from service, "labor of love" from "labor," nonetheless there are also huge political and social advantages to gain from changing these conventional divisions.

CARE AS A PUBLIC VALUE

If we take the necessity of care seriously, then the "importance of what we care about" (Frankfurt 1988) is not merely an individual matter. We can also use this account to think about what our collective values and concerns are as well.

When we think about it, it is not so absurd to say that care is a public value. Some functions that are quintessentially roles assigned to the state can be described as "caring": education, welfare, and in the language of the eighteenth century, "police." Even Aristotle, who distinguished between the public and private spheres and placed economic life and personal care within the private sphere, used parallel language to describe how mothers raised their children and how the good state should educate its citizens (Schwarzenbach 1996).

In social welfare states where citizens have a greater sense of solidarity, care is easily comprehended as a public value (Sevenhuijsen 1998; Waerness 1990). Given more individualistic assumptions in the United States, care is understood almost entirely as a private matter. Nevertheless, there are grounds on which even individualistic Americans do conceive of collective needs. The existing assumptions that block such an understanding are not too difficult to identify. Let me first describe some aspects of these assumptions, and then end by proposing an alternative conception that opens the possibilities for making care a part of furthering a democratic, egalitarian agenda instead of opposing it.

In the first place, the assumption that people are primarily *consumers* affects the logic of seeing individuals in relationship with each other. The logic of consumption is relentlessly individualistic. Juliet Schor (2004) reports how marketing and advertisers have always sought to peel off more and more members of families from traditional loyalties to create loyalties to their own products and brands: from women as targets in the 1920s until the present when the targets are children (who, researchers now reveal, can identify brands at the age of two and influence parents' buying between two to three years of age). Further, though marketing produces consumers' sense of loyalty, the discursive presumption about consuming is that it is all a matter of individual "choice." If one respects such individuality, then it is difficult to ask people to see fellow citizens as anything but consumers making their own choices.

In the second place, in addition to consumerist similarity, the logics of difference (African Americans, Latinos, immigrants, Jews, etc.) point toward a reason for Americans not to embrace a public value of care. Public care, after all, has to be shared with these "others," who have often been seen as incapable of taking advantage of it. Although some dimensions of public care have probably benefited rhetorically from a demand to make "many into one" (e.g., the need for assimilation produced support for public education), in general the process of "othering" has historically been harmful to those excluded. One of the consequences of failing to face up to this past is that it makes Americans more likely to dwell upon their fear of being misunderstood, forgotten, or excluded. If one believes in reciprocity, then it makes sense that when those who have been treated badly have an opportunity to do so, they will reciprocate by treating their former tormentors in the same way. As long ago as Thomas Jefferson's *Reflections*, a part of the American psyche has presumed that if God were just, then white Americans will someday pay for these often unacknowledged acts.

On the other hand, though, there is also empirical evidence to suggest that, at times, Americans ignore both their instincts to make people rely upon themselves and their dislike for the particular lives of others. Steve Kelman argues, for example, that despite the culture of individual self-interest, there is a lot of evidence to suggest that people do behave in a way that reflects a "public spirit" (Kelman 1988). Furthermore, he notes, the more people observe altruistic behavior, the more likely they are to behave altruistically (Kelman 1988, 52–3).

The question becomes, then, under what conditions is it possible to turn the vicious circles that flow when care is treated as an individual matter into virtuous circles, and thus to avoid what Nancy Folbre calls (contra the prisoner's dilemma), "the nice person's dilemma" (Folbre 2001)?

Although in a longer work we might provide an extensive justification for this claim and examine the justifications that have been offered by other scholars, for the purposes of this essay, let us assume a commitment to public care. Let us imagine that we committed ourselves, as a society, to provide the care necessary to guarantee equal access to care so that citizens could all be assured that their basic care needs would be met.[13]

If we believe that there is good reason to take care seriously as a public value, then we will need to make three presumptions to provide such care. First, we need to presume that everyone is entitled to receive adequate care throughout life. Second, everyone is entitled to participate in relationships of care that give meaning to life. Third, everyone is entitled to participate in the public process by which judgments about how society should ensure these first two premises. Although I cannot justify these premises here, I do want to end this essay by arguing that the three presumptions form a whole that should not be separated.

The first premise seems to be a restatement of a classic "social right," as T. H. Marshall asserted. My claims, however, require that we understand care as an ongoing social process, not as an entity that can be granted or withheld from citizens. The model of social rights often presumes a one-sided relationship in which the state provides a concrete benefit. T. H. Marshall himself described the model of seeing citizens as holders of social rights (i.e., as people who make claims on the state by asserting a right to social welfare benefits) as ultimately disempowering:

> As for social rights—the rights to welfare in the broadest sense of the term— they are not designed for the exercise of power at all. They reflect, as I pointed out many years ago, the strong individualist element in mass society, but it refers

to individuals as consumers, not as actors. There is little that consumers can do except imitate Oliver Twist and "ask for more," and the influence politicians can exert over the public by promising to give it is generally greater than the influence of citizens—or those who care about these things—can exercise over politicians by demanding it. (Marshall 1981, 141)

For these reasons, it is not enough to assert any entitlement to care as if it were a good to be distributed. Instead, we have to see care as an activity of citizens in which they are constantly engaged. The change advocated here is not that the state should become the provider of such services, but that the state's role in supporting or hindering ongoing activities of care needs to become a central part of the public debate.

The second presumption is critical because people's views of good care do vary by race, class, ethnicity, religion, region, ideology, and even personality. Thus, the notion that one model of care will work for everyone is absurd. Platitudes such that every frail elder person should be confined to a nursing home, or that every family should take care of its own violate the ways in which humans vary in their abilities to give and receive care. Just as no one should be forced to receive care of a type that he or she finds demeaning, neither in a good society would we insist that family members, for example, must provide care; Janet Finch calls this "a right not to care" (Finch 1996).

The third presumption is critical because simply to say that people will think of "others" when they are acting in altruistic ways (Kelman's language) is not to say that they will genuinely reflect upon the needs of others as opposed to imposing their own sense of the needs of others onto care provision. We have earlier seen how the practice of presuming that everyone's needs and desires are like one's own causes people to act in ways that currently perpetuate vicious circles of care. Such a posture can only be turned around through reflection upon people's real accounts of their needs. Democratic processes are required to assure that the voices of all people, not just the powerful, middle class, and so forth, are heard.

This requirement for democratic process may seem unrealistic given how unrepresentative most political institutions in the United States are. But most care is local: one does not need to think about democratic processes to create care as operating only on the highest level. Julie White has demonstrated that in specific care settings, those that are organized more democratically succeed more thoroughly (White 2000).

In this section I have argued that a public concept of care is possible, and would provide a basis for rethinking care relations, the value of care work (paid and unpaid). Let us conclude by considering this question: Why would making care a public value help to solve the problem of the growing gap of unequal care?

CONCLUSION

I have argued that it could be possible to turn vicious circles of care inequality into virtuous circles of care. This is not to say that care would become equal, but that the problem of care inequalities could become a collective problem that we care about.

In order to make such a shift, ironically, we must first recognize our essentially passive nature as recipients of care. To do so requires that we throw away many of the ascriptive categories that currently inform care policy: abled versus disabled, healthy versus infirm, adult versus child, productive adult versus frail elder, those who command service versus those who need care. Lurking in these distinctions as well are differences of gender, and of class and racial status. Instead, we need to see the ways in which all of us are constantly caring for ourselves and for those around us.

Ironically, to accept this weakness of always being among the cared-for provides us with the strength to recognize common cause in making certain that everyone is well cared for. The tasks of collective care that I have outlined here are not easily undertaken and make demands of citizens. These are demands different from the ones that political order often makes, choosing lesser evils among competing elites, though, so the assumptions of political sociologists that people will be unwilling to participate do not apply so forcefully.

If, as many other scholars have suggested, unequal care is a great harm to basic values such as equality of opportunity and fairness, then clearing the ground to see this inequality as a threat is an important step to take to realize change in the value of care. The current ways Americans see care allow many in society to have what W. O. Brown called "an inoculation against insight." We cannot easily see how our own private value of "doing the best for ourselves and our family" turns into greater social inequality. Transforming this vicious circle into a virtuous one requires that care be embraced as an account of the human condition, as a part of our public value, and as a part of our understanding of what citizens are and do.[14]

NOTES

1. The legal scholar Joan Williams (2001) has called this person the "ideal worker."

2. For example, after women's suffrage was achieved in the United States, an ongoing struggle continued until 1934 for a woman's citizenship status not to be affected when she married. See Bredbenner (1998).

3. For other arguments that describe the relationship of equality and care, see Harrington (1999) and Heymann (2000).

4. If this definition seems to conflate almost all of the distinctions that social scientists use to parse the world into analytical units, I do not find this to be a weakness. We should remember that ideas are also a result of the allocative effects of ascriptive categories; we might well expect that the intellectual categories of social scientists would be organized differently if they had been modeled on the lives of women. We shall leave that project for another day, however.

5. "Poverty is one of the firmest predictors of academic performance, not because low income, in and of itself, makes a child a dunce, but because the circumstances of poverty often erode the supportive and attendant expectations that would likely enhance learning." Yeakey and Bennett (1991): 14.

6. Heymann's example that government agencies have been slow to respond to the different temporal needs of citizens who engage in care is a powerful one. In Italy, feminists have worked to reform local governments so that *tempi della città* (urban time policies) are sensitive to the needs of care; see Mareggi (2002).

7. Arlie Hochschild has recently labeled this phenomenon "the empathy squeeze" (2005).

8. Incidentally, as Shapiro notes, Adam Smith had noted a similar tendency and worried about its consequences for republican virtues in *The Theory of Moral Sentiments.*

9. "You want someone who puts the children before herself," said Judy Meyers, 37, a mother of two in Briarcliff Manor, N.Y., who works for a health insurance company. "But to find someone for the right amount of money is not so easy" (Rubenstein 1993).

10. Thus, to continue this example, the ideology of what Sharon Hays has called "intensive mothering" (1996) is primarily a middle class phenomenon. Although Anita Garey found a way to classify mothers' activities across class lines, it is clear that the categories that she uses to define what is important for mothers will vary across class. For example, "being there" will have a different meaning to a middle class parent who can get leave from work to attend a child's school than to a working class parent who cannot (Garey 1999). Francesca Cancian has also explored the differences among working and middle class families in their accounts of "good caring" (Cancian 2002).

11. I am indebted to Henk Manschot, University for Humanist Studies (Utrecht, the Netherlands) for pointing out to me this important way to understand Foucault's project. I have also benefited from discussions of this point with Liane Mozère of the University of Metz (Metz, France).

12. Among other political philosophical scholars who also dwell upon human frailty and dependence, see MacIntyre (1999); Kittay (1999); Sevenhuijsen (1998).

13. Among some justifications for caring that have been offered, consider: Kittay's (1999) argument from a Rawlsian perspective; Folbre's version of a social contract (Folbre, forthcoming); Margaret Urban Walker's derivation of ethical requirements from responsibility (Walker 1999); and arguments from equal opportunity made by Harrington (1999) and Heymann (2000).

14. Earlier versions of this chapter were presented at the Annual Meeting of the American Sociological Association, 2002, at the CAVA Symposium at the University of Leeds, 2004, at the Conference on Women and Citizenship sponsored by the Basque government in 2004, and at the University of Kentucky, 2005. I am grateful

for insightful comments I received on these occasions as well as from Pamela Stone, Teresa Arendell, and presenters and members of the "Considering Care Seminar" at City University of New York. I also thank the editors of this volume for their suggestions and assistance. As always, I am entirely responsible for all errors.

REFERENCES

Beauvoir, Simone de. 1968. *The second sex*. 1st American ed. New York: Modern Library.

Bredbenner, Candice Lewis. 1998. *A nationality of her own: Women, marriage and the law of citizenship*. Berkeley: University of California Press.

Bridges, Amy. 1979. The other side of the paycheck. In *Capitalist patriarchy and the case for socialist feminism*, ed. Z. Eisenstein. New York: Monthly Review Press.

Brown, W. O. 1933. Rationalization of Race Prejudice. *International Journal of Ethics* 43(3): 294–306.

Cancian, Francesca M. 2000. Paid emotional care: Organizational forms that encourage nurturance. In *Care work: Gender labor and the welfare state*, ed. M. H. Meyer. New York: Routledge.

———. 2002. Defining "good" child care: Hegemonic and democratic standards. In *Child care and inequality: Rethinking carework for children and youth*, ed. F. M. Cancian, D. Kurz, A. S. London, R. Reviere, and M. C. Tuominen. New York: Routledge.

Duncan, Greg J., Mary C. Daly, Peggy McDonough, and David R. Williams. 2002. Optimal indicators of socioeconomic status for health research. *American Journal of Public Health* 92 (7): 1151–57.

Finch, Janet. 1996. Family responsibilities and rights. In *Citizenship today: The contemporary relevance of T. H. Marshall*, ed. M. Bulmer and A. M. Rees. London: UCL Press.

Finch, Janet, and Dulcie Groves. (eds.) 1983. *Labour of love: women, work, and caring*. London: Routledge.

Fisher, Berenice, and Joan C. Tronto. 1990. Toward a feminist theory of caring. In *Circles of Care*, ed. E. Abel and M. Nelson, 36–54. Albany, NY: SUNY Press.

Folbre, Nancy. 2001. *The invisible heart: Economics and family values*. New York: New Press.

———. Forthcoming. *Our children, ourselves: economics and family policy*. Manuscript, Department of Economics, University of Massachusetts.

Foucault, Michel. 1997. The ethics of the concern of the self as a practice of freedom. In *Ethics: Subjectivity and truth*, ed. P. Rabinow, 96–116. Harmondsworth: The Penguin Press.

Frankfurt, Harry G. 1988. *The importance of what we care about: Philosophical essays*. New York: Cambridge University Press.

Garey, Anita Ilta. 1999. *Weaving work and motherhood*. Philadelphia: Temple University Press.

Gilens, Martin. 1999. *Why Americans hate welfare: Race, media, and the politics of antipoverty policy, studies in communication, media, and public opinion*. Chicago: University of Chicago Press.

Han, Wen-Jui, Jane Waldfogel, and Jeanne Brooks-Gunn. 2001. The effects of early maternal employment on later cognitive and behavioral outcomes. *Journal of Marriage & Family* 63 (2): 336–54.

Harrington, Mona. 1999. *Care and equality*. New York: Knopf.

Hays, Sharon. 1996. *The cultural contradictions of motherhood*. New Haven: Yale.

Heymann, Jody. 2000. *The widening gap: why America's working families are in jeopardy and what can be done about it*. New York: Basic.

Hoagland, Sarah Lucia. 1988. *Lesbian ethics: Toward new value*. 1st ed. Palo Alto, Calif.: Institute of Lesbian Studies.

Hobgood, Mary Elizabeth. 2000. *Dismantling privilege: An ethics of accountability*. Cleveland: The Pilgrim Press.

Hochschild, Arlie. 2005. The chauffeur's dilemma. *The American Prospect* 16 (July).

Hondagneu-Sotelo, Pierrette. 2001. *Doméstica: Immigrant workers cleaning and caring in the shadows of affluence*. Berkeley: University of California Press.

Jencks, Christopher. 2002. Does inequality matter? *Daedalus* 131 (1): 49–65.

Johnson, Allan G. 2001. *Privilege, power and difference*. Mountain View, Calif.: Mayfield.

Kelman, Steven. 1988. Why public ideas matter. In *The power of public ideas*, ed. R. B. Reich. Cambridge, Mass.: Ballinger Publishing.

Kittay, Eva Feder. 1999. *Love's labor: Essays on women, equality, and dependency*. Thinking Gender, ed. L. Nicolson. New York: Routledge.

Lareau, Annette. 2002. Invisible inequality: Social class and childrearing in black families and white families. *American Sociological Review* 67 (5): 747–76.

MacIntyre, Alasdair C. 1999. *Dependent rational animals: Why human beings need the virtues*. The Paul Carus lecture series, vol. 20. Chicago, Ill.: Open Court.

Mareggi, Marco. 2002. Innovation in urban policy: The experience of Italian urban time policies. *Planning Theory & Practice* 3: 173–94.

Marshall, T. H. 1981. Reflections on power. In *The right to welfare and other essays*. New York: Free Press. Original edition, 1969.

McIntosh, Peggy. 1988. *White privilege and male privilege: A personal account of coming to see correspondences through work in women's studies*. Wellesley, Mass.: Wellesley College Center for Research on Women.

Mills, Charles. 1997. *The Racial Contract*. Ithaca, New York: Cornell University Press.

Narayan, Uma. 1995. Colonialism and its others: Considerations on rights and care discourses. *Hypatia* 10 (2): 133–40.

Nelson, Julie A. 1999. Of markets and martyrs: Is it OK to pay well for care? *Feminist Economics* 5: 43–59.

Omolade, Barbara. 1994. *The rising song of African American women*. New York: Routledge.

Ostrove, Joan M., Pamela Feldman, and Nancy E. Adler. 1999. Relations among socioeconomic status indicators and health for African-Americans and whites. *Journal of Health Psychology* 4 (4): 451–63.

Parreñas, Rhacel Salazar. 2001. *Servants of globalization: Women, migration, and domestic work*. Stanford, Calif.: Stanford University Press.

Postsecondary participation: The effects of parents' education and household income. 2002. *Education Quarterly Review* 8 (3): 25–32.

Ronsaville, Donna S., and Rosemarie B. Hakim. 2000. Well child care in the United States: Racial differences in compliance with guidelines. *American Journal of Public Health* 90: 1436–43.

Rubenstein, Caren. 1993. Consumer's world: Finding a nanny legally. *The New York Times*, January 28, C1.

Ruhm, Christopher J. 2000. Parental leave and child health. *Journal of Health Economics* 19: 931–60.

Schor, Juliet B. 2004. *Born to buy: The commercialized child and the new consumer culture*. New York: Scribner.

Schwarzenbach, Sibyl A. 1996. On civic friendship. *Ethics* 107 (1): 97–128.

Sen, Amartya. 1992. Missing women. *BMJ: British Medical Journal* 304 (6827): 587–88.

Sevenhuijsen, Selma L. 1998. *Citizenship and the ethics of care*. London: Routledge.

Shapiro, Ian. 2002. Why the poor don't soak the rich. *Daedalus* 131 (1): 118–29.

Shi, Leiyu, James Macinko, Robert Politzer, and Jiahong Xu. 2005. Primary care, race, and mortality in US states. *Social Science & Medicine* 61: 65–76.

Slater, Don, and Fran Tonkiss. 2001. *Market society: Markets and modern social theory*. Cambridge, UK: Polity.

Tilly, Charles. 1998. *Durable inequality*. Berkeley: University of California Press.

Tronto, Joan. 2002. The "Nanny" Question in Feminism. *Hypatia* 17, 2 (Spring): 34–61.
———. 1993. *Moral Boundaries: A Political Argument for an Ethic of Care*. New York: Routledge.

Waerness, Kari. 1990. Informal and formal care in old age: What is wrong with the new ideology in Scandinavia today? In *Gender and caring: Work and welfare in Britain and Scandinavia*, ed. C. Ungerson. London: Harvester, Wheatsheaf.

Wagstaff, Adam. 2002. Poverty and health sector inequalities. *Bulletin of the World Health Organization* 80 (2): 97–105.

Walker, Margaret Urban. 1999. Getting out of line: Alternatives to life as a career. In *Mother time: Women, aging and ethics*, ed. M. U. Walker. Lanham, Md.: Rowman and Littlefield.

White, Julie Anne. 2000. *Democracy, justice and the welfare state: Reconstructing public care*. University Park, Penn.: Pennsylvania State University Press.

Williams, Joan. 2001. *Unbending gender*. New York: Oxford University Press.

Yeakey, Carol Camp, and Clifford T. Bennett. 1991. The legend of school as the key to equality. *Education Digest* 56: 12–16.

Chapter Two

Caring and Social Policy

Nel Noddings

In *Starting at Home: Caring and Social Policy,*[1] I suggested that an examination of life in ideal or best homes might provide a starting point for social policy. Here, after briefly reviewing the relevant features of caring in such homes, I explore how our findings might contribute to more humane social policies.

STARTING AT HOME

All homes provide shelter, support certain attitudes about places, objects, and bodies, introduce the young to other selves and ways of interacting, and train them to some standard of acceptability. In addition, ideal homes provide protection as well as shelter, offer an adequate supply of material resources, encourage growth, have at least one adult who does the work of attentive love, and educate for a form of acceptability that is simultaneously adapted to and critical of the cultural standards of the society in which the home is located. (It should be noted here that when I refer to "home" or "family," I mean to include any group of persons who commit themselves to establishing a shared life under one roof; the description is not restricted to traditional husband-wife arrangements. I am, however, particularly interested in those homes that include children.)

In the Western liberal societies to which my analyses have been confined, each of these features can be described in more detail. Ideal or best homes in these settings are continually under construction. Most of their norms or ideals are not permanent or fixed beyond question. There is one fixed element, however, and that is that every member of such homes can count on the response, "I am here," when he or she expresses a need. Someone in the home responds.

I have suggested that ideal homes recognize and encourage a healthy attitude toward the body and its pleasures, toward material objects, and the buildings in which we live and work, and they give attention to the reasons why all of these things are important to us.

All good homes reject cruelty, but in the best homes every act of coercion raises a question. There are times when, because we are responsible, we must use coercion, but many such acts are artifacts of power and expedience, not of responsibility. When coercion is used in ideal homes, it is followed by negotiation. The person in control helps the one who is controlled to understand why coercion is necessary, and she negotiates conditions that make the use of force more palatable and profitable to the one who is coerced. The aim is always to shift control as nearly as possible to the one who is more dependent, but there is no denial of interdependence. Autonomy gives way to intelligent heteronomy.[2]

Again, all good homes put an emphasis on shifting the locus of control from the stronger and more mature to the weaker or less mature, but the best homes retain and promote the idea of shared responsibility. They do not divide the world into those who stand on their own feet and those who must lean a bit on others, nor into the entirely good and the thoroughly evil. Such homes make an important distinction between negative desert and bringing unwelcome things on ourselves, and they reject negative desert almost entirely. (By "negative desert" I mean the common notion that a person who does something bad deserves to have something bad done to him or her.) Adults in an ideal home believe that no one deserves the deliberate infliction of pain, but they recognize that we all sometimes do things that bring pain on ourselves. Then there is a lesson to be learned. When one person hurts another, the conversations and decisions that follow are aimed at restitution, at understanding what happened, how each party might have behaved differently, and how similar events in the future might be avoided. Healthy guilt is encouraged and followed by restitution. Unhealthy guilt—brooding on what cannot be changed—and shame are both minimized.

Intellectual growth and everyday competence are encouraged in all good homes, but the best homes have flexible ideals and an appreciation for a wide range of occupations and contributions to the family and society. Most middle class parents want their children to achieve a level of financial success compatible with contemporary standards for the reasonably well-to-do. This understandable desire, however, sometimes leads to coercion that is unhealthy for both the children who are coerced and the society in which they will live. Why should skilled tradespeople be less highly valued than members of a profession? The argument I offer has little to do with markets and salaries but more to do with self-esteem, job satisfaction, the recognition of interdependence, and social appreciation. A society that does not value all of its competent workers is a sick society, one mired in selfishness and self-deception. The home that denigrates a young person's well-informed choice of occupation injures both the child and the society.

The ideal home continually negotiates between expressed and inferred needs. Expressed needs—revealed verbally or in body language—arise in the one expressing them. In contrast, inferred needs are determined externally and imposed on the one said to have them. In homes and schools, a need is usually inferred by noting a gap between some norm and the current condition of a child or student. Indeed, almost all of the needs identified in schools are of this sort; they are not the needs expressed by children. In the best homes and schools, an effort is made to analyze both expressed and inferred needs. Sometimes, when an inferred need is challenged, it can be dropped or modified, and caring adults should be open to persuasion on this possibility. On the other hand, not all expressed needs should be met. Children do have impulses that need restraint; they sometimes misunderstand what is in their own best interest. Some children should be urged strongly to engage more fully with academic work; some should be encouraged to follow a different path. As John Dewey rightly pointed out, teaching and parenting are hard, time-consuming occupations. There are no recipes. Care demands listening, discussing, and responding.

Perhaps the greatest difference between "just good" homes and ideal homes is the emphasis in the latter on understanding how we are all socialized. The best families, like all families, socialize their children to acceptable norms, but ideal families also help their members to understand the processes of socialization. They do not flout social etiquette and rules of behavior, but they discuss—often with humor, sometimes with dismay—why it is usually best to know and follow these rules. They leave open the possibility that some rules should be broken and that some should be changed. They do not try to internalize the stern father as a conscience but, rather, to educate for critical thinking and caring responses.

The ideal home in a democratic society does not reject all of the liberal tradition; it would be foolish and hypocritical to throw away hard-earned rights and a tradition of open discourse. But it rejects the individualism and emphasis on autonomy that characterize much of liberalism and, in doing so, it also modifies the liberal attitude on coercion. The ideal home and the society built in its image are willing to use some coercion, even on adults, if the move is clearly for the good of those coerced. However, the ideal home and society would use far less coercion on children than most other homes and societies. The improvement offered here is an approach that puts realistic emphasis on interdependence, on understanding and appreciating the power of intelligent heteronomy, and on learning to care.

In summary, for purposes of this brief chapter, ideal homes are caring homes—places in which someone (preferably all of the adults) does the work of attentive love. This requires listening and responding, as positively as resources and values permit, to needs. In such homes, there is an emphasis on interdependence and shared responsibility. It is recognized that we often bring unpleasant outcomes on ourselves, but this does not mean that we deserve the resulting pain. Indeed, ideal homes reject almost entirely the notion of negative desert. Finally, ideal homes continually try to identify, evaluate, and respond to both expressed and inferred needs. What would a society look like if it modeled itself on ideal homes?

TOWARD SOCIAL POLICY

Having laid out a description of life in ideal or best homes, a temptation might arise to write a utopian tract on social theory, but my point is not to describe a perfect society, only one that might be better. To attempt a wholesale transfer of life in ideal homes to the wider world would be, in effect, to imagine a utopia, and the description would encourage both snorts of disbelief and the sort of wary dread produced by behaviorist and socialist utopias.[3] There is no such danger here. In describing best homes, I left room for mistakes and shortcomings—losses of temper, shared blame, acts of coercion not strictly necessary, doubts about the importance of inferred needs and the good of expressed needs. Further, to attempt a wholesale transfer would be to destroy the special nature of homes. The world at large, even the small community, is not a home. However, some of the attitudes acquired there—ways of responding, of controlling encounters, of coming to understand—may profitably be tried out in the larger world.

The basic attitude, one captured by the response of one doing the work of attentive love is, "I am here," and it is cultivated in the original condition, the ideal home. There we learn to feel secure or insecure, able to control events to a certain degree or unable to do so, willing to share both joys and burdens, or selfishly protective of our own good fortune. Gradually, we gain (or fail to gain) the capacity to respond to others: "I am here."

Social policy guided by this basic attitude would reject any principle or rule that makes it impossible for people in responsible positions to respond with care to those who plead for care or obviously need it. This basic attitude, as we'll see, should govern policy on abortion, euthanasia, capital punishment, and finding homes for the homeless. It should also guide policies on the personal use of alcohol, tobacco, and drugs. Lisbeth Schorr makes the important point that people in social services often complain that the system it-

self gets in the way of their best efforts. She says, too, that "In their responsiveness and willingness to hang in there, effective programs are more like
families than bureaucracies."[4] This means that professionals must be trained
to a high level of competence and trusted with a wide range of decisions. Social workers should be able to adjust (within limits) amounts, deadlines, eligibility requirements, and the like. In courts, there should be no mandatory
sentencing laws that effectively remove judgment from judges. (Even to say
"take judgment out of the hands of judges" is a verbal absurdity.) Schools
should not have adopted zero tolerance rules and, if they already have them,
they should abolish them. It is one thing to say that "we" will not tolerate certain kinds of behavior; it is quite another to insist on uniform penalties for infractions that cannot easily be categorized. If, for example, a child acciden-
tally brings a sharp instrument to school (picks up his mother's lunch box,
say), that child should not be subject to a penalty designed to reduce the threat
of violence. Educators, like judges, need to exercise judgment.

Often, rigid rules are justified in the name of impartiality. The same rules
and the same penalties are supposed to apply to everyone. At the practical
level, however, the administration of justice in the United States is not impar-
tial, and that is one strong argument that has been used against capital punishment. But so long as impartiality is held as the ideal, we will continue to tin-
ker with rules and penalties in the hope that reality can be made congruent with
the theoretical ideal. However, even at the theoretical level, there is something
obviously wrong with most applications of impartiality. Events that are similar on the surface involve very different selves and, thus, are really different
events. Further, the penalties fixed before the fact assume not only that no one
should commit certain acts but also that all persons are equally likely to perform them. This may be true for some small offenses—parking briefly in a
loading zone, exceeding the speed limit a bit, failing to renew the dog's license
on time—but it is not true for the great offenses against social order. There is
a story to be told about the construction of selves who commit horrendous
crimes, and this story should be taken into account both in the treatment of the
criminal and in programs of prevention. Of course there must be broad guidelines specifying the seriousness of various offenses and describing a range of
penalties for infractions, but within those broad guidelines, each offender must
be treated as a unique self. Professional discretion, coupled with cycles of coercion and negotiation, is necessary in both law and social work.

The clear danger in granting judgmental discretion to professionals is abuse
of individual professional power, but the prevention of abuse through the re-
moval of judgment institutionalizes abuse and leaves the whole system open
to a charge of absurdity. The utopian answer to the possibility of abuse is to
deny that it will happen—"that never happens here." In a utopia guided by care

theory, members of the caring professions would simply be immune to abuses of power. In actual life, however, provision must be made to curb both error and abuse, and one answer to the problem is the establishment of review boards or informal counseling groups. Judicial decisions are routinely open to appeal, but the process could be made more efficient and more instructive. Small groups of professionals in every occupation might be organized to monitor one another's work, make suggestions for reconsideration, and mediate disputes with clients. In teaching, for example, a teacher's grading might well be reviewed by two or three other teachers who might also make suggestions for remediation. Students, too, should be able to request a review when they are dissatisfied with a grade. Review boards should be regularly constituted in all the caring professions. These boards should provide protection for clients and both support and education for those making judgments.[5] A strong system of review boards, immediately accessible in the arena of decision making, should, in addition to increasing fairness, reduce litigation and increase the general feeling that agencies and institutions are responsive.

We have not made use of review boards in education. Instead, distrusting the judgment of individual teachers, we have put greater emphasis on high-stakes testing in deciding whether students should be promoted, graduated, or awarded various credentials. This move has weakened the integrity of teaching, damaged student-teacher relationships, encouraged dishonesty, and opened the system to mockery when large-scale errors are uncovered.[6] It would be far better to rely on teacher judgment strongly backed by the evaluative review of a competent professional board.

The basic attitude, "I am here," should be encouraged by flexible guidelines and backed by peer support. In the following sections, I apply care theory and what is learned in ideal homes to a few important social problems.

RESPONDING TO EXPRESSED NEEDS

One important set of expressed needs centers on health and medical care. Plans for socialized or nationalized medicine are no longer confined to utopian tracts. There are working models all over the postindustrial world. Sooner or later the United States will follow. What stands in the way? Besides economic issues, two attitudes remain strong in the United States. First, there is a lasting dread of communism and everything it represents. People seem unable to sort out and adapt ideas according to their current worth. Instead they choose ideological positions and stay close to party-like lines. This is a problem for education writ large; we need to educate for both caring and critical thinking. Second, there is an attitude toward competition that, in moderation, makes us inventive and prosperous. In its extreme version, however—in the "We're number one!" version—it makes us obnoxious, paternalistic, and shortsighted. Many Americans fail to see that people in other parts of the world compete successfully without insisting on being first and that these other people find our incessant bragging unattractive. The "top of the heap" attitude also makes our generosity paternalistic instead of genuinely cooperative. And, because this attitude blocks deep critical thinking, many Americans believe that we are "number one" in areas where this is simply untrue. It isn't unusual to hear someone proclaim that we have the best medical system in the world, but this is untrue if effectiveness is measured by the widely accepted standards of, for example, infant mortality, life expectancy, and adolescent motherhood. Almost certainly, however, we have one of the world's most technologically sophisticated medical systems. If you have an exotic problem, this is the place to come, but if you are poor or troubled, you might get better everyday care in any of several other nations.

In part, our failure to provide universal medical coverage is an issue of caring. An ethic of care is needs based. Carers listen and respond as positively as resources and moral evaluation will allow. At present, the care we provide is almost always in the spirit of charity, not in the recognition of interdependence. Edward Bellamy, in his very popular utopian novel of 1888, had some interesting words on this. Dr. Leete, his speaker from the year 2000, patiently corrects his young guest from the nineteenth century. Leete insists that in the society of 2000, the "incapable class" are not considered objects of charity. When his guest protests that they are, after all, incapable of self-support, Leete answers this way:

> Who is capable of self-support? . . . There is no such thing in a civilized society as self-support. In a state of society so barbarous as not even to know family cooperation, each individual may possibly support himself, though even then for a part of his life only; but from the moment that men begin to live together, and constitute even the rudest of society, self-support becomes impossible.[7]

I agree with Bellamy on our interdependence, but I disagree that this mutual dependency is based on our *deciding* to live together. Our interdependence is part of the original condition and in no way a product of some social contract. We would not be "men" at all if we did not have one another to call upon. Culture and individual prosperity sometimes lead us to believe that we are independent, but the reality is obvious to anyone who thinks deeply on it. An acceptance of interdependence is learned in the best homes, and it can be used effectively in making social policy. The idea, entirely compatible with liberal economics, is to shift the balance of control to individuals where this is possible, but to recognize that all of us remain interdependent both economically and morally. We must logically reject the independent/dependent dichotomy.

Care of bodies, whole organisms, requires more thoughtful consideration in education, too. Debate often arises over a distinction between early childhood education and child care. But every form of child care provides encounters of some sort, and these can be educative or miseducative. To suppose that child care can be responsibly provided without considering education is a mistake. A different sort of mistake is made by those who argue that we must feed inner-city children in schools so that they can learn. The mistake here is in elevating cognitive outcomes over physical ones. We should feed hungry children because they are hungry,[8] because that is the need to which a caring society should respond. In the same vein, there are those who demand proof that certain early childhood programs "work," but they seem interested only in academic gains and threaten to cut off funding if such evidence is not forthcoming. A caring society wants for all its children what the best homes provide for their own.[9] This means that no child should be deprived of basic legitimate expectations and that every child should be given opportunities to satisfy legitimate contingent expectations. It does not mean that every child should study the same curriculum, meet one preestablished standard, or prepare for college. On the contrary, every socially acceptable talent and interest should be respected and encouraged.

In today's world, any discussion of a society's ethical obligation to respond to bodily needs must include abortion and euthanasia. These topics provide an especially useful illustration of the application of care to social problems. First, an ethic of care does not lay down fixed rules for resolving these social problems; it leaves matters open for responsible decision making, and "responsible" is interpreted in terms of exercising the capacity and competence to respond to needs. In making decisions about either abortion or euthanasia, we must consider needs throughout the web of care, but we must also carefully identify the greatest needs and the consequences that may follow from meeting them. People who care may differ not only on their practical decisions but even on the ultimate reasons they offer. For example, some may develop their view of care from a religious base, and God may appear in their reasons.[10] The ethic of care, as I understand it, does not involve a god at all but depends entirely on the basic relatedness of human life. God may or may not be a reality, but deity in any form need not be invoked in ethical life.

Why should a care ethicist allow abortion? Our answer is not given in terms of rights. We may believe that such a right should be granted under law, but we do not believe that any right "exists" before it is granted. Indeed, if care theory had guided social policy from the start, there would be no need to declare a right, because no laws would have been passed forbidding abortion.

Instead, we consider needs. The pregnant woman's needs are primary because it is she who must bear both the bodily burden and the burden to self. The decision should not be made lightly, and it should be well-informed; it should be made early—before the fetus has developed the capacity to respond with its own characteristic human needs. If review and counseling boards are in place, the recommendation that a decision be well-informed should not conflict with the general rule that it should also be made early. Any young woman who resists counseling—"I just want to get it over with!"—should be gently coerced to accept the counseling. The purpose is not to make her feel guilty about whatever decision she makes. On the contrary, the purpose is to avoid guilt by helping her make a decision she can accept as responsible.

But is there no one else in the web of care whose needs must be considered? Religious ethicists will likely identify the fetus as the one to bear the greatest burden. If abortion is chosen, the fetus will not live to become a self. There is no denying this, and we should not pussyfoot about, using euphemisms. But what is killed is not a self; there has been no encounter-with-affect. Considering the prolificness of nature—all the animal embryos that do not come to full life, the seeds that do not germinate, the seedlings that die, the eggs that are never fertilized—should fill us with awe, but there seems to be no ethical issue here. A woman who aborts a preresponsive fetus is eliminating a potential life, but, for that matter, a woman who lives a life of celibacy or of carefully controlled contraception is eliminating a host of potential lives.

Critics might enter an interesting objection to the view just stated. Since I have said that expressed needs may be revealed in either verbal or body language, how can I deny the needs of the fetus—those needs expressed in continuous biological growth? The answer to this comes directly from an analysis of caring relations. A caring relation exists if and only if the cared-for responds with recognition to the efforts of the carer. If the potential recipient of care is constitutionally incapable of making such a response, the obligation to care for disappears. This test applies not only to abortion but also to euthanasia, as we will see in a bit.

Critics may now press the case by asking whether our obligation to care is removed when the cared-for is unconscious or even merely asleep, and the answer is of course not. A sleeping person is not constitutionally incapable of responding; he or she only needs to be awakened. Similarly, an unconscious person is usually incapable of response for only a short period of time; he or she is not constitutionally incapable of responding. If a person *is* constitutionally incapable of responding, the ethic of care would permit his or her life to be ended.

Still another objection may be raised to my defense of abortion. True, the early fetus is incapable of a characteristically human response but, if it is allowed to live, it will develop that capacity. It, like the person temporarily unconscious, will—in time—become capable of the responses treasured in infants. This objection is not easily brushed aside and leaves us with differences that cannot be reconciled by simply asserting that a position for or against abortion should become the absolute rule. Care theory recognizes the fetus's growing capacity to respond and finds late-term abortions troubling. It also recognizes and respects those who hold a religious view that life (however defined) is sacred, and it would not press a woman or group to accept abortion. But in every individual case, when the question arises, it asks: What conscious beings are suffering? Who will bear the burden of the decision?

Besides the pregnant woman, there may be an interested man involved in the decision, and his needs, too, should be considered, but cases in which the man desperately wants the child and the woman does not are probably rare. Similarly, there may be potential grandparents whose interests should be considered by the woman in making a well-informed decision. Full consideration of these interests might change her decision, but they should not be allowed to dictate it. The job of medical and social agencies is to draw attention to these possibilities so that the woman's decision is really well-informed.

The complete dependency of the fetus on its mother-host underscores the relational nature of all human life and of ethical life in particular. If a woman wants this fetus as a child, if she cherishes it, there is already encounter of a sort, but it is one-way; it is the mother who has encounters, mostly in imagination and anticipation, and these encounters will influence the baby when it is born. If the woman does not want a child, the fetus has no status as a pre-self. Other individuals cannot say, "Well, we want it!" because to insist on its continued existence would override and ignore the expressed needs of the woman. People who make this claim do not want the unique individual that the fetus will become. They are not responding to an individual who can, in turn, receive their care but either to a principle or to a personal need. But in the latter case, it is clear that no woman has a responsibility to bear a child for another. When a fetus is viable, however, the picture changes. Now others can respond directly to the infant's needs, and this increases the uneasiness of care theorists with respect to late-term abortions.

The ethic of care leaves us unwilling to prescribe final rules of action. It instructs us to respond to any organism in pain by relieving the pain and to respond to a human self by considering its needs and meeting them if possible. It does not pronounce once and for all that abortion is right or that abortion is wrong. It *suffers with* as it judges. If, after the help required to make a well-informed decision, a young woman says, "I want to get rid of it!" a carer's response has to be, "I will help you." A carer would give the same response to one who decides to see the pregnancy through. It is part of what is meant when we say, "I am here."

Suppose, now, that an infant is born with enormous handicaps. Should we allow infanticide? I think an ethic of care can responsibly say yes, sometimes. Our reasons would be somewhat different from those of Peter Singer, who offers a utilitarian rationale for allowing parents to make this decision.[11] First, we would not argue on the basis of a calculation of the greater happiness that might be produced by the birth of a later, normal child. Our basic argument is that a society should not insist that one or two people (or a small group, a family) should bear longtime suffering in the name of a principle—the alleged sanctity of life. It is easy to mouth such principles, and it may be a matter of justifiable pride for medical technology to keep babies alive despite handicaps and deformities, but it is another matter entirely to hand over such an infant to its parents. If there is no possibility that an infant can develop the responses characteristic of normal human life, it would be a compassionate and caring move to kill the infant mercifully and allow the parents to get on with their lives.

Now, obviously, I am not saying that parents should be allowed to kill any newborn they don't want. I have already pled the case for a near-term fetus. As carers, we must respond to the expressed needs of the infant. But we are concerned with both current and future needs. The immediate needs of a normal infant are food, warmth, cuddling, and mild stimulation. Satisfying these needs contributes to the child's growth and to parental satisfaction through the infant's response. If the child cannot grow and, especially, if it is in pain, then the merciful move is to end its struggle for life. It is not only the infant who must be considered here. There are parents who may be sentenced to a lifetime of suffering, siblings who may suffer neglect, and a whole circle of intimates who may be affected.

Several recent news stories and responses have dramatized the plight of parents struggling to care for severely handicapped children. The help that is said to be available to parents in this situation often requires still more effort on their part. In addition to caring for their child, they are often expected to join "help" groups, attend meetings, and give help to other sufferers. Further, the suffering of parents is often increased as the children get older, because the children suffer more, and what little hope might once have flickered has now faded entirely. One letter writer, responding in sympathy to the story of parents who had left their child at a hospital, wrote: "I have traded my freedom to be the primary caretaker of my daughter. In the nine years since her birth, my husband and I have never been away alone together."[12]

There should, of course, be safeguards. Cases such as these illustrate the obvious value of professional review boards. A medical team, not just one physician, should supply the prognosis of hopelessness, and the parents—not the state—should make the decision. Parents who, for religious reasons, want the child to be kept alive should be respected. So, too, should those who can't face the prospect of caring for a badly handicapped child or who see no point in doing so.

There will be debate on which conditions are so hopeless that infanticide should be allowed. Here Singer and I differ again. I would not name either hemophilia or Down syndrome as hopeless conditions unless they are complicated by other conditions that would make the construction of a human self impossible or would visit predictably intolerable pain on the child. Indeed, I would be slow to name any one condition that should evoke a decision to end life, although there are some conditions that will spontaneously end life in a short time. Every case must be considered in its fullness and specificity, and that means considering the capacity and convictions of the parents. The test care theorists should use is this: if an infant can never become a self—will not be able to communicate or in any recognizable way respond to human care— then it is probably best for everyone if that life is not continued. The body, after all, is the means of meaningful encounter, of making a self. If meaningful human encounter is impossible, then mere life may be terminated, and the unfortunate parents of the infant should not be made to feel guilty.

It is worth noting here that, although both Singer's utilitarian view and my care perspective allow killing a severely handicapped infant, there are important differences. Following the utilitarian argument to its logical conclusion, parents should feel *obligated* to terminate the child's life in order to secure the best possible ratio of happiness over pain. No such conclusion follows from the care view. Because we are primarily concerned with the needs of those suffering, we can support parents in either decision.

The case of incompetent, permanently damaged adults is similar in the problems it presents. The case must, of course, be medically hopeless and the patient permanently unresponsive. Now the family must be the concern of carers. Are they ready to let go? Will the patient's death release them from great stress and suffering? The needs of those actually suffering are the needs that must be met, and either decision—for continued mere life or death— must be supported.

The case for voluntary euthanasia is somewhat easier, but again, it is a decision requiring a team effort. The primary decision maker is the patient; medical staff give professional information and advice; family, too, contribute to the debate.[13] A stable, well-informed decision to die, when death is inevitable from the sufferer's condition, should be respected. Any other response rejects the expressed need of the patient and addresses itself to a rule or principle.

All of these cases are complex and difficult, and—by discussing them in this abbreviated form—I do not mean to suggest that I have solved problems that involve great suffering, mental agonies, and real tragedy. I only intend to describe an approach—one that makes it possible for human beings working together to care for one another and reach responsible decisions.

DESERT AND MORAL INTERDEPENDENCE

The approach can be illustrated also in considering the problems of moral interdependence. Earlier, I discussed shared blame and the important distinction between bringing pain on ourselves and deserving it. Young mothers, for example, often suffer confusion over this distinction. Our society expects mothers to control their young children and, paradoxically, also expects them to do it without using corporal punishment. Sometimes, predictably, tired mothers slap or spank their unruly children and then feel guilty about it because they have violated the rule against physical punishment. Many of these tired mothers are, at least implicitly, followers of care theory and do not believe that children deserve pain for their unruly behavior; yet there is a sense in which children bring the pain on themselves, and mothers should be helped to understand this. The mother's guilt is appropriate (the strong should not strike the weak), but her healthy guilt should not be aggravated by shame. Restitution is best made through a conversational analysis of shared responsibility; both mother and child learn how to avoid violent reactions in the future. A responsible education system should teach parenting and contribute to the understanding of shared responsibility.

The case of battered women is very different. A husband or male partner is no longer expected to control his wife, and he has many alternatives (e.g., leaving the house to cool off) that a young mother does not have. Therefore, even a slap or yank is a clear abuse and, because it demonstrates that one party is dominant and the other subordinate, it inflicts great emotional pain. Anything beyond a slap—any act that leaves bruises or other physical damage—cannot be allowed or excused whether the victim is a child or adult.

Should social policy, then, endorse shared blame or responsibility when a male partner batters a woman (or, rarely, when a woman batters her male partner)? Is any such approach a case of blaming the victim? In a very interesting study of informal adjudication, Navajo peacemaking, Donna Coker debates these issues.[14] To be sure, there are risks in openly analyzing cases of battering. The introduction of discussion may convey the false impression that the batterer's acts may be justified. Appropriately conducted sessions must make it clear at the outset that violence is not condoned. There must be no insistence on forgiveness. But it should be possible for the battered woman, both families (if they can be involved), and close friends to analyze their contributions to the problem and how they might help to prevent future occurrences. A procedure that involves a significant number of participants is hard for people in an individualistic culture to entertain. Coker is careful to point out that we need to use caution in borrowing from other cultures because the ways of one may not fit the ways of another. Although this is true, we should not forgo opportunities to learn from one another. Whether it comes from Navajo culture, African culture,[15] or a middle class ethic of care, the idea of moral interdependence and shared blame is worth exploring.

One of the most obvious ways that women share responsibility for their own battering is by staying with their batterers. Maintaining a caring relation does not require maintaining a formal relationship. It does not require one to continue living with a violent partner. But that means that women must have alternatives—places where they and their children will be safe and where they can learn how to support themselves. This much is commonly accepted even when resources are inadequate to act on accepted knowledge. Resources must be increased.

More needs to be done. The relation must be transformed to one of nonviolence and, optimally, to one of care. Even if the relation remains empty—no encounters—for a considerable period of time, the aim should be for each party to understand his or her role in battering or allowing battering to continue. The only lasting protection a woman has is for her batterer to feel genuinely guilty and give up the practice of battering. It is *his* only hope for future, amicable relations. Further, her understanding of her own role should help the woman form new, healthier relations. For a real transformation to take place, members of the couple's inner circle will have to work with sympathetic, well-trained professionals. Again, we will have to overcome our fear and distaste for intervening in the "private" lives of others. We intervene not just in the liberal spirit to keep a man from harming a woman, but in the spirit of care to save the woman from herself and the man from himself.

The process I have outlined, despite its challenge to autonomy and individualism, has much in common with liberal philosophy. It emphasizes process rather than fixed goods. Its one exception—the insistence on caring relations as fundamentally good—makes all the difference; it allows us to intervene to prevent harms to self as well as harms to others. It does not pronounce abortion or euthanasia good or bad in any final or fixed sense; instead, it asks about their effect on caring relations. It favors policies that allow choices, but those choices are collaborative, and they are not anchored in rights. This is not to say that care ethicists do not ever use the language of rights. I have already acknowledged that we often do. But rights have a way of becoming entrenched and inflexible. As a result, debates on abortion and euthanasia often deteriorate to a conflict of rights. The modification made by an ethic of care directs us to consider needs. In doing so, we must face up to the built-in conflict between expressed needs and inferred needs. This both broadens and deepens the practical debate and, in the best cases, leads to mutual understanding and a sense that participants have done the best thing for all involved.

Because care theory is based on needs and responses, it is also experience based in the sense that we must listen to what others are going through in order to respond as carers. Susan Behuniak argues that jurisprudence should be transformed to allow the inclusion of particular persons' experience.[16] She argues for an integration of care and justice in the context of abortion and physician-assisted suicide cases. Although I agree that a caring response to the plight of particular persons in their particular experience should be possible in law, I suspect that the transformation alluded to by Behuniak would go far beyond an "integration" of care and justice. Justice as a body of doctrine and practical guidance would itself be radically transformed if it were acknowledged that it arises from the "caring about" that is firmly anchored in "caring for."

The best homes have almost no use for the concept of negative desert; they do not establish rigid rules and fixed penalties for their infraction, because every human encounter has unique features that must be taken into account. Expectations are both high and reasonable. Adults, in agreement, expect children to be present at dinner, to come home at agreed-upon hours, to do the work assigned to them, to treat family members and guests with civility, and to respond with care to needs that they are competent to meet. In turn, all family members know that expectations associated with basic needs for food, shelter, clothing, medical care, and protection will never be denied. All members know, too, that some legitimate nonbasic expectations are contingent and may be withheld if a member fails to satisfy the basic requirements of acceptability.

No adequate social policy can ignore the bodily health and safety of its citizens. No good home would allow one of its members to live in misery because "he deserves it." Instead, it finds ways to reward the behaviors and attitudes it espouses. By providing care, doing the work of attentive love, it helps to teach care. Can a society use a similar approach in caring for its citizens?

A society based on what is done in ideal homes will certainly reject social Darwinism. It could not argue that the poor deserve their poverty because they are naturally less fit or that infant mortality among some groups is nature's way of eliminating the weak. Instead, we are committed to meeting the needs of all human beings capable of expressing needs.

The United States lags behind many other countries in providing health care for all of its people. We are even more backward in our retention and defense of capital punishment, and many of us are willing to execute even juvenile offenders. The United States joins just five other countries in having executed young offenders in the last decade, and some legislators in this country are arguing to make the age of eligibility for the death penalty even lower.[17] The most persuasive argument for the death penalty is deterrence but, as Alex Kotlowitz points out, the very young are least likely to be deterred by the threat of the death penalty, and there is considerable evidence overall that the death penalty is not effective as a deterrent.[18]

If deterrence is not a good argument, how about retribution? Do some people deserve to die? I used to think so but, even then, I argued against capital punishment because I believed that the rest of us do not deserve to live in a society marked by state violence. Now I would argue that no one deserves to die. The cruelty and suffering that inevitably accompany the death penalty are avoidable only by abolishing it. No rule should be so fixed that we cannot respond to another's cry for help. It is incongruous to respond to someone who wants to live with "I am here" and "I am going to kill you."

George Orwell commented on "the unspeakable wrongness of cutting short a life when it is in full tide."[19] Any chance a criminal might have to redeem himself in the world of humanity is ended. Given the obviousness of this end to all possibilities, one wonders why so many American Christians defend capital punishment. This is a dilemma explored by William McFeely.[20] He notes that today's seemingly paradoxical association of Protestant Christianity with the defense of capital punishment is not a new phenomenon. Lynching and increased interest in religion also appeared together in the 1890s, and McFeely looks to the historian Donald Matthews for a possible reason. Matthews suggested that torture and death are central metaphors of the Christian religion and that, perhaps, only death can atone for perceived sins. But what of the other central metaphors in Christianity—those of love and forgiveness? The correlation remains baffling. One would suppose that Christians would insist on giving every person a chance to redeem himself—at least as far as this is possible—in this world. Perhaps it is the otherworldly focus that stands in the way. Some Christians welcome confession, conversion, and the promise of divine forgiveness and go right ahead with executions. They might argue that only God knows whether remorse and conversion are genuine, but the horror is that the perpetrator—hopeless and filled with terror that he dare not admit—may not know himself whether his remorse is genuine. Caring families understand that genuine remorse—even for minor infractions—is shown over time in restitution and better behavior.

Governments have tried to find more and more fastidious ways of killing condemned criminals. One recoils in horror at accounts of people burned at the stake, gutted, torn into fours, decapitated, pressed, crucified, and otherwise tortured to death. We are aesthetically displeased when electrocution causes nosebleeds or minor fires and disgusted at stories of people choking on cyanide fumes. We reject public executions. But Albert Camus argued persuasively that executions should be public.[21] People should see what their government has been allowed to do. Camus's own father permanently rejected his initial endorsement of capital punishment after witnessing an execution by guillotine. Disgusted that France together with England and Spain was the only nation in Europe outside the iron curtain to retain the death penalty (in 1957), Camus argued that it must be discussed—that "when silence or tricks of language contribute to maintaining an abuse that must be reformed or a suffering that can be relieved, then there is no other solution but to speak out and show the obscenity hidden under the verbal cloak."[22] He believed that witnessing an execution, hearing a head fall, would cause people to repudiate the death penalty.

Camus considered reforming capital punishment—that is, killing by lethal injection or even allowing the condemned person to do it himself in Socratic style. This, he said, would bring "a little decency" to a "sordid and obscene exhibition."[23] But he suggested this only as a compromise prompted by despair. The compromise, now activated in the United States, has apparently made it easier to kill, and because the end itself is supposedly painless, we can more easily ignore the months and years of psychological suffering that precede the final moment.

Both Camus and McFeely (and Orwell) argue that proximity to a condemned person and/or attendance at an execution should produce moral loathing of the death penalty. Reviewing McFeely's book, Russell Baker notes that, as a journalist, he was saved from observing an execution when a colleague took the duty for him. "He saw three men dropped through the trap and was sick for days."[24] This underscores the argument I made earlier—that, if some criminals do deserve to die, the rest of us do not deserve what Camus calls the "weight of filthy images."[25] The effects on the entire web of care must be considered.

Does anyone deserve to be deliberately killed? I would not argue, as Clarence Darrow did, that criminals bear no responsibility for their acts, that what people do is solely a result of conditioning and genetic accident.[26] However, I would argue that prior conditions, the encounters on which selves are built, have much to do with the acts that are performed at any time. It is not a matter of sole blame or no blame. It is a matter of holding largely responsible, partly responsible, barely responsible; further, responsibility is rightly shared among individuals and by communities and whole cultures. Thus, offenders have not earned the kind of rewards they might legitimately expect in a condition of acceptability, but a caring society cannot deprive them of legitimate expectations that are unconditional; foremost among these is the protection of life itself. Further, restitution should be our main aim. A murderer cannot restore the life of one he has murdered, but he can spend his own life doing something to preserve and enhance other lives.[27]

When we reject capital punishment, are we forgetting the victims? This is an accusation often leveled at those opposing executions. The death of the perpetrator is said to bring closure and a sense that justice has been done for the victim's survivors. "Now it is finished" is a common reaction. But does an execution finish anything but the life of the perpetrator? Some of those who must participate are sick for days, haunted for years. Some of those who should be deterred are actually attracted by the possibility of being killed by a society they hate.[28] And all of us should be disgusted by people demonstrating enthusiastically outside prisons where executions are taking place: "Now he's going to burn, now he's going to fry, now he's going to shake, now he's going to die."[29] What sort of self accumulates and exudes such hatred?

The basic approach of an ethic of care, learned in the best homes, is one of response to the needs of the cared-for. It is captured in the response, "I am here." An expressed need cannot always be met. Sometimes resources are lacking, and sometimes the need is only contingently legitimate. Sometimes, also, needs conflict. We cannot responsibly allow a murderer his freedom because he expresses a need for it, but we can allow his life to continue so that he can earn the satisfaction of some other needs. Expressed needs and inferred needs often clash. When we feel justified in using coercion to satisfy an inferred need, we must follow up with negotiation that makes the need more plausible and more likely to become an expressed need.

The caring approach implies shared responsibility. Behind every good or evil act, there is always a story. Some selves are clearly incapable of certain acts. How did they get that way? What encounters contributed to the present state? What interventions contributed to the good? Which to the bad? What did the carers and the cared-fors do to sustain caring relations? How can child-rearing practices enhance the possibility that caring relations will develop more widely?

INTERPRETING NEEDS AND INTEGRATING RESPONSES

Most needs require interpretation. Even expressed needs are sometimes misleading, and carers have to watch and listen attentively to identify the underlying need. Children, for example, may cover over their need to belong with a show of aloofness or indifference, their longing to succeed with a pretense that success does not matter to them (what shows, then, may be thought laziness), their need to be relieved of fear by avoiding any task that might induce the fear of failure. These hidden needs are still *expressed* needs in the sense that, when uncovered, they come from the one having them, not from an external source. Inferred needs, too, require regular analysis and reevaluation. It is a mistake to establish uniform needs by observing a gap between a person's condition and a prespecified norm that may or may not apply to that person's situation. It is the mistake educators make when they decide that all children should study exactly the same curriculum and meet the same standards.

Some basic needs are expressed biologically, and their consideration is often the starting point for social policy makers.[30] We know, for example, that people need food, water, shelter, and medical attention when their lives are in danger. But times change, and cultures differ on the identification of needs. In today's liberal democracies, needs might rightly be named "basic" that would not once have been so labeled and might still not be called basic in other cultures.

Today the need for a home should almost certainly be considered a basic need, but so far in the United States, social policy has not recognized that need as basic. Instead, it has concentrated on supplying enough food to prevent starvation, shelter to prevent freezing, and medical attention in emergencies. Many homeless people must find their three daily meals (if they get three) in three different places, and their shelter at night may be in yet another place.

But consider the functions of a home. (By "home" here I mean a relatively stable place of residence for a family—however that family is constituted. Ideal homes of course, provide much more than basic needs.) It not only supplies shelter, food, and protection, but it also provides a place to keep our belongings, an address where others may find us, and a center of communication. It is the place where all sorts of needs are identified and the process of meeting them is launched. Few of us today receive medical attention at home, but our search for such attention usually begins at home with a phone call. When we are in need of a job, we may begin our search at home with the daily newspaper, and we hope to receive an answer to our applications at home. To be homeless in today's society is a genuine catastrophe.

Barbara Ehrenreich, in her fascinating attempt to live for a year as our poorest wage earners do, comments on the near hopeless situation faced by many:

> I need a job and an apartment, but to get a job I need an address and a phone number and to get an apartment it helps to have evidence of stable employment. The only plan I can come up with is to do everything at once.[31]

If we add to the problems of obtaining a job, apartment, and phone those of child care, transportation, and suitable dress, the needs really are overwhelming.

Our society still has not recognized the need for a home as a *basic need*. We persist in separating and fragmenting the functions of a home and attending only to those already identified as basic. In many of our states, for example, even the educational systems—staffed by people who should know better—have employed directors for the education of homeless children, and there are new courses for teachers focused on the problems of teaching the homeless. It is disheartening—and disgraceful—that educating the homeless is rapidly becoming a field of specialization. The caring response, of course, is to regard a home as a basic need and to ensure that there are no homeless children.[32]

There are signs that social thinkers are beginning to recognize the urgency of addressing the whole web of needs. Academic, occupational, health, and social problems are interconnected, and we cannot solve one without attending to others.[33] Citing interviews with clinicians in Massachusetts, David Shipler writes, "Eating and learning, housing and health, a mother's early nurturing and a child's later brain function are connected."[34] "That's why," Shipler observes, "Dr. Barry Zuckerman hired attorneys to work with his staff at the Boston Medical Center's pediatrics department."[35] Lawyers and social workers can help families to get better housing, and better housing can prevent or relieve asthma, earaches, lead poisoning, accidents, and even unemployment. A home should be regarded as a basic need.

Schools might serve as social agencies to integrate a community's responses to needs. People who are homeless or in danger of becoming so do not have the time or resources to chase all over town looking for help in meeting each basic need. School campuses could house dental clinics, social workers, and legal aides to help in finding homes, reliable child care, nonusurious check-cashing centers, parenting classes, and some job preparation centers. Instead of taking this reasonable approach, however, policy makers today insist that schools can teach the poor and homeless effectively if they just try hard enough—thereby performing a bootstrap operation for a society unwilling to meet its social obligations. The emphasis on academic proficiency regardless of overwhelming, unmet needs is wrongheaded. Indeed, as Richard Rothstein has suggested, school test scores might be boosted appreciably by taking care of children's dental problems.[36] Just as caring homes serve as centers in which a family's needs are identified, interpreted, and met in an integral series of responses, so some public institution must serve this integrating function for the larger community. The school might be the ideal institution to do this.

NOTES

1. Nel Noddings, *Starting at Home: Caring and Social Policy* (Berkeley: University of California Press, 2002). Much of this chapter is adapted from that book.

2. See Martha Albertson Fineman, *The Autonomy Myth: A Theory of Dependency* (New York: New Press, 2004).

3. Criticisms of B. F. Skinner's *Walden Two* (New York: Macmillan, 1948) included comments such as "a slur upon a name, a corruption of an impulse," "alluring in a sinister way, and appalling, too"—both from the back cover of the paperback edition. Criticism of Edward Bellamy's *Looking Backward* (New York: New American Library, 1960) is discussed by Erich Fromm in his foreword to the volume.

4. Lisbeth B. Schorr, *Common Purpose: Strengthening Families and Neighborhoods to Rebuild America* (New York: Anchor Books, 1997), 6.

5. Richard A. Posner has made such a suggestion in *The Problems of Moral and Legal Theory* (Cambridge: Harvard University Press, 1999).

6. See Linda McNeil, *Contradictions of School Reform* (New York: Routledge, 2000).

7. Bellamy, *Looking Backward*, 98

8. See the symposium on Kozol's *Savage Inequalities* in *Educational Theory* 43, no. 1 (1993): 1–70.

9. This is a paraphrase from a well-known comment by John Dewey in *The School and Society* (Chicago: University of Chicago Press, 1902), 3. It is often misunderstood, however, to mean that all children should have exactly the same education. Dewey clearly did not mean this. He believed that the best parents want for each child what that particular child needs.

10. Strictly speaking, these writers are not care ethicists because human needs and care are not fundamental for them. Their theory of care is God-based. See, for example, Morton T. Kelsey, *Caring: How Can We Love One Another?* (New York: Paulist Press, 1981). See also Donald P. McNeill, Douglas Morrison, and Henri J. M. Nouwen, *Compassion* (New York: Doubleday, 1983); William F. Lynch, *Images of Hope* (Notre Dame: University of Notre Dame Press, 1974).

11. See Peter Singer, *Practical Ethics* (Cambridge: Cambridge University Press, 1993); also Singer, *Rethinking Life and Death* (Melbourne: Text Publishing, 1994). For a sense of the pain and suffering of families, see also Renee R. Anspach, *Deciding Who Lives* (Berkeley: University of California Press, 1993); Helga Kuhse, *Caring: Nurses, Women, and Ethics* (Oxford: Blackwell, 1997); Robert M. Veatch, *Case Studies in Medical Ethics* (Cambridge: Harvard University Press, 1977).

12. The original story appeared in *Newsweek*, "A Family's Breakdown," 10 Jan. 2000. The quotation is from a letter by Elizabeth Levine Wandelmaier, *Newsweek*, 31 Jan. 2000, 15. For a study that documents the suffering of such families, see Ann Hallum, "The Impact on Parents in Caring for an Adult-Age Severely Disabled Child," Ph.D. dissertation, Stanford University, 1989.

13. For an excellent discussion of nurses' attitudes on meeting the expressed needs of sufferers, see Kuhse, *Caring*,

14. See Donna Coker, "Enhancing Autonomy for Battered Women: Lessons from Navajo Peacemaking," *UCLA Law Review* 47, no. 1 (1999): entire issue. Coker uses the word "autonomy" but makes it clear (10) that she is not using it in the classical liberal sense. Because the Navajo culture is a "partnership society," autonomy in that context is more nearly like "full partnership." This is compatible with care ethics.

15. For an interesting comparison of African morality and Carol Gilligan's approach to an ethic of care, see Sandra Harding, "The Curious Coincidence of Feminine and African Moralities," in *Women and Moral Theory*, ed. Eva Feder Kittay and Diana T. Meyers (Totowa, N.J.: Rowman and Littlefield, 1987), 296–315.

16. See Susan M. Behuniak, *A Caring Jurisprudence* (Lanham, Md.: Rowman and Littlefield, 1999).

17. See Alex Kotlowitz, "The Execution of Youth," *The New Yorker*, 17 Jan. 2000, 23–24.

18. On the inefficacy of capital punishment as a deterrent, see Albert Camus, "Reflections on the Guillotine," in his *Resistance, Rebellion, and Death* (New York: Alfred A. Knopf, 1969), 173–234; see also literature from Amnesty International. The best evidence for its lack of deterrence is that countries and states that have abandoned capital punishment do not record an increase in the number of murders.

19. George Orwell, *The Orwell Reader* (New York: Harcourt, Brace, 1956), 11.

20. See William McFeely, *Proximity to Death* (New York: Norton, 1999).

21. See Camus, "Reflections on the Guillotine."

22. Camus, "Reflections on the Guillotine," 177.

23. Camus, "Reflections on the Guillotine," 233.

24. Russell Baker, "Cruel and Unusual," *New York Review of Books*, 20 Jan. 2000, 13. On the effects of proximity, in particular getting to know the prisoner, see Helen Prejean, *Dead Man Walking* (New York: Vintage Books, 1996).

25. Camus, "Reflections on the Guillotine," 234.

26. See Kevin Tierney, *Darrow: A Biography* (New York: Thomas Y. Crowell, 1979).

27. Apparently, Nathan Leopold, one of the young murderers spared from the death penalty by the eloquence of Darrow, is evidence of such a possibility. He spent many of his prison years as a hospital assistant.

28. See the argument in James Gilligan, *Violence* (New York: G.P. Putnam's Sons, 1992).

29. Quoted in Baker, "Cruel and Unusual," 13.

30. For a discussion of basic needs and social policy, see David Braybrooke, *Meeting Needs* (Princeton: Princeton University Press, 1987); also Alison M. Jaggar, *Feminist Politics and Human Nature* (Totowa, N.J.: Rowman and Allanheld, 1983); Joan Tronto, *Moral Boundaries: A Political Argument for an Ethic of Care* (New York: Routledge, 1993).

31. Barbara Ehrenreich, *Nickel and Dimed* (New York: Metropolitan Books, 2001), 54.

32. See chapter 12 in Noddings, *Starting at Home*.

33. See J. P. Shonkoff and D. A. Phillips, eds., *From Neurons to Neighborhoods: The Science of Early Childhood Development* (Washington, D.C.: National Academy Press, 2000).

34. David K. Shipler, *The Working Poor: Invisible in America* (New York: Alfred A. Knopf, 2004), 219.

35. Shipler, *Working Poor*, 225.

36. See Richard Rothstein, *Out of Balance: Our Understanding of How Schools Affect Society and How Society Affects Our Schools* (Chicago: Spencer Foundation, 2002).

Chapter Three

Care and Order: State Reformation and the Feminization of Liberalism

Eloise A. Buker

THE LIBERAL STATE AND FEMALE CITIZENS: WHAT IS WRONG?

The ethic of care holds promise for the reformation of liberalism into a gender-inclusive theory that can support democratic institutions for both women and men. I will argue that the ethic of care can revitalize liberalism by feminizing it. While "feminizing" is often seen as a negative process, as found in the phrase, "the feminization of poverty," I am using the image here to suggest that "feminizing" is a laudatory step in developing a fuller and more robust, gender-inclusive understanding of public life. I will first argue that because of transformations within the modern state, it is now important that the state provide care to citizens in order to sustain social order. This care has been previously performed voluntarily by women, and the state was able to sustain order through the police and military. Second, I will interrogate some of the problems that feminists have suggested about the ethic of care as a base for public theorizing and the ways in which a public ethic of care may endanger female citizens. I will conclude by offering reflections on how the ethic of care can reformulate the liberal state by feminizing it and so can take account of not only how law creates order but also how care is now a necessary component to sustain that order.

Liberal political theory draws on the social contract to explain that citizens give up individual freedoms to the state in return for social order and security. Thus, the legitimacy for state power rests on the state's moral obligation to provide citizens with security. In this story, security means protection from deliberate harm from another person or group, so citizens expect that social order will be sustained through law and its enforcement in both domestic and international settings. This narrow definition of "security" does not make citizens secure but simply protects them from a particular type of danger. To experience a secure sustained life requires more than protection from such harms. The state acknowledges this and has expanded its protection to include other types of policing actions such as the regulation of food and drugs, environmental protections, and access to shelter. While this makes sense and does work, the liberal state still retains in its core, in its constitutional commitments, the more narrow definition of "security." Hence, citizens expect states to sustain a strong police and military protection but do not expect the state to offer them a secure, safe life with the basic necessities of food, shelter, water, and care. In fact, the U.S. Constitution does not obligate the state to provide for these types of needs, and so citizens do not have a right to food, water, health care, or shelter. Nevertheless, the state does make efforts to see that needy citizens get some of these basics.

So, while the liberal state takes on the duty to provide security through military and police protection, it does not guarantee that citizens will have enough to eat. Because these types of basic care—food, shelter, health care—have been provided by activities in the private sector (family, employers, religious groups, neighbors), the state has been able to avoid paying attention to them and so has helped citizens in so-called "crisis" situations. The current national story is that the welfare system takes care of crisis needs. An exception to this practice exists in Social Security and Medicare where the state does, through current legislation, assume some obligations for the care of the elderly and disabled. However, these funds are now often insufficient to sustain life, and some question whether the state should even continue such care. Thus, the liberal American state offers some care in times of need, but citizens should not look to the state for food, shelter, and health care. Put crudely, citizens expect the state to prevent people from killing them, but citizens are much more ambivalent about expecting the state to keep people alive. Jack cannot kill Jill, but if she dies of starvation, or from the lack of medical care, or as a result of homelessness, it is sad, but is it really not the obligation of the state to "intervene" in this case. I will argue that the current situation is now sufficiently different that the state needs to turn its attention to the problem of care in order to sustain social order and so fulfill the basic promise of liberalism, the delivery of security to citizens. It is no longer a matter of crisis "intervention" but a normal requirement for the state to maintain order.

It is true that this minimalist liberal state and its narrow definition of security has fostered a robust capitalism and rugged individualism, but it has also fostered indifference to others, to environmental problems, and to poverty. But such a narrow understanding of state responsibilities is consistent with the Enlightenment's emphasis on individual independence. The Enlightenment model argues that citizens know what is best for themselves and can provide for themselves, so the state should not "interfere." However, the liberal tradition has also had the premise that the state should provide for the general welfare of its citizens.

These two premises produce a tension between independence, leaving citizens alone to fend for themselves, and the practical need to take care of citizens unable to provide for themselves in order to sustain order. The tension is replayed throughout the twentieth and twenty-first centuries in the United States as a conflict between Republicans, who argue for reducing the welfare functions of the state in favor of investing state capital to support corporate growth, and Democrats, who argue for a more robust welfare state with reduction of capital investment in activities that favor corporate advantage. However, both Republicans and Democrats ascribe to the liberal political theory of the state, which itself offers a minimalist view of the state in comparison to other political theories such as socialism and fascism. The modern *liberal* state rests on the assumption that law will sustain social order and that, for the most part, families will take care of other types of everyday necessities of life.

In the past, the conflict between Republican and Democratic views about how involved the state should be in providing for citizens did create a workable tension for the American political system. Some citizens have been given care through such government programs as Medicare, Medicaid, welfare, and Social Security. While some individuals have not been given sufficient care, which has threatened and shortened their lives, there has been a level of care sufficient to sustain the political order. Middle class and even working class citizens have had a sense that the state sustains a basic minimum level of care for everyone. This is fast becoming no longer the case.

This minimalist liberal form of government has sustained the United States, so why is it now a problem? The answer lies in the transformation of the U.S. economy from agrarianism to industrialization to a service-based economy. In the agrarian and industrial periods women were able to work in both the paid economy and the unpaid sector as care providers in the home and in neighborhoods. The public/private distinction reinforced this gendered economy with "man" as the "breadwinner" and "woman" as the "homemaker," supplying care to her family, her extended family, and to her neighbors. With the rise of the service economy and the necessity of the two-paycheck family, women have entered the workforce in such large numbers that they can no longer be the stay-at-home caregivers for families and communities. The proportion of working women doubled in the latter half of the twentieth century. In 1950 about one-third (33.9 percent) of women were in the labor force, but by 2000 about three-fifths (60.2 percent) of women were in the paid labor force, and by the turn of the twenty-first century, 46.6 percent of the labor force has become female.[1] This changes the nature of work both at home and outside the home. Furthermore, the mobility of the U.S. workforce has changed communities so that extended family members and long-term neighbors no longer live close to each other and so cannot offer supplementary care in times of crisis.

Care functions are increasingly left undone or assumed at some level by professional service organizations. Without such care, communities are put at risk because the lack of these basic needs disrupts social order. One solution that has evolved is that women have taken lower-paying service jobs. In 2000 women earned seventy-six cents for every dollar that men earned. Women are now paid a minimum wage to give care to strangers. Previously they did this kind of work voluntarily for relatives and friends. Many women continue to do so and find themselves with a double or even triple burden. But in many ways women can no longer provide care on an unpaid basis because families need two incomes to survive and single women with and without children need to work to survive. In earlier times, poor white women and women of color provided care at low, or even no, wages. Because of the stressed economy and gender social awareness, citizens can now see how women are caught between the necessity of working to provide food for their families and giving other types of care to their children. Furthermore, day care facilities are costly and often offer an indifferent, less personalized quality of care. Even fictive kin are unavailable for neighborhood cooperative care. Working poor women have been caught between needing work to earn food for their children and their ability to care for them after school for some time, and African American women experienced this tension even before the turn of the twentieth century. The number of families caught in this tension has increased and now, middle class women are wondering how they can both provide a paycheck and care for their families. Long-term fears bleed into short-term fears when parents fear that a sick child may cause them to miss work and lose their job.

While the minimum wage has offered some temporary relief for families, it did not solve the problem. As the postmodern world has extended the lives of the elderly and created more complex lives for children, the need for care has risen, making the problem more severe. It is not only that today's women are the sandwich generation but also that the nation has become a sandwich society, torn between child care and education for the young and medical assistance and care for the elderly. Latchkey children are endangered. Middle-aged persons struggle to meet daily needs and worry that a health disaster will destroy them. The strained economy and shrinking care system have created a fearful citizenry. How did we get into this situation?

Feminist political theorists such as Carole Pateman, Zillah Eisenstein, Nancy Hartsock, Susan Moeller Okin, and Jean Bethke Elshtain have shown how the history of liberal theory demonstrates that male privilege has been an integral part of it from its beginning.[2] In response to that history, Eisenstein turns to a left socialist view of liberalism, Elshtain turns to a communitarian solution, and Okin turns to a restructuring of family responsibilities and paid work. Feminist political theorists have demonstrated that liberalism has failed to take account of one-half of humanity: women. If liberalism can be changed so as to take account of women's contributions to the social order, citizens may be able to continue to use liberal ideals to shape state activities. Other major political theories for guiding state activity, such as fascism, totalitarianism, and socialism, are not attractive alternatives for U.S. citizens, so it seems important to examine how liberalism might be reformed to enable the state to provide a minimal amount of care so that it can sustain order.

THE OLD SOLUTION: WHY IS LAW AND ORDER NO LONGER ENOUGH?

Contemporary American culture has relied on a liberal model of law, just punishment, and order, under the belief that law will produce order. This belief grows out of the theories of two of the architects of liberalism: Thomas Hobbes, who argues that the state must produce order even if it requires totalitarian means, and John Locke, who argues that order is best achieved through laws framed by the consent of the governed. This consent makes sense in the context of a social contract that gives over some aspects of individual sovereignty in exchange for state protection. In the nineteenth and early twentieth centuries, these guiding principles sustained modern democratic nations and allowed the welfare state to evolve.[3] America continued to develop even though the economy failed in the 1930s, and the nation held together despite the ugly aspects of racism and sexism that defied Constitutional amendments.

But by the mid-twentieth century it became apparent that democracy worked a lot better for some than for others; liberalism lost some of its shining glory. Civil rights leaders offered a richer dream of society, and religious leaders cautioned that social justice is vital for a democratic society. Their cries did not go unheard. These social movements took hold because their issues got at a central problem of liberalism, the problem of a minimalist liberal state that depends on nonstate activity to sustain it. Nevertheless, the state has given aid to poor families with children; Social Security has provided support for the elderly and disabled; and unemployment benefits have given resources to those who have lost their jobs. These care functions are now insufficient, and even the small amount of care that the state offers has been questioned. As it turns out, the state has provided just enough care to suggest that it could be a source to sustain the life of needy citizens. The benefits provided through these social welfare institutions demonstrated that the state could provide the basics for needy citizens. So citizens who find themselves and their neighbors without such basic life needs have become critical of government and of the state. If the state provides some care, why did it not provide enough to take care of the basic needs for all—or for at least the majority? The state's success at providing some care sharpened the critique when it became obvious that the state welfare system was not providing sufficient care for those in need.

This has made way for critical voices from the new left and other socialist positions. In the latter part of the twentieth century, the right also raised objections by offering a different critique of the liberal state with a set of alternative solutions. These concerns were taken up in presidential politics. President Ronald Reagan called for more social volunteers, and President George W. Bush created funding for religious-based community services. But the problems have persisted, and now the nation is faced with an endangered Social Security and Medicare system. The future of America has become increasingly insecure.

The social contract legitimized the state on the grounds that it offered citizen safety. But what happens when the state can no longer keep its citizens safe? Consumers have gained a measure of protection in the area of food and drugs, but they also continue to ingest unsafe food and drugs. Corporations deliver not only products but mass pollution as well. Terrorism exists in poor neighborhoods, and 9/11 underscored its presence at the international level. The economic order has become much more fragile and threatening. Security seems elusive. The state does not keep citizens secure; law has not produced order. The old "law and order" mantra rings less true.

It may be that American citizens have too much faith in social institutions and their ability to provide a secure, safe enclave for them. Robert Bellah explains how middle class citizens have attempted to create a sphere of safety in gated communities.[4] But the gates are not enough because the problem goes beyond safety in the home; it is a national problem. The early founders may have had a more vigorous understanding of human limitations, which came from their sense of a divine presence, a cosmos bigger than "U.S." Religions offer a narrative about human limits and so explain part of the problem. The secularization of a mobile America can no longer provide the nourishing communities that propped up the thin liberal model of the state's duties with social responsibilities for needy community members. Who can help those in need—the sick, elderly, children, poor families, the mentally ill, and citizens in crisis?

Citizens are becoming increasingly aware of this and are fearful about it. It may well be that the popularity of the television drama *Law and Order*, represents a desire on the part of citizens to reassert this old maxim in hopes that if they say it often enough, it will become true again. Murray Edelman has explained that the media offer citizens symbolic reassurance that things really do work.[5] Even this reassurance seems no longer to work. Social order seems to require some basic level of public care. Can that care be delivered in such a way as to avoid state-based paternalism, which is inconsistent with democratic values? How can citizens find ways for the state to offer care? Can the modern state sustain order or is the state itself a worn-out institution?

Michael Sandel argues that part of the problem comes about because liberalism has offered a thin understanding of citizens as persons. He suggests that replacing it with a more robust understanding of the citizen, which includes elements of care, would move citizens toward a systematic solution.[6] Feminists have seen this problem emerging for some time and so have been arguing that the public needs to provide care and that an ethic of care offers a theoretical framework for such a solution. The ethic of care draws from the everyday duties formerly ascribed to women (such as nurturing, feeding, providing emotional support, and producing services), to reformulate the state by infusing it with a new authority principle that expands the notion of security to include basic aspects of care.

ENGAGED CONCERN: WHAT DOES THE ETHIC OF CARE OFFER TO THE LIBERAL STATE?

The ethic of care, developed by feminists, challenges two basic assumptions of liberal theory. The first assumption is a challenge to the private/public split, which has placed women in the private sphere with a focus on care for others, and men in the public sphere with a focus on competition with others. The second assumption is a challenge to the source for moral authority that liberalism has located in the individual's consciousness. The ethic of care relocates a portion of this authority in the collective political community and argues for a moral imperative to provide care for those in need. This moral obligation extends to the state, to local communities, and to public institutions. In this way, the ethic of care offers a new principle for justifying state authority. This reformed principle draws on the left's understanding of the state as a body empowered to regulate the economy to distribute resources and on the right's vision of the state as an ethical community.

For this reformed liberalism to work, care will need to become a broad-based state concern with each citizen committed to seeing the state carry out this obligation. There are two reasons for states and citizens to do this. The first reason comes from the utilitarianism that underpins American self-interested politics. To be useful, the state must sustain order. The volunteer work that was once performed by women for families, neighborhoods, and communities can no longer be done by them. The economy now depends on women for 47 percent of its workforce.[7] If all women quit the paid labor force and focused only on caregiving in the home, the economy would come to a halt. But without some level of care for the sick, elderly, children, temporarily poor, and injured, cities and states cannot stabilize their communities. Ghettoes suggest possible futures for the members of the middle class, who can slip from relative prosperity into poverty with the high costs of health care and housing. While the suburbs continue to grow, poverty continues to follow families as they move out of the inner cities.

This problem has been evolving for some time as the mobilization of the citizenry has shifted care activities from extended families to public institutions — education, health care, elder care, emergency financial assistance, adult education. Moreover, security now depends on people watching out for their neighbors. Neighborhood watches try to reduce crimes, and the president has called on all citizens to scrutinize their environment to help reduce international terrorism. Citizens need to be mindful of both foreign terrorism and the problem of crime, the terrorism inflicted by citizens on one another. The two problems of alienated citizens who commit crimes and international terrorists can create a population that is afraid to fly because of international terrorism, afraid to drive because of carjackings, and afraid to walk down the street because of drive-by shootings. Without care, order may not be sustained and political chaos may follow.

The second reason that care needs to be built into the system comes from the ethical premise that legitimates the state's exercise of power. For the American democratic society this means that the community of citizens has a moral obligation to live together in such a way as to enable each person to pursue the American dream — "life, liberty, and the pursuit of happiness." If the lives of citizens are threatened by the lack of basic needs, not only can they be prevented from pursing their own goals, but they will also be unable to fulfill their duties toward the state or even their neighbors. Reducing life to a struggle for survival creates a desperate citizenry. States in such situations have difficulty sustaining democratic institutions because the normal obligations of law and order are sacrificed to obtain food, shelter, and other basic life necessities. The work of responsible active citizenship gives way to the work of mere survival.

DANGERS FOR FEMALE CITIZENS: HOW CAN THE ETHIC OF CARE BE A TRAP FOR WOMEN?

Creating an ethic of care for the liberal state is problematic. Four social practices can create a "care trap," which simply once again constructs care as women's work and keeps both women and care out of the public sphere.

The first practice develops out of popular cultural self-understandings of womanhood. Giving care is a satisfying and important activity. But it also involves a special kind of sacrifice, which at this point relegates the caregiver to secondary political status. Is this necessarily a part of care? Women have been willing to offer care and compassion as a part of their workday. The research on comparable worth illuminates how the care fields (often predominately female fields like nursing, day care, and elementary teaching) earn less than masculinized noncare work, which demands similar educational levels, skills, responsibilities, and risks.[8] There are good reasons to believe that women, including feminists, like giving care, but it might be too much to say that women are in love with the image of themselves as good people, who do things in a more caring way than men do. This image can easily become a "trap," and women are aware of this. The image of woman as "server" evokes images of servants and subordinates. Women's social contributions in terms of care have been treated as secondary or, even worse, have gone unnoticed. It is simply expected but not rewarded. Sometimes women's contributions have been privately acknowledged but publicly unappreciated. Taking care of people is a habit that needs to be developed and acknowledged by all citizens. It is not the exclusive duty of female citizens. The call for care needs to be an equal opportunity employment.

The second practice is that women rely on other women to assist them in the work of serving others. There is almost a silent agreement that emerges as a duty to take care of the men in the room, whether this is a business meeting, an academic conference, or a social organization. The women care for the men collectively, which cuts down on the work of any one woman but leaves in place the assumption that the care functions are "women's work." Marilyn Frye and other radical feminists address this issue by arguing that the only way of breaking this habit of care is for women to work only in all-female organizations to undo this patriarchal socialization.[9] Women, in caring collectively for others, satisfy not only their learned desire to serve but also their learned desire to work collaboratively. There is a certain amount of silent rectitude that comes with knowing that "we women" did something together, even if it does not result in promotions, additional pay, or professional credit.

The third practice that serves as a care trap for women is the replication of the private/public split within the informal structure of organizations so that women end up performing informal private functions and emotional labor while men are placed into policy-making positions. Organizations seldom recognize or reward emotional labor. Secretaries and administrative assistants often function as caregivers in a semiformal way, but more care is needed than they can give. So when women in other professional positions perform such tasks, this not only detracts from the performance of their formalized duties but can also lower their status by reducing their image to functional "assistants"—secretary types rather than potential corporate leaders. One solution for women has been to refuse those duties that are the symbolic equivalent of serving the coffee. But if a woman refuses to perform such emotional duties, she may be punished and designated an "immoral, selfish person" by her peers. The gendered corporate structure mythologizes the female as an employee who is supposed to provide emotional comfort to male workers, whether it is in the job description or not. While all employees perform informal tasks as a part of their work, the gendered division of emotional labor endangers women's opportunities to create a profile of a successful professional. Women prove themselves by serving; men prove themselves by asking to be served. The double bind is that to perform their jobs, women may need to refuse the image of the "emotional assistant" while actually assisting those below and above them. While the formal structure attempts to create gender equity based on employment responsibilities and expertise, the informal structure creates a gendered hierarchy with the expectation that women will serve men.

The fourth mechanism that sustains the "care trap" is liberalism's narrow or minimalist view of community. Charles Taylor and Michael Sandel have shown how liberalism draws on a very thin version of the self and a minimalist view of law and order to structure the state.[10] The thin political view of an autonomous individual depends on a silent view of persons as connected to others. The work of connecting persons with each other and supplying their needs is performed by women in ways that escape recognition. Even though care is a requirement for human existence, the popular saying "take care of yourself" suggests how much care is needed and how hard each citizen must work to gain needed care. Robert Putnam points out the lack of community spirit in contemporary America. He explains that the fact that people no longer bowl in leagues but go alone or with families is one clear illustration of the changes in the last fifty years.[11] But bowlers still depend on bowling alleys. The difference is that these exchanges of goods and services can be done in a bureaucratic mechanical way, rather than a social communal way. Citizens pay and then play, but they do not do that with each other. If they cannot pay, they cannot play. It is an exchange rather than a human interaction. But how could the bowler generate community at the alley? The old way was bowling leagues. Is there a new way? Making this type of isolation visible is important, but it permits an examination of the informal work women have done in the past to sustain communities.

This community-building work has gone unrecognized because the original understanding of the state was that of a bond based on male-to-male relationships in which the social contract was between males who "represented" families in the public realm. Carole Pateman explains that the liberal social contract itself rests on a prior contract in which women agree to serve men when they marry. The democratic state was created on the premise of an undemocratic family in which the man/husband assumed so much authority for the family that the woman/wife could not even appear in court, sue for divorce, be sued, vote, retain ownership of her own property or wages, or seek custody of her children. Pateman refers to this marital state as the sexual contract.[12] This means that in the social contract that founded the state, women are invisible because they are situated in a prior family sexual contract that subordinates them to their husbands. This contract suggests that all real citizens are autonomous, free, and equal. Therefore, women are not full citizens if they are dependent. This helps to explain why women in liberal states like the United States had a hard time obtaining the right to vote and gaining access to politics. In terms of the "care trap," liberalism continues to privilege the citizenship of men by arguing for autonomy as the basis for participatory citizenship. When women are considered as those who serve, as servants, they cannot also be considered as those who rule. The activity of care denigrates all women because it undermines their autonomy as citizens by reducing them to servants. Pateman asks citizens to consider how to reframe policies publicly so that care is not relegated to the private realm and the sphere of women. If care is restricted to the private realm, those who give care will be subordinated, and their participation in public policy that regulates care will be limited. This further reduces the ability of the public sphere to develop an ethic of care.

A CONCERNED LIBERALISM: HOW DO FEMINISTS CONSTRUCT A STATE-BASED ETHIC OF CARE?

Carol Gilligan, in *In a Different Voice*, demonstrates that women tend to make moral decisions based on issues related to persons rather than simply in terms of principles, while men tend to make moral decisions by applying abstract principles to situations.[13] The modern American liberal state used the principle-based approach to structure the U.S. Constitution and the judicial system that sustains it. In contrast, Gilligan and her followers argue for an ethic of care that infuses the state with a new moral code that uses both principles (presently embedded in the legal system) and relationships (presently practiced within families). I am arguing that Gilligan's position is necessary for revitalizing public life. In this sense, political theorists have used her work to update liberalism so that it will serve contemporary situations and offer more accurate interpretations of public life.

In some respects, this update has been attempted by the twentieth-century welfare state in so far as it has moved some of the care duties from the private unpaid labor force to the public labor force. Foster care is an example of this sort of move. However, this does not reform the state at the level required to adopt an ethic of care. An ethic of care requires more than simply performing care tasks. *It requires that a community understand that its survival depends on caring for its citizens.* Presently citizens understand national military security in this way, but they do not yet understand care in this way. It requires understanding care as a foundational component of the modern state.

Communitarians like Jean Bethke Elshtain want to accomplish this transformation of the state by building communities based on care.[14] Ethicists like Nel Noddings are drawn to the care model which also builds politics on the values of care, a view advocated by many religious traditions.[15] Gilligan's model is consistent with liberal views that key gender differences are cultural and not biological, and her model offers a way to reform families and the state to socialize both women and men into both relational- and principle-based ways of thinking.[16] In this regard, her work supports the liberal ideology that everyone is "just" a person and difference does not need to be given any special attention except as a social construct. This premise appears to simplify public life and public policies, but it does so at the cost of justice.

Furthermore, Gilligan's explanation is consistent with the everyday practices of American culture. Women are the nurturing, soft "caregivers"; men are the tough "breadwinners." The terms are telling. Care is a "free" extra gift; bread must be "won" because the basic needs of food will not be met by the state. Gilligan's explanation fits neatly into the current gender ideology. But for someone who is continually hungry, the breadwinner metaphor is cruel. The saying goes, "Just treat everyone the same, and all will be fine." When the hungry are treated similarly to the well-fed, things are not fine. When people are sick and will die without care, care is no longer one of life's little extras.

Gilligan's arguments and Nancy Chodorow's work on childhood development suggest that the state would do better if citizens were socialized into both principle-based and relational-based moral reasoning.[17] This socialization would require that children in their early years be nurtured equally by both women and men. While that sounds like a small move, it invites the radical restructuring of families, child care centers, and elementary schools so that men spend as much time nurturing children as women do. Drawing on both this understanding of childhood development and women's need to participate in public life, Susan Okin argues that families need to be structured so that at an early age, children witness equality between adults rather than domination.[18] By restructuring its relationship to care, the state can evolve into a more ethical system that does deliver both justice and care.

Even so, for some feminists, the ethic of care comes dangerously close to being a new version of the years-old status quo for women—women's primary work is in household type tasks while men do the real work of governance by constructing social institutions that embody the primary features that create and sustain the system. In brief, women create and nurture individuals (children), and men create and nurture social systems. The large number of women in service-type employment, nursing, elementary school teaching, office staffing, and counseling reify this pattern because even employed women deliver care. It is "women's work."

Feminist scholars like Catherine MacKinnon and Judith Baer argue that the care model is dangerous because it allocates care to women and so burdens women without giving them the authority that would generate policies that could support care.[19] Women become those who prepare food for the hungry, and men are the ones who set economic and food policies that regulate the number of hungry people. Put more bluntly, men make the dirt; women clean up the mess, one mess at a time. As Zillah Eisenstein, Nancy Hartsock, and Jean Elshtain have pointed out, this policy depends on a private/public split and a long tradition of representing women as private persons, such as moms, and men as public persons, such as presidents.[20] Martha Minow, drawing on Seyla Benhabib, argues that one way out of the problem of privatization is to develop a public model of decision making that is based on the "moral feelings of solidarity, friendship, love and care" for particular persons, rather than on abstract or generalized others.[21] The problem is how to do this in such a way that the obligation to deliver care is not limited to one's own family, friends, and intimate associates.

Julie White draws on Gilligan's ethic of care to solve this problem. She corrects liberalism. White shows how Americans have relied on a set of principles that avoid care because they mistakenly assume that care will evoke state paternalism and enhance state power. She reframes common understandings of state "intervention" to suggest that the problem is not that the state "intervenes" in people's lives because that is what states do in regulating public life. But the problem is that some citizens are given a privileged position to "speak for others" and to determine the needs of the poor and citizens in crisis.[22] Intervention on behalf of benefits for corporate operations are commonplace in providing roads and other resources while intervention on behalf of the medical needs for poor children are less forthcoming. Liberalism is based on the assumption that each of us, poor and rich alike, can identify our own needs. To fully address this problem requires that citizens acknowledge that democracy depends on giving voice to all citizens to determine what the state should do. White, evoking the work of Kathleen Jones, Selma Sevenhuijsen, and Joan Tronto, develops an ethic of care that is not only compatible with deliberative democracy but also serves as a necessary complement to it in the reformation of liberalism.[23] By incorporating storytelling and testimonies along with other arguments more rooted in Enlightenment notions of reason, a wider variety of citizens can participate in political conversations. This lays the groundwork for integrating deliberative democracy and the ethic of care.[24]

White argues that a key component in these deliberations is not that care displaces principles of justice but that adding an ethic of care enables those employing principles of justice also to take account of the ways in which persons exist in different situations in terms of their power and autonomy. More importantly, infusing justice with an ethic of care enables citizens to see how all citizens are in some regard "dependent" on others; that is, that the state is composed of a network of "different relationships of *interdependence.*"[25] White is arguing that all citizens receive some types of care from the state. The problem is that some citizens are seen as receiving care while the care given to others such as corporations and wealthier citizens goes unnoticed.

Joan Tronto argues that "taking care of" is masculinized and ascribed to public life, while "caring about" has been a feminized activity, to be found in private life. Tronto demonstrates how taking care of things evokes power while receiving care evokes disenfranchisement.[26] Tronto politicizes care by showing how it has been used to subordinate women and to relieve the state of this key social responsibility.[27] Care-type duties fall to women, and this results in women's triple-duty work—working during the day for wages, performing emotional labor for fellow employees as an informal and unrecognized part of the work day, and caring for family members and neighbors during the evening hours. Raja Halwani makes a similar argument by situating care within virtue ethics and proposing that care is a virtue that makes a moral claim on citizens.[28] By politicizing care, Tronto argues for moving it from the private sector to the public, and once this conceptual move takes place, it is possible to interpret care as a political virtue that avoids paternalism. Tronto explains that a public ethic of care for the public arena contains five attributes: attentiveness, responsibility, competence, responsiveness, and integrity.[29]

White, Tronto, and Halwani show how the state can and does *take care of* both powerful and weak citizens by providing the infrastructure, institutional practices, policing regulations, and communication networks that support a robust economy and an effective state. However, the American myth is that some citizens receive care while others do not. Large rich corporations receive benefits from the state just as do poor working mothers. Both are dependent on the state to spend money to sustain them. But citizens have failed to notice the dependence of large and small corporations and focused attention only on the dependence of the single mom.

White, Tronto, and Sara Ruddick argue that citizens need to see how care is a political matter so that it can be addressed more directly in public deliberations. Drawing from a different body of theory but reaching a similar solution, Ruddick argues that the activity of mothering can be used to reconstruct politics in a way that promotes peace rather than war as a primary way of solving world conflicts.[30] The implication is that Carol Gilligan's argument about the ethic of care and the model of relational thinking that is linked with thinking about mothering is important for public political decisions. Care is part of who we are as humans and so cannot be eliminated from individual, state, or international ethical deliberations. Care is essential for social order and for human existence.

Gilligan recognizes the importance of locating the ethic of care in the public realm to develop a relational understanding of justice. She argues that by making care a public matter, citizens can avoid paternalism and the limits of rights talk, which has reduced justice to "equality, fairness, reciprocity—or in terms of contractual obligation, neither of which had much bearing on many women's situation."[31] Gilligan politicizes the ethic of care by arguing, "In developing a different voice as a key to a new psychology and politics, I found that human voices and also relationships become more resonant and more vibrant."[32] This makes care a public matter for all citizens who receive benefits from the state in order to sustain their individual prosperity and their collective need for order. The problem rests not with Gilligan but with contemporary understandings of liberalism, which privatize care. The mistake of an unfeminized liberalism is that it assumes an autonomous citizen, when in fact all citizens are semiautonomous. The mistake is confounded by then assuming that some citizens receive care from the state and others do not.

A FEMINIZED LIBERALISM: HOW CAN THE STATE GIVE CITIZENS CARE AND ORDER?

But what sort of society would exist if persons did not perform care activities? As I have suggested, it is a society that does not work. Liberalism worked in the past because care functions were provided by women. There was a silent, unseen workforce of women who made liberalism a workable theory even though they were not included in its premises. Now this no longer works. Women cannot sustain the levels of care that they provided in the earlier histories of the states. Liberalism needs a new story that writes care into the social contract. Is that possible?

In this new story, social order requires both "law and order" and "care and order." Societies work to the degree that citizens find that social and political institutions provide the structure in which they can gain the basic elements of life, housing, clothing, food, education, art, health care, work, justice, and recognition. This is not a new principle. Native Americans have suggested this, religious leaders have suggested this, and even the early Greeks suggested this principle. Without basic life-sustaining care for all citizens, a society will not be able to sustain order. If only a few citizens can "gain" these basics, or if these basics are so badly distributed that some have a great deal more than others, societies can become dysfunctional and order can be lost. Modern complex societies require order, but the law is insufficient to sustain order. It is only when citizens voluntarily cooperate to live peacefully that order is sustained, and while a minimum amount of law helps this to happen, it happens only because citizens choose an orderly life. They choose it because they believe it will work.

As the social order has become more complex through citizens' mobility, citizens have come more and more to rely on laws and principles rather than personal relationships to create justice. As women's lives have become increasingly filled with the obligations of employment, the social sector has withered. PTAs and women's clubs find themselves devoid of members, and churches scurry around to find volunteers. Citizens, both women and men, are less involved in social relationships and more involved with each other through economic relationships. In this economically focused life, citizens appeal to principles and the law to settle disputes. It is not simply that America has a litigious society that creates the high cost of malpractice insurance for doctors; it is because America is a society that has come to rely on the law in ways that law cannot deliver. Order is increasingly fragile and the old bonds are dissolving. *The ethic of care does not arise from nostalgia for the old ways when service was there for more of us, but from yearning for a society that works.* It calls citizens forth to be engaged with others and so can infuse neutral bureaucratic practices with concern. Can care be provided by both genders?

A glimmer of hope might be found in the response to 9/11 when so many citizens were depicted as helping others without a view to profit. Of course, profit did appear as a motive for some, but there was real service as well by men and women. In times of crisis, American citizens have always told about how citizens rally and help each other and, in fact, they do. But it is ordinary times that really count in reframing social values in a gender-inclusive way. Radical feminists argue that women should withhold care activities until the social order can redistribute these types of duties. Psychoanalytic feminists argue that it is especially important that men as well as women be involved in early child care. Postmodern feminists argue that citizens need to tell new stories about the deconstruction of gender to open the way for cross-gendered activities that will liberate all genders. So, the story needs to be told of how men take care of babies and women make laws; how men cook at home and women are restaurant chefs; how men's images include crying and women's images include military action. Some of these new stories already are circulating.

Can the social contract be reformed to include a commitment to care for and sustain the lives of citizens? Can citizens agree to care for each other as a part of their agreement to participate in the state? Is a care contract already in place and only needs to be given more press? Can nations socialize their citizens into the ethic of care, generating work that depends on both women and men to deliver care?

Building on the tradition of liberalism, Theda Skocpol calls on an understanding of universal citizenship to develop policies designed to enable citizens to help themselves and at the same time help each other. She infuses an element of care into the national agenda. Her progressive policies argue for a "universal health care system, employment training and retraining open to American workers at all levels of the employment structure; and policies to support the incomes of single parents and low income workers."[33] Her vision advocates a national care policy that builds on the Social Security system to create other institutional practices that can deliver care to a broad-based group of citizens. Although she does not draw on feminist scholars who employ the ethic of care, Skocpol's policy conclusions have a kinship with them. She offers a set of policies designed to create a "family-friendly America."[34] Skocpol demonstrates how a historical review of American public policy can be used to develop a more robust state that is able to address the needs of children, middle class parents, those in need of health care, the partially employed, child care for employed parents, and the elderly (grandparents).[35] She explains that the minimum wage has not worked to provide the resources needed by families, and she argues for a thirty-five-hour work week that would then support both women and men offering some family care functions themselves. She refers to this plan as a "moral vision"[36] and thus infuses her reading of liberalism with an ethical stance.

Skocpol does not elicit feminist discourses and does not directly advocate for women, but her argument supports such advocacy because of the way she focuses on families. Her rhetoric fits more neatly into traditional liberal discourse because she makes no special case for women. She simply moves some of the functions of the family, formerly performed by women, into the public arena. Since her rhetoric does focus on the family and not on women, it may have broader appeal to both the left and the right. Nevertheless, her policies build on an ethic of care rooted in moral decision making similar to that articulated by Carol Gilligan, in which political moral decision making incorporates considerations of relationships among citizens and between citizens and the state rather than merely abstract principles of law and regulation.

It is only by reforming policies and political practices as well as the institutions they support that an ethic of care can become a political ethic that motivates the actions of citizens. Rather than frightening citizens into obedience, the state would entice them into obedience by creating the appropriate funding to make this possible. The threat of external enemies motivates the allocation of financial resources to the military, but the threat of internal unrest needs to be more fully understood to motivate citizens to fund care. Care that has been delivered silently by women whose work is unseen and undocumented by even the gross national product can no longer be depended on to secure the commonwealth.

The image of the *welfare state* helps to redefine the state's responsibilities. However, as long as care is symbolically linked with the family or the private sector or even with private organizations, it may well be continued to be considered a "feminine" activity. Care cannot be simply left to volunteers and yet its professionalization cannot be sustained without financial resources. To do this requires that care become part of the political value system in the same way that military defense has come to be a financial priority in the United States.

To realize a care ethic requires a new way of thinking about the state. Such a change requires letting go of the familiar law, order, and punishment model to catch hold of a new idea that links care with order. It may be only when the social order has further decayed that citizens will be ready to take this risk. But some are ready today. Perhaps those citizens who are less confident that "liberalism with care" will work can find a way to try it before the social order loses its center.

To make this work, citizens will consider care a part of the primary obligations of the state; it will be as important to provide care as it is to provide for national defense. While the caregivers might come from the private realm, the obligation for sustaining care and creating the necessary conditions for its delivery will be part of the state's obligation. To keep citizens safe, the state will provide care because care is an essential element for sustaining the order in a nation-state system. Care will enable all citizens to participate more fully in the democratic system, and citizens who receive care will not be considered in any way inferior. This system will aid citizens in recognizing how all citizens depend on the state for care and end the stigmatization of some citizens who receive care. Understanding ourselves as interdependent persons who are dependent on the government infrastructure and institutional practices is a first step toward a more realistic vision of the state. The care the state offers needs to become visible so that all citizens can more fully participate in shaping the forms of those interdependent relationships. American citizens now need to understand the connection between "law and order" and "care and order" to effectively sustain American public life.

NOTES

1. Cynthia B. Costello, Vanessay R. Wight and Anne F. Stone, eds., *The American Woman 2003–2004* (New York: Palgrave MacMillam, 2002), Table 4-1, 242, data from Bureau of Labor Statistics.

2. Zillah R. Eisenstein, *The Radical Future of Liberal Feminism* (New York: Longman, 1981); Jean Bethke Elshtain, *Public Man, Private Woman: Women in Social and Political Thought* (Princeton, N.J.: Princeton University Press, 1981); Nancy Hartsock, *Money, Sex, and Power: Toward a Feminist Historical Materialism* (Boston: Northeastern University Press, 1985); Susan Moeller Okin, *Justice, Gender and the Family* (New York: Basic Books, 1989); and Carole Pateman, *The Sexual Contract* (Stanford, Calif.: Stanford University Press, 1988).

3. Theda Skocpol, *Social Policy in the United States: Future Possibilities in Historical Perspective* (Princeton, N.J.: Princeton University Press, 1995).

4. Robert N. Bellah, et al., *Habits of the Heart: Individualism and Commitment in American Life* (Berkeley: University of California Press, 1985).

5. Murray J. Edelman, *Politics as Symbolic Action: Mass Arousal and Quiescence* (New York, Academic Press, 1971) and *The Symbolic Uses of Politics* (Urbana: University of Illinois Press, 1985).

6. Michael J. Sandel, *Democracy's Discontent: America in Search of a Public Philosophy* (Cambridge, Mass.: Belknap Press of Harvard University Press, 1996).

7. Costello, *The American Woman 2003–2004,* 242.

8. Rita Mae Kelley and Jane Bayes, eds., *Comparable Worth, Pay Equity, and Public Policy* (New York: Greenwood Press, 1988); and Sara M. Evans and Barbara J. Nelson, *Wage Justice: Comparable Worth and the Paradox of Technocratic Reform* (Chicago: University of Chicago Press, 1989).

9. Marilyn Frye, *Willful Virgin* (Freedom, Calif.: Crossing Press, 1992); and *The Politics of Reality: Essays in Feminist Theory* (Trumansburg, N.Y.: Crossing Press, 1983).

10. Michael J. Sandel and Charles Taylor, *Sources of the Self: The Making of the Modern Identity* (Cambridge, Mass.: Harvard University Press, 1989).

11. Robert D. Putnam, *Bowling Alone: The Collapse and Revival of American Community* (New York: Simon & Schuster, 2000).

12. Pateman.

13. Carol Gilligan, *In a Different Voice: Psychological Theory and Women's Development* (Cambridge, Mass.: Harvard University Press, 1982).

14. Jean Bethke Elshtain, *Power Trips and Other Journeys: Essays in Feminism as Civic Discourse* (Madison, Wis.: University of Wisconsin Press, 1990), and *Democracy on Trial* (New York: Basic Books, 1995).

15. Nel Noddings, *Caring: a Feminine Approach to Ethics and Moral Education* (Berkeley: University of California Press, 1984).

16. For a full explanation of this model see Carol Gilligan and Nancy Chodorow, *The Reproduction of Mothering: Psychoanalysis and the Sociology of Gender* (Berkeley: University of California Press, 1978).

17. Gilligan and Chodorow.

18. Okin.

19. Judith Baer, *Our Lives Before the Law: Constructing a Feminist Jurisprudence* (Princeton, N.J.: Princeton University Press, 1999); and Catherine A. MacKinnon, *Toward a Feminist Theory of the State* (Cambridge, Mass.: Harvard University Press, 1989).

20. Eisenstein; Hartsock; Elshtain.

21. Martha Minow, *Making All the Difference: Inclusion, Exclusion and American Law* (Ithaca, N.Y.: Cornell University Press, 1990), 209–11.

22. Julie Anne White, *Democracy, Justice and the Welfare State: Reconstructing Public Care* (University Park: Pennsylvania State University Press, 2000), 136.

23. White, 145–52.

24. White, 145–52.

25. White, 156.

26. Joan Tronto, *Moral Boundaries: A Political Argument for an Ethic of Care* (New York: Routledge, 1993), 117–23.

27. Tronto.

28. Raja Halwani, "Care Ethics and Virtue Ethics," *Hypatia* 18, no. 3 (Fall 2003): 168.

29. Tronto, 127–37.

30. Sara Ruddick, *Maternal Thinking: Toward a Politics of Peace* (Boston: Beacon Press, 1989).

31. Carol Gilligan, "Hearing the Difference: Theorizing Connection," *Hypatia*, 10, no.2 (Spring 1995): 121.

32. Gilligan, "Hearing the Difference," 121.

33. Skocpol, *Social Policy in the United States*, 311.

34. Theda Skocpol, *The Missing Middle: Working Families and the Future of American Social Policy* (New York: W. W. Norton & Company, 2000).

35. Skocpol, *The Missing Middle*, chapter 5, "Reaching for the Middle," 140–71.

36. Skocpol, *The Missing Middle*, 163.

Chapter Four

South African Social Welfare Policy: An Analysis through the Ethic of Care

Selma Sevenhuijsen, Vivienne Bozalek,
Amanda Gouws, and Marie Minnaar-Mcdonald

Since the fall of the apartheid system the South African government has embarked on the arduous task of designing new forms of social policy that can address problems of poverty, housing, health, violence, and welfare in a coordinated and inclusive manner.[1] This is an urgent matter since the South African welfare sector has since its inception been strongly racialized.[2] In 1937 the Department of Welfare was established with the goal of dealing with the problem of "poor whites." This department was established as a result of a study on white impoverishment funded by the Carnegie Corporation in New York. Poverty among other disenfranchised groups was largely ignored. In place of any ameliorative measures for addressing black poverty, a process of systematic dispossession of land from indigenous peoples was put in place with legislation such as the 1913 Land Act, which reserved 86 percent of land for white use and taxes, which forced the migration of workers to the mines. The Native Urban Areas Act of 1923 confined Africans to rural reserves. These reserves formed the basis for the homeland policy of the apartheid government. This policy designated ten small areas as homelands to Africans, who formed the majority of the population, resulting in widespread poverty and an inability of inhabitants to sustain subsistence farming.

In 1948, the apartheid government consolidated and institutionalized the Afrikaner nationalist ideology of separate development, which translated into practice, meant racial discrimination and inequality. This racial discrimination was affected by means of disparities in terms of training, practice, legislation, and provision of social welfare to various "racial groups" constructed by the apartheid regime—whites, Africans, Coloureds, and Indians. In the 1950s the Departments of Bantu Administration and Coloured Affairs and in 1961 the Department of Indian Affairs were established to deal with African, Coloured, and Indian welfare issues, respectively. The homeland policy was

designed to deal in an inferior manner with African welfare, with each homeland setting up its own department of welfare. In 1983 those who were constructed as Coloured and Indian under the apartheid regime were accommodated within a new constitutional dispensation, the Tricameral Parliament,
and permitted to manage their own welfare departments. Under the apartheid
government the state maintained and protected certain vulnerable groups of
people, particularly those who were constructed as "poor whites," at the expense of all others. Welfare was seen as a form of remediation for whites (and
more recently to a limited extent, Coloureds and Indians) of individual
pathologies or deficiencies such as child abuse, drug dependence, etc.

So the current process of renewing and restructuring social policy is a pervasive one. It entails not only setting up and supporting new measures, provisions, institutions, and projects but also a search for new normative frameworks: social and political value systems that can serve as a guideline for the
new policies. In the wake of the new South African constitution, accepted in
1996, arguments of equal rights, social justice, and social development have
been prominent in setting up new frameworks for social policy. Recently,
however, the ethic of care has also become a serious candidate as a guideline
for policy making. In January 2000 Zola Skweyiya, the minister of social development, launched a ten-point action program, aimed at addressing South
Africa's most pressing social problems. The first point is as follows:

> Restoration of the ethics of care and human development into all our programs.
> This requires the urgent rebuilding of family, community and social relations in
> order to promote social integration.[3]

From the text of this ten-point program it is by no means clear, however, what
the assumptions and the details of an ethic of care look like and how it could
be promoted as a framework for designing and implementing of social policy
in a South African context.

In this chapter we want to contribute to the discussion on what the ethic of
care could offer by analyzing the South African *White Paper for Social Welfare* (WPSW), a document that has since its publication in 1996 formed the
basis for several discussions on social policy making and that also forms the
basis of future policy and legislation in this field.[4] We use the feminist political ethic of care as a lens to trace the normative framework of this report and
to judge it in relation to its adequacy for dealing with issues of care and welfare.[5] We start from the assumption that policy texts display authoritative
ways of speaking about care, and that in doing so they assign meaning to sexual difference. Also, they contain a range of gendered assumptions, in the way
they represent social practices of care, or in the way they substantiate leading
values and assign them to certain practices.[6]

In the first section we shortly contextualize the WPSW, in order to trace its leading policy definitions and normative concepts in the second section. In the third section we subject the normative framework of the WPSW to a more in-depth evaluation, by looking through the joint lenses of gender and care. In the fourth section we discuss the question of what the ethic of care can contribute to solving some of the problems we have established in our analysis.

CONTEXTUALIZING THE *WHITE PAPER*

The writing of the WPSW coincided with a complex policy formulation process that was influenced by a unique combination of political/legal, socioeconomic, and international factors, and that resulted in three basic documents.

The first important policy document was, of course, the new Constitution, creating the space for the first nonracial, nonsexist government of South Africa. The equality clause in the Constitution allows for the redress of past disadvantage and includes seventeen grounds on which no discrimination may take place, five of which are very important from a gender perspective: sex, gender, sexual orientation, marital status, and pregnancy. Albertyn and Kentridge have argued that equality in the Constitution can be interpreted as embodying substantive equality.[7] Interpreting equality in the Constitution as substantive equality opens the way to take women's disadvantage into consideration during policy making. It could therefore be argued that the broad principles of equality and the redress of disadvantage on basis of race and gender as embodied in the equality clause should inform all policy making, including social welfare policy.

The second important document that had an impact upon the writing of the WPSW was *Reconstruction and Development Programme* (RDP), which was published in 1994.[8] The first drafts of this program had been relatively influenced by COSATU, the Congress of South African Trade Unions, and were aimed at strengthening of public ownership, at redistribution of wealth, and at state regulation of the economy.

The RDP proposed to develop five ways to combine growth with development: 1) meeting basic needs, 2) upgrading human resources, 3) strengthening the economy, 4) democratizing state and society, and 5) reorganizing the state and the public sector. The basic needs strategy was stated as resting on four pillars: 1) creating opportunities for all to develop their full potential, 2) boosting production and income through job creation, production, and efficiency, improving conditions of employment and opportunities for all to sustain themselves through productive activity, 3) improving living conditions through access to better social services (health care, education, etc.), and 4) establishing a social security system and other safety nets to protect poor, disabled, and elderly people and other vulnerable groups.

During the policy process African National Congress (ANC) economists began, however, to shift ground because of attempts to reconcile left-wing demands for redistribution with neoliberal demands for market-driven growth. Suggestions were made for a reduction of the public sector, the legal protection of property rights, and most important, an adaptation of the South African economy to the requirements of international competition, which involved the repayment of debts inherited from former apartheid governments. The RDP as a coherent document became undermined to the extent that Marais concludes that in essence, it has become a social containment program that acts as a quasi-welfare cushion, while purportedly self-adjusting market forces run their course.[9]

The tendency toward neoliberalism, started off in the RDP, was further strengthened by the third document that set the tone for the WPSW and subsequent policies, namely the *Report on Growth, Employment and Redistribution* (GEAR), adopted in 1996. It was accepted by the Mandela government on the initiative of Thabo Mbeki, then deputy president, despite considerable opposition within the ANC and its alliance partners (South African Communist Party and COSATU). GEAR noted a marked shift from promoting "growth with equity" to being "pro-growth." This shift to GEAR confirmed the RDP's malleability as well as its compatibility with a development path influenced by the needs of capital.[10]

We will now proceed with an analysis of the actual text of WPSW to show how these different approaches feed into the normative framework of this report.

THE WPSW: TRACING THE NORMATIVE FRAMEWORK(S)

Problems and Solutions

When trying to trace a normative framework of a specific policy paper it is important to first look at the definition of the policy problem that is adopted by the report: usually these definitions are by no means value neutral but contain several normative assumptions that feed into their overall text.[11] In the opening paragraphs of the WPSW the declining economic growth and national income and the increasing poverty over the last few decades are constructed as the main problems for social welfare. Declining gross domestic product, decreasing per capita income, declining job opportunities, and increasing inability to meet basic needs and increasing poverty levels, resulting in extreme inequalities between rich and poor, urban and rural, and men and women, are all raised as issues that the new social policies will have to deal with. It would therefore appear that the welfare system is in fact under pressure from two sides. On the one hand more people are (potentially) dependent on welfare for income maintenance and social support, while on the other hand the system as a whole lacks financial resources to meet these needs. This is probably one of the main reasons that the WPSW adopts, following the RDP, the notion of developmental social welfare as the overarching guideline for solutions.[12] It is in fact one of the first South African government papers that elaborate the principles of the RDP for a specific field. In accordance with the notion of developmental social welfare the most prominent solution for poverty is sought in leading as many persons as possible to the organized labor market and to other forms of income generation, so that the degree of economic self-reliance can be enhanced. Or to quote the vision and mission statement of the WPSW:

> Vision: a welfare system which facilitates the development of human capacity and self-reliance within a caring and enabling socio-economic environment. Mission: to serve and build a self-reliant nation in partnership with all stakeholders through an integrated welfare system which maximizes its existing potential, and which is equitable, sustainable, accessible, people-centred and developmental.[13]

The WPSW further emphasizes the need for an integrated and intersectoral approach. It substantiates this need with reference to the lack of literacy, education, and access to services like health care, housing, and basic services like water and nutrition. These have in the recent past deprived many people of their dignity and the ability to look after themselves. According to the developmental social welfare approach the future social welfare system is conceptualized as a two-tier system. It should distinguish between, on the one hand, a system of cash transfers, social relief, and developmental services that aim at protection during times of unemployment, ill-health, maternity, childrearing, widowhood, disability, and old age, so that "households can adequately care for their members," and, on the other hand, a system based on the human and social rights of vulnerable groups of people with special needs, who "cannot participate." In this way social welfare would not only contribute to social development but also to social integration, which has been considerably strained by "social problems caused by the policies of the past."

The WPSW also claims that the proposed system would accord with a wide array of sociopolitical values, ranging from the securing of basic welfare rights, equity, nondiscrimination (in terms of tolerance, mutual respect, diversity, and inclusion), democracy (in terms of consultation and participation) and respect for constitutional human rights and fundamental freedoms, to "people centred policies," investment in human capital, sustainability, transparency, accountability, accessibility, appropriateness, and, last but not least, Ubuntu, the African concept of caring for each other's well-being.

When examining the WPSW as a whole we may conclude that there are different normative vocabularies at play that do not always fit easily together. The overarching framework can certainly be characterized as neoliberal: this is shown in the emphasis on (economic) self-reliance, the development of human capital, and the respect for human rights. The neoliberal vocabulary is joined, however, by more social- and democratic-oriented values of needs, equity, and basic welfare rights. But there is also an outspoken communitarian influence at play, stressing the family in the community (i.e., women) as primary locations of care, and that is potentially reinforced by invoking the principle of Ubuntu.

Looking through the Lens of Gender and Care

At the most general level, care figures in the WPSW as an element of what is perceived as a good society. It is mentioned in the preamble of the report, where it is stated that it is the goal of developmental social welfare to create a "humane, peaceful, just and caring society." It is also mentioned in the vision statement, where it argues for a "caring and enabling socio-economic environment." In the elaboration of this societal model the provision of care is, however, conspicuously absent, while self-reliance, the meeting of basic needs, and the upholding of welfare rights are mentioned as its central elements. By looking, successively, at how care is conceptualized as social, moral, and political practice, we can come to a better understanding of the question of if and how the WPSW actually substantiates its claim of developing a "caring society."

Care as a social practice, the practice of caring work, is mentioned at several places in the report. Social relief programs are promoted with the argument that they enable impoverished (mostly previously disadvantaged black) households to provide adequate care for their members, especially children and "those who are vulnerable." It is also acknowledged that caring obligations themselves often make individuals vulnerable to hardship, or, to quote the report:

> Urban and rural poverty has affected the capacity of families to survive and meet the needs of their members. Families caring for members who are elderly, chronically ill, disabled, or who have special needs and problems, are often faced with additional caregiving roles. This in turn could lead to financial vulnerability and increased psychological stress.[14]

The WPSW is indeed informed by a familialist understanding of care. Care is first defined as caregiving, then is relegated to a separate, private sphere of "households" and "families." This is more explicitly so in the sections on the family. It is, for example, stated that "the family is the basic unit of society" and that it will be strengthened and promoted through family-oriented policies and programs.[15] It is striking in this respect that family life is described in gender-neutral functionalist and moral terms. This is, for instance, the case when the family is praised for guaranteeing survival, development, protection, and participation for children, for creating a sense of belonging, for imparting values and life skills, for creating security, for providing spiritual foundations, and for instilling notions of discipline.[16] These functions are then assembled under the denominator of "parenting and social support roles," without referring to the gendered divisions of labor and to the power constellations in which these roles are embedded, and without also referring to the hands-on work of care presupposed by these "functions," which is overwhelmingly performed by women. Women's work in the family is mentioned, however, in a later chapter on women, in the context of their caregiving roles in the community:

> Women's contribution to development has generally been invisible to social planners and policy makers and has been underreported in social development studies. In the main, women are the key providers of unacknowledged social care to the sick, the physically and mentally disabled, the young and the elderly. In addition to their roles in the family, women in communities contribute voluntary time to social and development programmes.[17]

In the guidelines for strategies of this chapter it is stated that community programs should take into account that women as caregivers have special needs in terms of employment opportunities and financial support. When reflecting on these statements, it is noticeable that they are rather more linked to a communitarian moral vocabulary than to norms of gender equity. Women, it is argued, should be supported in their caring roles, without the gender divisions in care being questioned in the light of gender justice or of promoting caregiving as an aspect of the quality of men's lives. On this issue, too, the report uses the language of partnership, by stating that "policies and programmes will promote the partnership between women and men in domestic, parental, family and reproductive health responsibilities." This can in fact imply anything, ranging from joint discussions to joint parental rights to the sharing of actual caring responsibilities.

Finally, care as a social practice is mentioned in the chapter on aging. Under the argument that the white community has too much emphasized institutional and government responsibility for the elderly, the report argues here for a shift away from the notion of "care for the aged" toward a policy perspective that regards aging as natural phase of life, but "without denying the special needs of older persons." Older people should be enabled to live active, healthy, and independent lives as long as possible, but with the family as the core of their social support system. Again, we can see here the dominance of familialist notions of care, while self-reliance is also positioned as the opposite of being dependent on social caring arrangements.

Apart from care as a social practice the WPSW also constructs care as a moral practice. It does so not only by defining the family as the primary locus for imparting values and instilling discipline, but also—and more openly—by referring to Ubuntu as a principle for social welfare policy. To quote the explanation the text gives of this principle:

> The principle of caring for each other's well-being will be promoted, and a spirit of mutual support fostered. Each individual's humanity is ideally expressed through his or her relationship with others and theirs in turn through a recognition of the individual's humanity. Ubuntu means that people are people through other people. It also acknowledges both the rights and the responsibilities of every citizen in promoting individual and societal well-being.[18]

It is striking, however, that Ubuntu is only featured as the last of the seventeen principles of the WPSW, while it is also without further thought inscribed in a rights framework. It is featured as an afterthought that is not in the mainstream of the vision and mission of the policy framework throughout the document and thus also is not in its representations of care as a social and political practice.

This brings us to our third point: care as a political practice, the question of how public responsibilities for care are structured in the report. This is in fact the most underelaborated aspect of care in the WPSW. This shouldn't come as a surprise, given the centrality of the notions of self-reliance and independence as guidelines for policies for poverty and for the situation of elderly people. In fact these notions are constructed as opposites against a too-strong reliance on support by the state in terms of social services and institutionalized care. On the other hand, the state is attributed a positive role in several respects. It should support families in order to care well for its dependent members, and should provide for the "special needs" of vulnerable groups. But by not elaborating on these collective responsibilities in terms of care, both care and Ubuntu can indeed preserve their privatized overtone.

As a consequence, the question of who should perform these more public supporting roles is also rather unclear. While issues like providing for basic health care, maternity care, child rearing, and disability are constructed as the focus for social partnerships between government agencies and nongovernmental organizations, it remains quite vague in the end who should be responsible for the availability and quality of care on a social scale. By framing the role of the state primarily in terms of facilitation and coordination of partnerships, and of the executing of the Constitution and international conventions, a potentially more direct role in the setting up of care provisions is indeed denied.[19] In fact only in the absence of stakeholders the state is accorded a more proactive enabling and providing role. This is certainly at odds with, if not ignoring, the language of needs that is also present in the WPSW, where it, for example, states that social welfare should be responsive to the needs of people and where equity and accessibility of welfare for members of society who find themselves in need of care are stated as important political values.

CONTRADICTORY SUBJECT POSITIONS

The contradictions in the WPSW regarding gender and care may also be highlighted by summarizing the subject positions that the report attributes to specific social groups: In which social roles are they addressed, which identities and social problems are ascribed to them, and how are these fitted into specific normative vocabularies?

As noted above, women are addressed in a rather contradictory manner. In the chapter on social security it is stated that women should be "fully integrated into the economy," while in other chapters their role as caregivers in the family and the community is praised. It is clear that this last role gets more prominence in the WPSW, while their caring work is, without further elaboration of the complexities that go with it, deemed as necessary to uphold the special needs strategy of the report. In the absence of a more fully fledged collective responsibility for basic needs, women are the first resort for providing for the needs of dependent persons. The seriousness of this contradiction may become even more clear once we realize that it wouldn't be possible to "fully integrate women into the economy" without actively promoting a thorough change in the division of labor in families/households and without providing networks of subsidized child care and other public care facilities. But this wouldn't fit easily in the privatization strategy espoused by the WPSW.

The normative assumptions about women's positions as caregivers are in fact combined with the negative way in which children and youth are constructed in the report. It is stated that 75 percent of the South African youth of all races are marginalized or at risk to be marginalized, that is, are forced beyond or are on the periphery of the social and economic mainstream.[20] They are positioned as involved in substance abuse, engaged in or the victims of violence and abuse or in criminality, living on the streets, burdened by teenage pregnancy, and suffering from HIV/AIDS. Without trivializing these problems, it should be noted that these constructions serve the way in which families (i.e., women) are held responsible for educating youth in the right direction. These constructions support in fact a traditional sociological discourse of "functional versus dysfunctional families" that runs through the document as a whole. In this discourse children can only be perceived on the receiving end of care, which overlooks the fact that children actively participate in caring work. This is especially pertinent in the South African context where children in black families are often the main caregivers for their siblings and elderly relatives, when their mothers have to go out for their work or are "absentee" mothers, such as domestic workers who live at their places of work.[21]

Similar contradictions are visible in the way elderly people are addressed in the WPSW. While the elderly are constructed as a group that should be independent, their roles as both care receivers and caregivers are underexposed. Again, the family is in this respect perceived in a rather unilateral manner. While the family is positioned as the primary locus of care for elderly people, it is not mentioned that elderly persons are in many cases primary caregivers in family networks. The WSPW does not acknowledge that aging women, in their roles as parents, grandparents, and aunts have been and still are daily caregivers to children and destitute family members due to the migratory labor system created under apartheid and the family disintegration caused by this system, especially in the rural areas. Not only does this pertains to the daily work of care like preparing food, washing, cleaning, and supervising children, but in many cases entire families are also dependent on the pensions of their aged members for financial sustenance. The WPSW acknowledges this dependence in its statement that for black South African families each pensioner's income helped five other people in the household; it does not, however, elaborate on the consequences of these insights for its normative framework. For how would it be possible to relegate care for elderly people to the community, if in reality care is organized the other way around: elderly people as principal caregivers in communities?[22]

With regard to disabled people, who are at this moment overwhelmingly dependent on family care, the report takes a mixed strategy of, on the one hand, securing them more independence by promising a wide range of measures to make the labor market and public facilities open to their special needs, while, on the other hand, announcing that it will explore the possibilities of providing financial support for home caregivers in respect of people with disabilities. It is striking, however, that this intention is mentioned at the bottom of the list of strategies for social security for disabled people. It thus seems to figure as a measure of last resort, rather than being considered as a full-fledged alternative for the measures directed at securing independence and self-reliance for disabled people.

Compared to the relative space that is devoted to women and other "special groups" it is in fact rather astonishing how little is said about men as a social group. Apart from the passages where they are addressed as "stakeholders" in domestic and familial responsibilities, the WSPW is silent on the social problems caused by masculine behavior. Despite mentioning family violence against women and children, a problem that is indeed highly prevalent in South Africa, the report doesn't discuss how this might be caused by specific conceptions of masculinities. There is no thorough discussion of male negligence and neglect (refusal to pay child support, for example) and the abandonment of wives and children. Child abuse and neglect and street children are mentioned without mentioning the agents of abuse and neglect. This gender blindness also prevents an examination of the transferral of the HIV virus in a sub-Saharan context (where 70 percent of the world's AIDS cases reside). The constructions of male sexuality that justify many sexual partners and an unwillingness to practice safe sex are not addressed.

By this invisibility of men in the document, women are in fact targeted as the individuals who have the responsibility of solving large-scale social and political problems, while men remain relatively off the hook. But in spite of the fact that men are little mentioned as such, one can say that male normativity is clearly underlying the discourse of the WPSW. Behind the face of the independent, self-reliant citizen, who figures as the normative subject position in the document, one can perceive the male breadwinner who is supposed to perceive his caring duties in terms of financial maintenance of his family, so that "the family" can serve as an adequate locus for daily care for dependent individuals.

All in all it must be concluded—again—that the WSPW, in spite of its promise to support the notion of a caring society, draws heavily on a familialist model of social caregiving. Furthermore it would appear that, in spite of some gestures in the direction of gender equity and addressing women's needs, the WPSW is seriously biased in the direction of traditional gender divisions in familial responsibilities and daily caring practices. Because the family is positioned as the preferred unit for reintegrating society the report cannot address the contradictions with which women are currently faced in an adequate manner. The argument for women's economic independence may seem laudable from a feminist perspective, but it also must be said that the WPSW aims at integrating women into the model of self-reliance and independent citizenship in a one-sided manner, without investigating the moral and practical complexities of this model.

SOCIAL (IN)ADEQUACY OF THE WPSW'S FAMILIALIST APPROACH

The above analysis already shows in itself that the policy of indicating the family as the preferred social location for care is riddled with complexities. It not only adds to the burden of women by relegating the care for persons with "special needs" to them, but it is also inadequate since a wide range of social problems are inherent in the persistence of gendered asymmetrical power relations in family life.

But the familialist strategy is even more inadequate since it doesn't respond to the situation in which the majority of South African families find themselves. The report draws heavily on a (normative) construction of the family, which is implicitly constructed as the heterosexual nuclear family; other types of "family units" are referred to, but never conceptualized at any length. At this point it is striking that the WPSW does not elaborate on how gender, race, and class intersect to produce a wide variety of kinship patterns and caring practices and also huge social unbalances in the giving and receiving of care. A 1989 survey showed, for example, that 36.9 percent of urban black households were living in a nuclear arrangement, and 44.6 percent are to be regarded as extended households. Percentages for white households are 46.3 and 6.9, for "Coloured" 40.3 and 37.6, and for Indian households 55.1 and 30.5 respectively.[23]

But, it should also be realized that studies that are based on "household" as meaning "shared residence" have to be reviewed critically when assessing South African caring practices. This is because of the fluidity and movement between households due to the migrant labor system under apartheid and coping with the exigencies of everyday life. To examine discrete households would be problematic in that individuals are moving on a regular basis between rural and urban households, as many South African anthropologists have reported.[24] According to the report of the Lund Committee on Child and Family Support published in 1996, the majority of households living in poverty contain three and often four generations, particularly in rural areas.[25] This report also noted that in many female-headed households the middle generation is missing, with high numbers of children being born out of informal unions and being left with relatives. An estimated 20 percent of South African children are reported as not living with their parents. In 1991, 900,000 women, the majority of them African, were employed as domestic workers. It is the biggest source of employment for rural, uneducated black women. Because of long distances of travel between their homes and place of work many domestic workers stay on the property of the employer, which means that they are separated from their husbands, children, and other family members.[26]

As Le Roux points out, mothers do not always care for children in single-parent units.[27] The role of the extended family remains important. Extensive assistance patterns have developed due to detrimental socioeconomic circumstances. The extended family helps to provide assistance for working mothers but also sustains the link with the rural communities. It is not a single-parent family that develops but a female-headed household that is often multigenerational. Relationships of dependency on family members are developed by and are sustained by a system of migratory labor. Care in these circumstances is provided by extended family members to the children of the domestic worker, who on her part provides care for the children of her employer.

By positioning the family as the preferred locus of care and social integration on a political level, the WPSW reproduces powerful (gender-laden) dichotomies between "functional" and "dysfunctional" families, between self-sufficiency and dependency, and between rights and needs.[28] By seeing care as an "environment" for the development of self-reliance, the *White Paper* accepts the male model of the independent, self-reliant citizen of modern justice theories as the normal subject position, while caring is defined as outside the sphere of normal social participation. In spite of the fact that care is mentioned now and again, it remains subsumed under the normative paradigm of justice in the WPSW.

The practical consequences of this gendered dichotomy of care underscore the saying by Carol Gilligan that care construed within a justice framework becomes "the mercy that tempers justice."[29] Gender remains an add-on in the WPSW document, and a gender consciousness only shows itself where women can be conceptualized in its language of social groups with "special needs" or where they can be unproblematically constructed as "normal" participants in the labor market; in that respect the neoliberal economic perspective clearly dominates the discourse of the WPSW. If an integrated gender approach had informed the text of the document, normative concepts and unquestioned sociological statements would have been interrogated. Shifting relationships of care, responsibility, and security embedded in kinship systems, communities, and state structures would have been taken as the focus of analysis, instead of questionable notions of the family.[30] We shall now more explicitly turn to the literature on the ethic of care in order to answer the question of what it can contribute to changing the focus in the discourse on social welfare in this respect.

THE CONTRIBUTION OF THE ETHIC OF CARE

Definitions and Values

As Joan Tronto has stated, an ethic of care refers to a moral disposition and a set of moral sensibilities, issues, and practices that arise from taking seriously the fact that care is a central aspect of human existence.[31] Against this background Tronto and Fisher have proposed defining care as

> a species activity that includes everything that we do to maintain, continue and repair our "world" so that we can live in it as well as possible. That world includes our bodies, our selves and our environment, all of which we seek to interweave in a complex, life-sustaining web.[32]

In this approach care is viewed as a continuous social process, which is characterized by several phases or dimensions, each with a corresponding value or virtue. "Caring about" requires the recognition that care is necessary: there is a need that should be met. Caring about requires the moral quality of attentiveness to these needs. Once a need is recognized, the problem of who and how to meet that need also arises. "Caring for" is an assumption of the responsibility for the meeting of the need. "Taking care of" or caregiving is the actual practice and work of caring. The corresponding value consists of competence. The person or group who does the caregiving may or may not be the same people who did the "caring about" or the "caring for." Competence becomes a moral question since the ones who take responsibility have to see, together with the caregivers, whether or not that work is done well. The fourth phase, "care receiving," requires that care receivers respond to the care received. Those engaged in caring will have to use that response to determine whether or not the care has been completed, whether more or different types of care are necessary, and so forth. Therefore, this phase of care raises the moral question of responsiveness.

Using an approach of an ethic of care reminds us that the process of care should be seen in a holistic manner, and also from the perspectives of both caregivers and care receivers. Since care is understood as a process of human existence it concerns not only privatized relations but also social and political institutions and cultural values. The ethic of care departs from the individualistic image of human nature that underlies neoliberal policy programs, and instead starts from notions of relationality and interdependence: the basic idea that humans are engaged in each other's lives in a myriad of ways.

The Four Phases: Do They Make a Difference?

Let's look now in more detail at the four phases of care: What difference would it make if applied to the discussions as contained in the WPSW?

If the value of attentiveness is integrated into social policy frameworks, this would imply that policy makers would found their proposals more on "on the ground" knowledge of actual needs for care, instead of only relying on statistics about their scale. This would refine policy insights about what actually is the problem as experienced by those who are implied in these practices, as both givers and receivers of care in a broad sense. The discourse of the WPSW as it is now is, as we saw, in its basic assumptions informed by the work ethic: the normalizing idea that economic self-sufficiency is necessary in order to raise poor individuals to a state of nondependence.[33] An approach using the ethic of care requires being attentive to the actual needs of South African citizens. This approach would bring about a democratization of processes of need interpretation. This approach is initiated in the WPSW's argument for consultative processes and for community organizations as mediators toward social policy making on a macro level. The ethic of care would ground these links in the policy process on a more permanent basis. In a more general sense institutionalized attentiveness can counter imminent forms of objectifying and stereotyping, as for example when it is assumed that the poor are always black, or when "dysfunctional families," teenage mothers, or drug addicts are constructed as the target of normalizing policies.

What about the notion of responsibility, then? The dichotomy between dependence and independence as inscribed in the WPSW conceals a notion of ascribed responsibility. It implies that "responsible" citizens are self-sufficient and not dependent on welfare. An ethic of care would instead start from more "on the ground" knowledge of how responsibilities for caring are actually practiced, and from deliberations about how these can be supported and enhanced. Social regulations would be held up to democratic standards, as for example access and voice, sustainability, nondiscrimination, etc. Again this is relevant in the context of the proposed partnership model for social welfare. The idea of partnership runs the risk of shifting the ball around between welfare, education, housing, and labor departments and business organizations with the result that in the end nobody is responsible, or that there are considerable gaps in chains of care. The core questions of the ethic of care, like who exactly is responsible for fulfilling which needs under which circumstances and with what resources may counter institutionalized patterns of privileged irresponsibility.

The notion of competence is a logical corollary of this. It gives substance to an understanding of what people need to be able to perform care work in specific situations. It places a responsibility with decision makers to make resources available for care to proceed well ("as good as possible") in terms of time, money, and expertise. Many individuals in the welfare system are in fact in a double position. They are care receivers insofar as they are dependent on welfare for the sustenance of their lives. But they are even more so caregivers since they are the ones who are responsible for translating resources into the basic needs of food, clothing, shelter, safety, education, etc. In the eyes of the welfare system they may seem "incompetent" in earning their own living, but in their own accounts this may in fact be the opposite, since they have to be quite inventive in combining different resources to take care of themselves and their relatives. Social policies should, again, care about how competencies can be enhanced and persons can optimally develop their capabilities.

Lastly, the value of responsiveness further contributes to constructing both informal and professional caring practices in relational terms. Care is indeed relational through and through: together caregivers and care receivers can make social practices into caring practices. Communicative moral dispositions like active listening and the willingness for common deliberation contribute to making caring practices responsive. They enable care receivers to respond to the care received so that caregivers can ascertain that the care provided indeed meets the needs of the care receivers. Although responsiveness is primarily a value for the care receiver, the inherent power differential in caring practices places a responsibility with caregivers to organize responsiveness adequately. This is important for preventing open or hidden forms of paternalism in caring practices, and also the notion that inheres in the WPSW that care should be reserved for "really dependent" or pathological individuals. As we argued above, pathologizing notions of care easily turn women into a group with special needs that deviate from those of normal citizens. The ethic of care instead recognizes that women are vulnerable because of the way society deals with caring responsibilities. The value of responsiveness can deal with this vulnerability since it acknowledges care as an everyday practice of human life and thus accommodates women's needs as caregivers in the designing of social policy.

CONCLUDING REMARKS

Both in our critical analysis of the WSPW and in the more constructive part about the contribution of the ethic of care we hope to have shown that a thorough inclusion of care in the considerations of current social policy would imply a rethinking and redrafting of some of the basic assumptions and proposals in this document. Linking the ethic of care with notions of human development, as proposed by Zola Skweyiya, the minister of social development, supposes not just that care is acknowledged as an element of family and community life, but that it is positioned in the heart of citizenship practices. It remains to be elaborated what this would imply in terms of concrete policy measures, that is, with regard to child allowances, elderly pensions, health care politics, domestic service work, community work, etc. We do hope, however, that our analysis may bring a gender-sensitive perspective to the discussions on these topics, which acknowledges care as a central element of human life, and which enables policy makers to reflect on the moral viewpoints and the normative criteria that they adopt and disseminate in their documents. In this way the ethic of care may make a small but indispensable contribution toward building a South African society that considers both justice and care as hallmarks of this new century.

NOTES

1. This chapter was first published in *Critical Social Policy: A Journal of Theory and Practice in Social Welfare*, 23, no. 3 (2003): 299–321. We thank the editorial collective and SAGE Publications for their permission to reprint it.

2. The historical remarks in this section are based on E. S. van Eeden, E. H. Ryke, and I. C. M. de Necker, "The Welfare Function of the South African Government before and after Apartheid," *Social Work/Maatskaplike Werk*, 36 (2000): 1–24.

3. www.welfare.gov.za/Statements/2000/October/why.htm.

4. Ministry of Social Development, *White Paper for Social Welfare* (Pretoria: Government Printer, 1996).

5. Guiding literature here: J. C. Tronto, *Moral Boundaries: A Political Argument for an Ethic of Care* (New York: Routledge, 1993); S. L. Sevenhuijsen, *Citizenship and the Ethics of Care. Feminist Considerations on Justice, Morality and Politics* (London: Routledge, 1998); F. Robinson, *Globalizing Care: Ethics, Feminist Theory, and International Relations* (Boulder: Westview Press, 1999); E. F. Kittay, *Love's Labor: Essays on Women, Equality, and Dependency* (New York: Routledge, 1999). Our approach is further based on Trace, a method for analyzing policy documents from the perspective of care, developed by Selma Sevenhuijsen: S. Sevenhuijsen, "Trace: A Method for Normative Policy Analysis from the Ethic of Care," in *The Heart of the Matter: The Contribution of the Ethic of Care to Social Policy in Some New EU Member States*, ed. S. Sevenhuijsen and A. Svab (Ljubljana: Peace Institute, 2004), 13–46.

6. Sevenhuijsen, *Citizenship and the Ethics of Care*, 30.

7. C. Albertyn and J. Kentridge, "Introducing the Right to Equality in the Interim Constitution," *South African Journal on Human Rights* 10, no. 2 (1994): 149–78.

8. African National Congress, *The Reconstruction and Development Programme—A Policy Framework* (Johannesburg: Umanyano Publications, 1994).

9. H. Marais, *South Africa—Limits of Change: The Political Economy of Transformation* (Cape Town: Cape Town University Press, 1998), 192.

10. Marais, *South Africa—Limits of Change*, 191.

11. C. L. Bacchi, *Women, Policy and Politics: The Constructions of Policy Problems* (London: Sage, 1999).

12. This notion is developed by the American sociologist James Midgley, an international exponent of the approach and special adviser to the South African Department of Welfare by the time of writing the WPSW. In the seventies and early eighties the idea of social development was inserted into models as promoted by international agencies like the UN, the ILO, the WHO and the World Bank, which all argued, al-

though in different modes, for an attuning of economic and social aspects of development policies. Midgley defines developmental social welfare as "a process of planned social change designed to promote the well-being of the population as a whole in conjunction with a dynamic process of economic development." J. Midgley, *Social Development: The Developmental Perspective in Social Welfare* (London: Sage, 1995), 25.

13. Ministry of Social Development, *White Paper for Social Welfare*, 5

14. Ministry of Social Development, *White Paper for Social Welfare*, 37.

15. Ministry of Social Development, *White Paper for Social Welfare*, 8.

16. Ministry of Social Development, *White Paper for Social Welfare*, 39.

17. Ministry of Social Development, *White Paper for Social Welfare*, 51.

18. Ministry of Social Development, *White Paper for Social Welfare*, 6.

19. This low ranking of state responsibility is also noticeable in the order of priorities that the WPSW sets for social security. This order runs as follows: first, private should be used, second, a system of social insurance sustained by employers and employees, third, a tax-based system for the "really needy," and fourth, there could be social relief for short-term problems.

20. Ministry of Social Development, *White Paper for Social Welfare*, 47.

21. V. Bozalek, "Contextualizing Caring in Black South African Families," *Social Politics: International Studies in Gender, State and Society* 6, no. 1 (1999): 85–99; T. Le Roux, *"We Have Families Too": Live-in Domestics Talk about Their Lives* (Pretoria: Human Sciences Research Council, Co-operative Research Programme on Marriage and Family Life, 1995); V. Bozalek, *Recognition, Resources, Responsibilities: Using Students' Stories of Family to Renew the South African Social Work Curriculum* (Ph.D. thesis, Utrecht University, 2004), http://igitur-archive.library.uu.nl/dissertations/2004-1203-094505/index.htm (9 Sept. 2004).

22. The WPSW in other passages in fact addresses the elderly in this community role when it states that the spread of HIV/AIDS will lead to an increasing role for elderly people as caregivers, without, however, substantiating what this will look like (Ministry of Social Development, *White Paper for Social Welfare*, 33). This passage also mentions the expected increase in the demand for foster care and adoptive care for children orphaned by AIDS, without mentioning, however, that a considerable part of this care will probably "logically" fall on the shoulders of elderly family members (i.e., women).

23. A. Steyn, "Urban Household Structures in the Republic of South Africa," in *Family Formation and Dissolution: Perspectives from East and West*, ed. C. Yi (Taipei: Academia Sinica, 1996), 169–204.

24. C. Murray, *Families Divided: The Impact of Migrant Labour in South Africa* (Johannesburg: Witwatersrand University Press, 1981); C. Murray, "Class, Gender and the Household: The Developmental Cycle in Southern Africa," *Development and Change* 18, no. 2 (1987): 235–49; F. Ross, *Umntu ngumuntu ngabanye abantu: The Support Networks of Black Families in Southern Africa* (Pretoria: Human Sciences Research Council, Co-operative Research Programme on Marriage and Family Life, 1995); F. Ross, "Diffusing Domesticity: Domestic Fluidity in Die Bos," *Social Dynamics* 22, no. 1 (1996): 55–71; A. Spiegel, "Fluidity of Household Composition in

Matatiele, Transkei: A Methodological Problem," *African Studies* 45, no. 1 (1986): 17–35; A. Spiegel, V. Watson, and P. Wilkinson, "Domestic Diversity and Fluidity among Some African Households in Greater Cape Town," *Social Dynamics* 22, no. 1 (1996), 7–30; C. S. van der Waal, "Rural Children and Residential Instability in the Northern Province of South Africa," *Social Dynamics* 22, no. 1 (1996): 31–54

25. Lund Committee, *Child and Family Support* (Pretoria: Government Printer, 1996).

26. T. Le Roux, "*We Have Families Too*," 1995, 2.

27. Le Roux, "*We Have Families Too*," 6.

28. See Vivienne Bozalek's extended critique of these notions, based on her empirical research on family practices of South African social work students: V. Bozalek, *Recognition, Resources, Responsibilities*.

29. C. Gilligan, "Moral Orientation and Moral Development," in *Women and Moral Theory*, ed. E. Feder Kittay and D. T. Meyers (Totowa: Rowman and Littlefield, 1987), 24.

30. R. Palriwala and C. Risseeuw, *Shifting Circles of Support: Contextualising Gender and Kinship in South Asia and Sub-Saharan Africa* (New Delhi: Sage, 1996).

31. Tronto, *Moral Boundaries*.

32. Tronto, *Moral Boundaries*, 103.

33. See also J. Tronto, *The Care Ethic and Welfare Policy* (Unpublished paper, 1995).

Chapter Five

The Potential of Same-Sex Marriage for Restructuring Care and Citizenship

Dorothy C. Miller

> Will you do me the honor of paradoxically reinscribing and destabilizing hegemonic discourse with me?
>
> —Allison Bechdel[1]

An important subtext to the gay marriage debate in the United States is the threat of fundamental changes to liberal society. Sanctioning same-sex marriage has the potential of calling into question both the gendering and the location of care and ultimately the autonomy of the ideal citizen. Contemporary marriage bequeaths countless benefits that reinforce a social norm that places most care in the private space of the heterosexual family. Care practices are not only situated in the family, ignored, and made invisible in the liberal political tradition, but also must remain so if the assumptions of that political tradition are to stand. Thus the cultural and political stakes in maintaining a heterosexual-based dichotomous mythology of care are high.

Should same-sex marriage become legally widespread, same-sex couples are likely to become "normalized," challenging both gender roles and the liberal ideal. Within the social upheaval resulting from these redefinitions there may be new opportunities for the socialization of care within public policy. The enactment of same-sex marriage as a legal right could effectively aid in bridging the gap between the accepted application of care ethics in the home to the very difficult intrusion of care ethics into the public realm. In this chapter I will discuss the linkages between gendered behavioral norms, public policy, and the liberal concept of citizenship. I will argue the benefits of legalizing same-sex marriage and contrast my views with those of lesbian feminist scholars who oppose the fight for gay marriage.

CARE THEORY

Both research and theory provide evidence that the care that men provide or don't provide is culturally assigned and has at least the potential of radical change. Men can and do care for others and are perfectly capable of performing such care in ways similar to the care given by women.[2] Indeed, some of the present-day gendered assumptions about care ethics (if not about the practice of housework) can be seen to reflect a historical shift.

Joan Tronto suggests that the public morality of justice and the private morality of care began in the eighteenth century. As the distance between people who had to relate to each other increased, there needed to be rules developed to guide them on how to do this. Kant's model of morality, the "moral point of view," grew out of an "erosion of confidence in the peculiar moral values of situated political orders."[3] It was only at this historical moment that men embraced reason and eschewed connection to community and attachment to others as a basis for moral sentiment, giving over such basis to women, who were increasingly confined to the home. This historical insight challenges the notion that gendered expectations of moral sentiments are biologically or even psychologically inherent.[4]

Carol Gilligan's landmark work attached care to a gendered feminine attention to connection, relationship, and context in the process of moral reasoning. In contrast, she found a gendered masculine orientation toward a paradigm of detached principles of justice.[5] However, the relationship of gender to moral reasoning is complex, and Gilligan's subsequent research indicated findings that many women have a justice orientation and many men can and do embrace an ethic of care when it is presented as an alternative.[6] Other researchers have found cultural and class differences in the expression of care, regardless of gender.[7] In the face of these findings, Gilligan identifies gendered influences but nondichotomized attributes of care and justice ethics in moral reasoning. Consequently, practices of care among women and men, married and unmarried, can be characterized as culturally driven.

GENDERED CARE AND THE
INSTITUTION OF MARRIAGE

The political debate over gay marriage ostensibly focuses on the nature of commitment between two people in love, the inviolability of religiously sanctioned marriage, and the interest of the state in defining and shaping the institution. Within the debates the question of the state's right to regulate marriage has been raised, often to minimize its importance. In this discourse, it is useful to understand that the state has always had a stake in defining and controlling marriage and to consider the values related to this stance.

Settlers and early statesmen considered marriage a cornerstone of a civilized democratic society. Native Americans were quickly indoctrinated with Christian teachings regarding marriage.[8] Freed slaves, forbidden to marry when enslaved, were exhorted to wed by officers of the Freedmen's Bureau.[9] A fierce and ugly struggle over Mormon polygamy, lasting decades, didn't stop until laws against it were passed and the Mormon Church itself changed its rules in 1890.[10] Patriarchal and traditional Christian views of marriage prevailed, as did the related conviction that the citizenship of men included men's responsibility to represent the family to the state. Indeed, the change in marital prescriptions with regard to black slaves versus nonslaves turned on the issue of citizenship, a status taken on with freedom.[11]

Although some might argue that contemporary culture fosters a marital ideal of equality, few would deny the history of marriage as a patriarchal institution, dating from the paterfamilias of Roman times. Men have traditionally ruled families, represented the family to the state, and up until recently, had more legal rights in marriage than did their wives. While it has become more common for married couples in the United States to declare themselves of equal status within the marriage, certain asymmetrical practices remain. Wives' greater share of household duties reveals at least a continuance of gender role demands and suggests a normative male dominance in marriage today.[12] Moreover, groups such as the Southern Baptists exhort women to submit to their husbands in the household,[13] and the Promise Keepers explicitly encourage men to reclaim the authority in marriage that they believe is due them.[14]

Perhaps the most common practical example of inequality and masculinist norms in marriage is housework. Social studies indicate that men's hours doing housework have increased slightly in recent years and women's hours have decreased, resulting in a relative proportional rise in men's contributions. Still, marriage increases housework hours "for women, but not for men, with marriage associated with a five-hour-per-week increase in housework for women."[15]

Even among dual-career couples women still do about two-thirds of the household labor.[16] There is also evidence that housework duties are related to gendered ideation. Conservative Protestant wives in evangelical households, for example, do more "female-type" labor (i.e., care duties) than men.[17] Likewise, one study found that men's likelihood of performing "feminine" tasks in the home was negatively related to their own subordination in the workplace.[18] These practices, contradicting commonsense economic assumptions, are surely driven by the demands of a masculinist patriarchal system.

Although most heterosexual married persons "care about" each other, women do most of the "caring for" in heterosexual families. They "take care of" husbands and children in most of the traditional ways, via cooking, cleaning up, care in times of illness, and seeing to others' needs. They tend to do the "kin work," that is, making the connections with extended families. Care in heterosexual marriage, the recognized site of care reflected in social norms and public policy, is constructed via a gendered framework.

In contrast to heterosexual couples, gay and lesbian couples are more likely to divvy up household and social roles according to skills and preferences rather than predetermined understandings about how one should behave.[19] In Kath Weston's study of forty gays and lesbians, *Families We Choose*, even those who identified as "butch" or "femme" did not divide their work tasks accordingly. Some relied on individual talents to divide up the work, while others rotated tasks.[20] A recent survey of 341 lesbian, gay, bisexual, and transgender (LGBT) New Yorkers age fifty and older found that nearly half of these are heavily involved in caregiving, both for members of the families they grew up in and for same-sex partners and close friends.[21]

Since homophobia is frequently based on a disdain for "men acting like women," variations of tasks and the amount of caregiving in the gay community are potentially threatening to the gendered expectations of society. Concomitantly, female "breadwinners" threaten conventional notions of femininity. As policy scholar and lesbian activist Urvashi Vaid has commented about the existence of queers, "we disrupt the sexist order that decrees women exist for the pleasure and service of men. In this we are a potentially transcendent movement; our full acceptance would necessitate a change in the status of women."[22]

I suggest that achieving acceptance of queer marriage would deeply threaten patterned heterosexual marital behavior through the normalization of alternative ways of living. Heterosexual women in particular would come to notice these variations and perhaps no longer accept the necessity of being the primary caregivers in a family. Men would of necessity take on more caring tasks.

THE SAME-SEX MARRIAGE DEBATES

William Eskridge has identified three thematic strains in the marriage debates.[23] The traditionalists or "premodernists" object to same-sex marriage based on reasoning from "nature, history or authority, including scriptural authority." This stance is recognizable to most who are familiar with the "anti" arguments. In contrast, most proponents of same-sex marriage are "modernists" who argue that "people should not be treated differently because of traditional status distinctions." This stance is the one taken by the Freedom to Marry organization, led by lawyer Evan Wolfson, who argued the Hawaii same-sex marriage case *Baehr v. Lewin*.[24] These two strains are the most commonly identified views before the public.

A third strain, however, led by lesbian feminist theorists and characterized by Eskridge as the "postmodern" view, is less well known outside of scholarly discourse. This perspective questions the advisability of same-sex marriage as a progressive strategy. Scholars argue that promoting gay marriage is equivalent to adhering to patriarchal, state control of women's lives. True liberation for women, and indeed, all people, involves opening up government benefits to everyone, thus discontinuing the privileging of heterosexual marriage as the basis of the welfare state. Opening up the barriers just to let in same-sex marital partners constitutes co-optation, giving in. More important, it will likely lead to a dichotomous social view of gays and lesbians, the acceptable married ones and the unacceptable promiscuous ones. Conformity with social mores will restrict, rather than liberate, gays and lesbians by inviting the state to regulate their lives.[25] They argue that same-sex marriage will mostly benefit privileged white gay men.

Such theorists often pit their arguments against those of Andrew Sullivan, author of *Virtually Normal*, and Bruce Bawer, author of *A Place at the Table*.[26] Both Sullivan and Bawer take the modernist view that gays and lesbians are no different from heterosexual people, are "normal," and only want "a place at the table." Their feminist sisters argue that many white gay men have no reason to think beyond their admittance into the final realm of acceptability in American life. Gay men like Sullivan and Bawer believe, rightly or wrongly, that marriage will give them the entrée that they need and want. They are not interested in redesigning the table but simply want a place at an already acceptable (to them) social order.

I would argue that Sullivan and Bawer are too optimistic even for the incremental empowerment that they seek. As James Baldwin once said, "A fag is a homosexual gentleman who has just left the room." But even if they are right, that same-sex marriage will afford them the status that they desire, it will not do the same for most, namely, lower-class men, lesbians and gays of color, and white women (except perhaps for the privileged white women who happen to share some of the advantages of men like Sullivan and Bawer). The rest, especially women, will continue to face discrimination.

Claudia Card is among those opposing the struggle for same-sex marriage. She states, "I would rather see the state deregulate heterosexual marriage than see it begin to regulate same-sex marriage."[27] She believes that "married victims of partner battering and rape have less protection than anyone except children," and furthermore asserts that she does not "see how this vulnerability can be acceptably removed from the institution of legal marriage," and anyhow, polic-ing this situation would only encourage more encroachment from the state.[28]

Valerie Lehr in *Queer Family Values: Debunking the Myth of the Nuclear Family* discusses the textured way in which gay and lesbian communities have created families and ties that in no way mirror the social structures of the larger society. She claims that queer lives suggest possibilities for alter-native understandings of relationships that have the potential of liberating everyone.[29] Furthermore, she questions the compression of gays and lesbians by norms that not only don't fit them but also don't seem to fit heterosexuals. As a punch line of a cartoon in *The New Yorker* says, "Marriage for gays and lesbians? Haven't they suffered enough?" The divorce rate alone would surely constitute a caution to those wishing to join this club.

Betsey Brown proposes the concept of designated next-of-kin (DNOK), a chosen domestic partnership that could include or exclude a biological relative or a sexual relationship, as one wished. With your DNOK you would have all the rights and privileges granted to married couples, and of course your DNOK could be your spouse in the usual sense of the term. DNOK would be the offi-cial couple designation offered by the state, with marriage a religious choice not tied to state sanction.[30] Such a policy would acknowledge that people are inter-dependent and often form dyads in helping each other. It also gives these dyad "couples" an opportunity to be aided and recognized in their care for each other.

Critiques of the heterosexual nuclear family are not confined to those who oppose the legalization of same-sex marriage. For example, social work scholar K. Sue Jewell asserts that social welfare policies of the 1960s and 1970s that purported to bring African American families into mainstream American life were destructive because of the incentives toward a value sys-tem in the broader society that stressed the importance of individualism, the acquisition of material goods, and the centrality of the nuclear family. Strong mutual help and kinship networks were prematurely replaced by government sources of aid.[31] Since black families have not been fully integrated into the economic structure of American life and the sources of government aid have been curtailed, many black families are worse off than they were before. She calls for a renewal of the black family's "propensity for interdependent rela-tionships" and "the values of cooperative collectivism" over that of individu-alism.[32] Her arguments are echoed among opponents of gay marriage who fear the loss of community among lesbian and gay familial groups.

AN ALTERNATIVE LESBIAN FEMINIST VIEW: CARE PRACTICE, POLICY, AND CITIZENSHIP

I recognize, as Card does, the continued oppression of married women who are battered and raped by their husbands. But I would argue that this is not because of the laws, which have changed considerably in the past twenty years, but because of our continued association of masculinity with dominance and violence. Furthermore, cohabiting heterosexual and GLBT couples and even those who are dating are subject to battering and rape. The problem of violence in intimate relationships is likely related to gender as well as our society's tendency to use violence as a solution to conflict. Restricting or even eliminating marriage is not likely to be a significant remedy.

Brown's suggestion of the DNOK is compelling as is Lehr's claim that alternative understandings of relationships are possible and desirable. Indeed, social statistics about cohabitation, a reluctance to marry among many people, and the continued extended kin and non-kin relationships in many ethnic communities and LGBT communities indicate an appreciation for relationships outside of marriage and the nuclear family. Perhaps behavioral changes toward alternative relationships will modify the culture enough to influence alterations in public policy. Yet it seems imprudent and unfair to suggest that gays and lesbians wait for radical reform when incremental policy change that could open the door to more radical change seems possible.

In her discussion of how to create a caring society, Nel Noddings attempts to bring the behavioral practices and intentions of the "best homes" into the educational system, thus influencing public policies of caring.[33] Thus caring practices at home can enter the public world via school systems. As both men and women develop more varied practices of care, their children will learn these practices and bring them into the schools and eventually the public world. I argue that the diversification of the definition of "best homes" will change the discourse of care, ungendering it to the extent that men's tendencies to care will become more expressive. But it is not only via personal practice in the home that care may become more public. As public policy changes, the discourse necessary to bring about that change will necessarily expand the possibilities of socializing care.

Susan Moeller Okin sums up the essence of possible change when she says, "The kinds of changes that would reduce the salience of gender and enable women to become equal with men would also lead to greater equality between homosexuals and heterosexuals."[34] The reverse is also true in that greater equality between homosexuals and heterosexuals would reduce the salience of gender. Same-sex marriage can do this by normalizing new forms of relationships between spouses.

Same-sex marriage would benefit heterosexual women by offering a challenge to the underlying patriarchal nature of marriage. The issue of who takes care of whom, who supports whom, who cares for the children and the household will increasingly be determined by criteria other than gender. I envision a gradual and reciprocal acceptance of same-sex couples and ungendered marital relations as "normal." Such normality would also need to be recognized by our existing social welfare systems.

In all there are more than a thousand federal benefits and responsibilities encoded in U.S. law that pertain to married people.[35] They do indeed regulate the lives of people who choose to become legally married, but they offer benefits and privileges as well. Potential changes in the Social Security system provide an important example of the public policy effects of federalizing same-sex marriage. Social Security retirement benefits currently go to both earners and their spouses. When one spouse has not had earnings or has had considerably fewer earnings than the other, the lower earner receives either her own benefit or one-half of her husband's, whichever is greater. The lower earner in these situations is usually the wife. This provision is in many ways a throwback to a time when most wives were the family caregivers and spent most of their adult lives out of the labor force entirely. While a provision for care, it nonetheless stood for dependency. Today, ironically, usually only the most well-off couples are eligible for this benefit.

The "higher earner—lower earner" designations in the law have heretofore safely gendered the protocols of Social Security without having to do so explicitly. The "lower earner" is the caring, more homebound, spouse. Thus the social order of care has been contained at least in terms of individual roles and behaviors. With the legalization of gay and lesbian marriage, no longer would the higher earners and lower earners be predominantly one sex.

Provisions in Social Security also benefit divorced dependent spouses and families of deceased or disabled workers under certain circumstances. Extending these benefits to gay and lesbian married couples and their children would be an enormous help to their well-being.[36] And while it is true that female couples would have fewer total benefits than male couples, for many lesbian couples the benefit structure would be an overall increase in financial security compared to what they would have had without it. Additionally, the benefits would be based on care as well as earnings, not just nominally so. Means-tested welfare laws, if maintained, would also have a different outcome for those eligible. Currently there is pressure for unwed women on welfare to marry. What if they married women? The inclusion of same-sex couples in all relevant social welfare provisions could force the issue of honoring care beyond heterosexual norms—for survivors, children, and male retired spouses. Perhaps a change in the marriage laws would result in a letting up of the heterosexual gender role bias of the U.S. welfare state.

Toppling the gendered nature of federal benefits and responsibilities could, in turn, problematize gender and perhaps provide sites for care considerations in public policy. As Tronto has remarked, insofar as a feminine approach to caring reflects the gender divisions of society and women's devalued role, "caring will always remain as a corrective to morality, as an 'extra' aspect of life, neither suggesting nor requiring a fundamental rethinking of moral categories."[37]

If, however, the gendered divisions become problematized, denormalized, then perhaps care will no longer be "extra" and perhaps no longer private. From a reformist point of view, this seems good enough reason to promote the fight for same-sex marriage. Making care "public," however, has embedded meanings related to political and social citizenship in liberal society.

HIGHER STAKES: CITIZENSHIP, SAME-SEX MARRIAGE, AND CARE

I move now to the fundamental infrastructure of liberalism and its political arrangements, which I believe would be threatened by the gendered political consequences of legalized same-sex marriage. British social theorist T. H. Marshall conceptualized three successive notions of citizenship: civil/legal citizenship, political citizenship, and social citizenship. Social citizenship establishes the right of all citizens to the state's care. Thus Marshall outlined the obligations and legitimacy of the welfare state. However, in the United States the status of "citizen" has been a contested one.[38] Citizenship has often been conceptualized as a status that must be achieved rather than simply assumed, and citizenship is integrally associated with the undertaking of paid work.[39]

As the welfare state, and presumably social citizenship, expanded, some groups were left out, notably African American women from the first welfare programs and many women and people of color from unemployment insurance.[40] The intermittent work patterns of black men and the unpaid caregiving functions of all women precluded their achieving the same status ascribed to white male citizens. The welfare state shores up the needs of earners and their dependents. With their primary responsibility for unpaid work, women have qualified mostly as dependents. In this way, care has remained categorically both private and female, and a barrier to full citizenship for women.

As for civil and political citizenship, Eva Kittay and Wendy Brown have written about the absence of women in the liberal concept of "the citizen," mainly due to the fact that women's roles as caregivers preclude the possibility of being the autonomous, independent citizen of the liberal state. Indeed, men's ability to perceive themselves as autonomous and independent citizens depends on the invisibility of interdependence in the public realm. As Kittay remarks,

> Liberalism constructed an equality for heads of households (wherein dependencies exist within the household and are attended to by women), and then counted the head of household as an *individual* who is independent and who can act on his own behalf.[41]

Wendy Brown's analysis of the foundations of liberal political thought illuminates the status of care as a subordinated function situated primarily in the family and denigrated when it has emerged undisguised in the public domain. According to Brown, the liberal political tradition hinges on the subordination of women whose task is to maintain necessary human relations (that is, care) that, paradoxically, must be eclipsed at the same time that it is essential to the perpetuation of human life and harmonious social relations. Care practices are not only situated in the family, ignored, and made invisible in the liberal political tradition, but must also remain so if the assumptions of that political tradition are to stand. Thus the cultural and political stakes in maintaining a dichotomous mythology of care are high.

Brown cites certain markers of citizenship in the liberal tradition: autonomy, independence, liberty, and rights. All of these markers support the notion of a free-standing, independent being without encumbrance. She sets these values as dichotomies with: necessity, dependency, needs, and family, all of which are associated with women and private life.[42] Crossing these constructed boundaries, acknowledging the interdependence of family and community, state, and globe, requires a reconceptualization of the meaning of political citizenship. It also necessitates the reconfiguring of social citizenship. Insofar as women represent care practice and care ethics, such a change represents a further inroad of care ethics into the social, public system of care, via the embodiment of women as citizens.

The legalization of gay marriage elevates married lesbians to full-fledged citizenship as undisputed heads of household, disrupting the gendered boundary of discourse about citizenship. The semblance of husbands mediating the family's relationship to the state would be demolished. (Although single women already have a direct individual–state connection, they continue to be widely viewed as social anomalies and/or in-between marital partners, and thus their numbers have not caused the kinds of change that I foresee.) Likewise, the interdependence of all people will become more evident as men care for men and women for women.

From a practical standpoint, this change could lead to greater political participation among women, notably the numbers of women in elected office. Since we know that women on all sides of the political spectrum in fact pay more attention to care issues, this would further aid in the introduction of care issues, practice, and policy into the fabric of public life and provision.

As social benefit systems change and the definitions of dependency and interdependence become more elastic, so could many gendered connections gradually disappear. Men as dependents have heretofore been few in number and usually associated with disability. Presumably, as same-sex couples have children and one spouse decides to stay home to perform unpaid work, the normalcy of interdependence and its association with the public realm will come to the fore. Thus, the starkly amusing marriage proposal from the cartoon *Dykes to Watch Out For*, quoted above, presents the reality of what lies before us—"paradoxically reinscribing and destabilizing [the] hegemonic discourse" of marriage.

A POPULAR CALL

In addition to the political and policy arguments for same-sex marriage, surely it is important and appropriate to consider what gays and lesbians actually desire. It is difficult for social scientists to know what most gays and lesbians want, since many are closeted and many live in suburbs and rural areas out of reach or interest to researchers.[43] Most research has been conducted in coastal cities among people who are relatively "out." By definition, research rarely gets to people who are closeted. While social scientists admit the limitations of their samples, generalizations are nonetheless inevitable, and I argue that some of these generalizations are likely untrue. My personal observations of gays and lesbians in Kansas and elsewhere in noncoastal cities and towns indicate that there are many lesbians who are not feminists, and many gays and lesbians who do not think theoretically about the institution of marriage. Students of mine in Kansas have pointed out that the "lesbian community" about which lesbian feminist theorists have written bears no relation to them. No doubt many of the lesbians who are choosing to get married when given the chance are not familiar with the theoretical lesbian and gay arguments against it.

About 10,000 U.S. same-sex couples have been legally married, although some of these marriages have been declared invalid. Some have married in Canada, others in San Francisco, Massachusetts, and small towns and cities whose officials have chosen to defy the law. In every instance in the United States, where scores of couples have gathered to obtain marriage licenses and get married, lesbian couples have been in the majority.[44] Clearly, many lesbians and gays harbor a desire to be part of mainstream culture, and this means getting married. Women in particular are socialized from a very early age to look forward to marriage, and this cultural impetus doesn't go away just because one is a lesbian.

Countless pictures of happy couples have been sent over the Internet, smiling faces of all sorts, one after another. These couples are performing a political act, but their accounts of their experiences demonstrate a groundswell of preferences, a burning desire to express their love in a way that is highly honored in our culture. These faces form a linkage from theory to reality. They are "on the ground," as we say.

Card makes the point that opposing the struggle for same-sex marriage doesn't justify the state's policy of denying it.[45] I would reverse the sentiment and say that promoting the struggle for same-sex marriage doesn't necessarily connote an acceptance of marriage as an ideal institution. Gay and lesbian persons have indicated that they want to work for marriage even more, it seems, than job security. David Mohr has suggested that lesbians and gays want to marry because they view marriage as "a way of experiencing the world."[46] Job security, in contrast, is something that everyone has and no one has. Perhaps a collective cynicism has overtaken us all with regard to the work world. What we have left are love and care.

Much like the progression described in *The Radical Future of Liberal Feminism* by Zillah Eisenstein, I have come to believe that the achievement of same-sex marriage in the United States, seemingly a reformist or even regressive goal, has the potential of introducing a new notion of care into the public realm. Eisenstein contended that the contradictions between liberalism and feminism would lead to a radical women's movement.[47] I argue that institutionalizing same-sex marriage in the public realm would create ideological contradictions that could force fundamental paradigm shifts. Public systems would officially recognize and compensate care by men for men and children, care for women by women, and care in heterosexual relationships equally, side by side, as part of the fabric of American life. This recognition has the potential of weakening patriarchy by means of the increasing awareness of how gendered behavior is a culturally constructed choice, a collective decision that can be changed, that does change, over time. It may also problematize the liberal notion of the autonomous, independent citizen, shifting our very notions of political identity.

Citing Barrington Moore, Tronto, in *Moral Boundaries*, says that "change occurs when people recognize that their predicament has been created by human action and that therefore the situation can be changed." She goes on to say that "Care's absence from our core social and political values reflects many choices our society has made about what to honor."[48] Perhaps these elements — the recognition that human choice can and does change things, and the challenge to make a shift in what we "honor" — form the crux of the political problem in this struggle.

Lehr claims that the end to laws barring interracial marriage did not stop discrimination against such couples and suggests that married gays and lesbians won't fare any better. As a test, Lehr asks the question of whether or not the change in the law has led parents to encourage their children to see interracial marriage as a "positive option."[49] I would suggest that a beginning has occurred in that there are many interracial couples who have succeeded in maintaining positive relationships with their parents and in-laws. *Their* children are an example to others and problematize racial distinctions. It is not unusual in my college classes to have several biracial students in a single class, some of whom are not recognizably so, and many of whom refuse to accept racial categorization or restricted choices. Although their lives may be more complicated than most, they have accepting friends of all races, and they do not often experience the kinds of hostile, dangerous situations that would have been commonplace fifty years ago. Likewise, a similar partial acceptance of gay and lesbian couples could prevail in society, with more acceptance from parents, families, and neighbors, although it would be short of a transformation in cultural values.

My argument is incredibly optimistic and far-reaching. Yet the opposition to gay marriage proposals among feminist theorists is also broad. Bell hooks once said that we cannot create what we cannot imagine. In this chapter I have imagined a rosy picture, which, in reality, will likely not end up quite so rosy. But I choose to imagine the possibilities.

NOTES

1. Allison Bechdel, "Dykes to Watch Out For," *Lesbian Connection* 27, no. 1 (July/August 2004): 31.

2. Carl Hirsch and Judith L. Newman, "Microstructural and Gender Role Influences on Male Caregivers," *Journal of Men's Studies* 3, no. 4 (31 May 1995): 309–34.

3. Joan Tronto, *Moral Boundaries* (London: Routledge, 1993), 51.

4. Tronto, 57, 59.

5. Carol Gilligan, *In a Different Voice: Psychological Theory and Women's Development* (Cambridge, Mass.: Harvard University Press, 1982).

6. Carol Gilligan, "Moral Orientation and Moral Development," in *Justice and Care*, ed. Virginia Held (Boulder, Colo.: Westview Press, 1995), 31–46.

7. Marilyn Friedman, "Care and Context in Moral Reasoning," in *Women and Moral Theory*, ed. Eva Feder Kittay and Diana T. Meyers (Totowa, N.J.: Rowman and Littlefield, 1987), 190–204; Sandra Harding, "The Curious Coincidence of Feminine and African Moralities: Challenges for Feminist Theory," in *Women and Moral Theory*, ed. Eva Feder Kittay and Diana T. Meyers (Totowa, N.J.: Rowman and Littlefield, 1987), 296–315.

8. Nancy F. Cott, *Public Vows: A History of Marriage and the Nation* (Cambridge, Mass.: Harvard University Press, 2000), 26.

9. Cott, *Public Vows*, 85.

10. Cott, *Public Vows*, 120.

11. Cott, *Public Vows*, 33.

12. Suzanne M. Bianchi, Melissa A. Milkie, Liana C. Sayer, and John P. Robinson, "Is Anyone Doing the Housework? Trends in the Gender Division of Household Labor," *Social Forces* 79 (Sept. 2000): 215.

13. Southern Baptist Convention website, www.sbc.net/aboutus, www.sbc.net/bfm/bfm2000.asp (24 June 2005).

14. "The first thing I did when I got home was to sit my wife and two daughters down. I got on my knees and apologized to them for not being the father, husband and leader I was supposed to be. Thank God they forgave me and so did God." Tim, Greensboro, The Promise Keepers website, www.promisekeepers.org/meet/meet12.htm (6 Sept. 2004).

15. Scott Coltrane, "Research on Household Labor: Modeling and Measuring the Social Embeddedness of Routine Family Work," *Journal of Marriage and the Family* 62 (Nov. 2000): 1223.

16. Bianchi, "Is Anyone Doing the Housework?" 211.

17. Christopher G. Ellison and John P. Bartkowski, "Conservative Protestantism and the Division of Household Labor among Married Couples," *Journal of Family Issues* 23 (Nov. 2002): 950–85.

18. Barbara A. Arrighi and David J. Maume, Jr., "Workplace Subordination and Men's Avoidance of Housework," *Journal of Family Issues* 21 (2000): 464–87.

19. Phillip Blumstein and Pepper Schwartz, *American Couples: Money, Work, Sex* (New York: William Morrow and Company, 1983), 148.

20. Kath Weston, *Families We Choose* (New York: Columbia University Press, 1991), 149.

21. Marjorie H. Cantor, Mark Brennan, and R. Andrew Shippy, *Caregiving among Older Lesbian, Gay, Bisexual, and Transgender New Yorkers* (New York: National Gay and Lesbian Task Force Policy Institute Pride Senior Network, Fordham University Graduate School of Social Service, 2004), 1.

22. Urvashi Vaid, *Virtual Equality:The Mainstreaming of Gay and Lesbian Liberation* (New York: Doubleday, 1995), 193.

23. William N. Eskridge, Jr., "Channeling: Identity-Based Movements and Public Law," *University of Pennsylvania Law Review* 150 (Nov. 2001), 419.

24. In this case, *Baehr v. Lewin*, the supreme court of Hawaii declared that the prohibition against same-sex marriage in the state of Hawaii was sex discrimination according to the state constitution. The state appealed, and while the case was pending it was made moot by the legislature's change in the constitution. Nevertheless, this case marked a turning point in the campaign to achieve legal sanctions for gay marriage while it also served as a red flag for its opponents. See Elizabeth Kristen, "The Struggle for Same-Sex Marriage Continues," *Berkeley Women's Law Journal* 14 (31 Jan. 1999).

25. Paula L. Ettelbrick, "Legal Marriage Is Not the Answer," *The Harvard Gay and Lesbian Review.* 4 (31 Oct. 1997), 34.

26. Andrew Sullivan, *Virtually Normal: An Argument about Homosexuality* (New York: Random House, 1995). Bruce Bawer, *A Place at the Table: The Gay Individual in American Society* (New York: Simon & Schuster, 1993).

27. Claudia Card, "Against Marriage and Motherhood," *Hypatia* 11, no. 3 (Summer 1996): 1–23.

28. Card, "Against Marriage," 15.

29. Valerie Lehr, *Queer Family Values: Debunking the Myth of the Nuclear Family* (Philadelphia: Temple University Press, 1999), 73.

30. Betsey Brown, "A Radical Dyke Experiment for the Next Century: 5 Things to Work for Instead of Same-Sex Marriage," *Off Our Backs: A Women's Newsjournal* 30 (Jan. 2000): 24.

31. K. Sue Jewell, *Survival of the Black Family* (New York: Praeger, 1988), 131.

32. Jewell, *Survival*, 142.

33. Nel Noddings, *Starting at Home: Caring and Social Policy* (Berkeley, Calif.: University of California Press, 2002), 283–300.

34. Susan Moeller Okin, "Sexual Orientation, Gender, and Families: Dichotomizing Differences," *Hypatia* 11, no. 1 (Winter 1996): 30–37.

35. Cott, *Public Vows*, 2; U.S. General Accounting Office, *Defense of Marriage Act: Update to Prior Report*, GAO-04-353R (Washington, D.C.: USGPO, 23 Jan. 2004).

36. David L. Chambers, "What If? The Legal Consequences of Marriage and the Legal Needs of Lesbian and Gay Male Couples," in *Queer Families, Queer Politics: Challenging Culture and the State*, ed. Mary Bernstein and Renate Reimann (New York: Columbia University Press, 2001), 306–37. Chambers indicates that not all the consequences of marriage would be beneficial and discusses the potential advantages and disadvantages in detail.

37. Joan Tronto, "Care as a Basis for Radical Political Judgments," *Hypatia* 10, no. 2 (Spring 1995): 141.

38. Michael B. Katz, *The Price of Citizenship: Redefining the American Welfare State* (New York: Metropolitan Books, 2001), 342–44.

39. Wendy Sarvasy, "Social Citizenship from a Feminist Perspective," *Hypatia: A Journal of Feminist Philosophy* 12, no. 4 (Fall 1997): 54–73.

40. Katz, *Price of Citizenship*, 346–47.

41. Eva Feder Kittay, "Taking Dependency Seriously: The Family and Medical Leave Act Considered in Light of the Social Organization of Dependency Work and Gender Equality," *Hypatia* 10, no. 1 (Winter 1995): 8–29.

42. Wendy Brown, *States of Injury: Power and Freedom in Late Modernity* (Princeton: Princeton University Press, 1995), 135–65.

43. "Lesbian Couples Reside in Nearly Every County in the U.S.," *Marketing to Women* 15, no. 6 (June 2002): 3.

44. Statement by Attorney Evan Wolfson, Executive Director of Freedom to Marry, in a speech made to the Cleveland City Club, July 2004. See also "Survey Finds Women in the Majority," *The Boston Globe*, 18 May 2004.

45. Card, "Against Marriage," 5.

46. David D. Mohr, "The Stakes in the Gay Marriage Wars," *The Gay and Lesbian Review Worldwide* 7 (31 July 2000).

47. Zillah R. Eisenstein, *The Radical Future of Liberal Feminism* (Boston: Northeastern University Press, 1981), 3.

48. Tronto, *Moral Boundaries*, 179.

49. Lehr, *Queer Family Values*, 37.

Chapter Six

An Inverted Home:
Socializing Care at Hull-House

Maurice Hamington

In defining care ethics, political theorist Joan Tronto recognized that our means for understanding care is usually personal, relational, and often dyadic. Such an understanding makes sense given that most people first learn about care through the experience of being cared for by a parent or guardian. There is a danger, however, in limiting the notion of care to the private sphere because it can help perpetuate the perception of parallel and sometimes conflicting moral tracks: the public sphere being largely guided by a morality of rules and principles of adjudication while the private sphere is dominated by the relational morality of care. This moral dichotomy is perhaps best evinced in the "get tough" movement that dominates current public discourse and is characterized by mandatory sentencing, record-breaking incarceration rates, and a disregard for human dignity as witnessed in the treatment of prisoners and detainees following the U.S. invasion of Iraq in 2003. Coexistent with public tough morality is the idealization of the private sphere as the locus of relational morality.

Some care theorists have fueled the identification of care with the private sphere through the use of parent-child examples as paradigmatic of care. There is nothing inappropriate about such examples as they resonate with many people's experiences. These identifications can, however, inadvertently marginalize care theory as having a largely personal domain rather than a social role in morality. Tronto and Berenice Fisher offer a definition of care that specifically avoids the public/private dichotomy:

> On the most general level, we suggest that caring be viewed as a *species activity that includes everything that we do to maintain, continue, and repair our "world" so that we can live in it as well as possible.* That world includes our bodies, our selves, and our environment, all of which we seek to interweave in a complex, life-sustaining web.[1]

Tronto explains that this definition does not "presume that caring is dyadic or individualistic."[2] She views an ethic of care as having the potential for guiding social policies and practices. Accordingly, care should not be limited to that which is private or personal in a holistic understanding of social morality. Furthermore, Tronto contends that an analysis of care ethics is incomplete unless its social entanglements are considered: "We cannot understand care until we place such an ethic in its full moral and political context."[3] She goes on to claim, "For a society to be judged as a morally admirable society, it must, among other things, adequately provide for care of its members and its territory."[4] For Tronto this is a normative assertion as elements of care, including attentiveness, responsibility, competence, and responsiveness, should be integrated as an organic whole for effective caring to take place.

While Tronto's analysis is compelling on a theoretical level, can it realistically be applied to institutional or social behavior? Care literature (including much of my own work) continues to offer numerous personal examples of care and a general lack of social examples. In this article I will suggest that the writing and work of Jane Addams (1860–1935) and the Hull-House residents provide a tangible example, as well as theoretical insight, into the possibility of socializing care that is instructive for modern institutions steeped in a world seemingly hostile to caring. I will begin with a brief description of the unique social experiment that was Hull-House. Then I will address how Addams and Hull-House applied and developed an ethic of care that is a model of socializing care in a manner not steeped in the metaphors of parent-child relations.

In 1889 a small group of women faced bleak social circumstances marked by widespread uncaring. Chicago, in the waning years of the nineteenth century, was a powder keg of social unrest ready to erupt. Unprecedented immigration had transformed the city into an uneasy amalgamation of the world community. Free-market capitalism reigned supreme with few labor, health, or safety laws to rein it in.[5] Many parts of the city were blighted by uncollected garbage and squalor. The labor riots of 1877 and the Haymarket bombing, as well as the subsequent trial of 1886, demonstrated how quickly violence and injustice could arise given the underlying tensions of the city. Into this dark picture came two women without much of a plan beyond the conviction that greater social knowledge—knowledge of one another's lives—would foster care and connection that had the potential to transform society for the better. They would succeed beyond their wildest dreams and, although largely forgotten and discredited, they left a legacy of, and a model for, socializing care.

The two women were Jane Addams and Ellen Gates Starr, and they are best known for founding the Chicago social settlement community known as Hull-House.

HULL-HOUSE

Hull-House is difficult to describe succinctly because of the variety and quantity of its endeavors and accomplishments. It was one of the first social settlements founded in the United States. Social settlements were the most radical reform-minded manifestations of the Progressive Era, which lasted roughly from the late 1800s to World War I. Progressive ideals were characterized by the belief that intelligent collective effort could improve the quality of life for all. Social settlements were created and operated by progressives, many of whom were first generation college-educated women who believed so strongly in social improvement that they dedicated their lives to it by forming intentional communities located among the oppressed. At their height, more than four hundred social settlements existed across the country.[6] Hull-House rapidly assumed a leadership position among them because of the level of activity, innovation, and dynamism of its residents, particularly of Jane Addams.

From the beginning, Hull-House residents maintained a commitment to reciprocal relations among people of different identities. Addams believed that society was made stronger through better understanding among diverse people: "Hull-House was soberly opened on the theory that the dependence of classes on each other is reciprocal."[7] Better knowledge of the rapidly growing immigrant population would infuse new vitality and possibilities into the established culture while facilitating the prosperity of those new to this country. The projects that Hull-House residents engaged in emerged from the transactions between its residents and the community. Hull-House would sponsor a public bathhouse, a kindergarten, child care, sex education programs, parks and recreation programs, a labor museum, adult education courses, social clubs, public speakers, community theater, and whatever else the community needed.

A who's who list of U.S. female social activists of the early twentieth century were associated with Hull-House during the Addams era. Alice Hamilton, Florence Kelley, Charlotte Perkins Gilman, Rachel Yarros, Mary Kenney, Sophonisoba Breckinridge, Edith Abbott, Grace Abbott, and Julia Lathrop, as well as many other residents and volunteers, made significant contributions to advancing social progress in medicine, politics, law, labor, and education. Yet all of them would readily agree that it was Jane Addams who provided the leadership and vision to make Hull-House and its endeavors possible. She supplied material leadership as well as intellectual leadership. Addams was a public philosopher of the first order. She authored a dozen books and five hundred articles for both academic and nonacademic audiences. William James described Addams as having a "deeply original mind" and characterized aspects of her

work as "revolutionary in the extreme."[8] Addams could engage the faculty at
the University of Chicago one moment and the latest immigrant child to arrive
on Halsted Street in the Hull-House neighborhood the next.

A CARING DEMOCRACY

Perhaps Addams's most important philosophical contribution was her commitment to a robust notion of democracy. For Addams, being a citizen in a democracy required much more than voting and occasional jury duty. Democracy was a way to lead a moral life through a conscious effort at
understanding others, no matter how different those others are. Addams believed that for democracy to be successful, our shared investment in one another had to be cultivated: "surely the demand of an individual for decency
and comfort, for a chance to work and obtain the fullness of life may be
widened until it gradually embraces all the members of the community, and
raises a sense of the common weal."[9] Addams understood democracy to presume human connection as fundamental. Because of this connection, social
resonance, empathy, understanding, and action on behalf of one another made
democracy effective. Knowing one another through social transactions was a
moral imperative for Addams, not for knowledge's sake, but for the proper
development of human sympathies.

> We are learning that a standard of social ethics is not attained by travelling a se-
> questered byway, but by mixing on the thronged and common road where all
> must turn out for one another, and at least see the size of one another's burdens.
> To follow the path of social morality results perforce in the temper if not the
> practice of the democratic spirit, for it implies that diversified human experience
> and resultant sympathy which are the foundation and guarantee of Democracy.[10]

Like later feminist care ethicists, Addams assumes that moral agents are fundamentally connected in a web of relationships as opposed to traditional
moral theories of atomistic individuals freely entering into contracts or exert-
ing personal rights. Further direct knowledge of others will lead to renewed
understanding of our shared human existence, which in turn fosters sympathetic feelings. Ultimately, if fully cultivated, sympathetic understanding will
lead to action on behalf of others.

A key element of Addams's robust understanding of democracy was what
she referred to as "sympathetic knowledge." Addams links epistemology with
ethics in positing that in better knowing one another, the potential for caring
and action increases. Socializing care is brought about bit by bit or relationship by relationship as unknown others are transformed into known others

through an increase in the quantity and quality of transactions. For example, Hull-House sponsored numerous social clubs, including those for specific cultural groups, political discussion, or age-specific interests. These clubs were not frivolous to the work of Hull-House but were central to its mission of increasing the depth of social interaction and thus contributing to social understanding.

ADDAMS'S CONTRIBUTION TO CARING

While "caring" is such a common notion that Virginia Held has suggested that it is the basis for all of morality,[11] "care ethics" as an organized field of study is a sometimes marginalized newcomer to moral philosophy. The term was coined by feminist theorists in the 1980s and developed by Carol Gilligan, Nel Noddings, Tronto, and others. Care ethics is an approach to morality that emphasizes relationships over rules and rights. Care is a concrete approach to morality that includes context and the web of relational entanglements that all moral agents find themselves in. For a care ethicist, a principle such as "thou shalt not steal," while a useful tool of ethics, does not capture the entire moral scope of any given situation. Relationships, power dynamics, and other elements of context must also be considered. Care ethicists do not dismiss rules and duties, but neither do they place all of their moral stock in them.

I suggest not only that Addams was a care ethicist even before the term was developed but that she makes original contributions to care theory as well. Addams's epistemological approach emphasizing direct concrete experience is perfectly suited for care ethics. Her social approach to morality emphasized caring relationships, and she foresaw democracy as entailing a caring disposition among its citizenry. While Addams was not opposed to invoking rules or rights, she thought morality was more than that. For example, when she addressed the plight of African Americans, Addams recognized that a civil rights movement was necessitated because whites had failed to extend civilities in social interaction. In an article for the *Crisis* edited by W. E. B. DuBois, Addams states, "We stupidly force one race to demand as a right from the other those things which should be accorded as a courtesy."[12] Here Addams implies that a richer social morality of care might mitigate the need for demanding explicit individual rights. Note that she fought vigorously for those civil rights, but she lamented that the need for them had arisen in the first place.

Furthermore, Addams, although an admirer of the founding fathers of the country, thought it was time to update their morality. She viewed the application of the traditional, individual-oriented ethics of the eighteenth century as mismatched to the social needs of her contemporary context. Her views were radical given that morality is not something that is widely considered capable of progressing. According to Addams, modernity brought with it new social problems that demanded a new morality that matched the times: "Without the advancement of the whole, no man can hope for any lasting improvement in his own moral or material individual condition."[13] Addams's robust approach to morality did not preclude rights and duties, but she found a social ethic marked by care to be the missing voice of morality in the late nineteenth and early twentieth centuries.

I will not delineate the characteristics and criticisms of care ethics here, but I do want to at least gesture toward how Addams is an original thinker in this field. One contribution that she made is a certain assertiveness reflecting the overlooked radical edge to her philosophy. Care ethics, as Noddings constructs it, involves caring for those who come into one's sphere of knowledge. "Indeed, the caring person, one who in this way is prepared to care, dreads the proximate stranger, for she cannot easily reject the claim he has on her."[14] Noddings's original formulation of caring is challenging but can be interpreted as somewhat passive: when happenstance or volition brings people into some degree of proximal relationship to me, I have some obligation to care for them. Addams takes this idea one step further by suggesting that we as good citizens in a democracy have an obligation to seek out unknown others for the purpose of understanding them and potentially caring and acting on their behalf. We have to actively bring others into our proximal relations. Caring exchanges between people was a major focus of the settlement movement. According to Addams, a settlement's "social relations are successful as it touches to life the dreary and isolated, and brings them into fuller participation of the common inheritance."[15] For Addams, morality is ultimately about social ethics, therefore making care a social practice and not merely a personal virtue.

SOCIALIZING CARE

The notion that "the personal is political" might be relegated to a slogan from a wave of feminism whose time has passed. However, the philosophical depth of this statement is, perhaps, not fully appreciated. Connecting experience at the level of personal interaction with experience at the level of public policy and the actions of social institutions requires a delicate balance between theory and action that many moral theories are ill-equipped to make. The legacy of the Enlightenment's glorification of the individual coupled with the rise of capitalism has hampered the ability of theorists in the Western tradition to address communal ideas of morality, epistemology, and action. Some, such as theologian and social commentator Reinhold Niebuhr, have asked whether it is even possible to have a viable social morality.

> Individual men may be moral in the sense that they are able to consider interests other than their own in determining problems of conduct, and are, on occasion, capable of preferring the advantages of others to their own. They are endowed by nature with a measure of sympathy and consideration for their kind, the breadth of which may be extended by an astute pedagogy . . . . But all these achievements are more difficult, if not impossible, for human societies and social groups."[16]

Niebuhr's realism, expressed here in the post-Progressive Era (1932), has largely held sway in popular beliefs until the present, with perhaps a respite during the 1960s. Note that Niebuhr, far from being a care ethicist, couches his notion of morality in terms that resonate with care: consideration for others and sympathy. Yet, he dismisses the idea that society can act morally in these terms.

In *Starting at Home: Caring and Social Policy*, Nel Noddings challenges Niebuhr's claim by proposing that if small groups, such as households, can be moral then perhaps that model of morality can be extended to larger groups: "What might we learn if . . . we start with a description of best homes and then move outward to the larger society?"[17] Rather than take moral ideas that arise in social and political theory and apply them to the home, Noddings asks us to examine the caring that takes place in functional and flourishing homes to see what can be useful in the social arena. The personal is political, or at least morality among intimates has implications for public morality.

Hull-House was an analogue to Noddings's reversal of the philosophic tradition both in its physical manifestation and as a symbol of the evolving social power of women. As mentioned, Addams and Starr began Hull-House as a home in the midst of the poverty of Chicago's West Side. It was decorated and furnished as a home and had regular residents who lived there. One did not merely go to work at Hull-House; those who worked there usually made it their home, sometimes for decades. Nevertheless, Hull-House was not just any home; it was a home turned inside out. The private, and all it entailed, including the nature of the relations between residents, was made public. As Beatrice Webb sardonically observed in her diary upon visiting Hull-House in 1898, "Hull-House itself is a spacious mansion, with all its rooms open, American fashion, into each other. There are no doors, or, more exactly, no *shut* doors: the residents wander from room to room, visitors wander here, there and everywhere; the whole ground floor is, in fact, one continuous passage leading nowhere in particular."[18] Neighbors were welcome at Hull-House at all hours. One of Addams's biographers recounts the story of Addams's confrontation with a burglar one night at Hull-House, "Discovering that he was not a professional but an amateur out of employment, she told him to go away and come back at nine the next morning, when she would see what she could do about getting him a job. He came, and she got him work."[19] Even when the private sphere was materially violated, Addams applied care that engaged a public solution. At Hull-House, the public sphere was continually allowed into the private sphere with the expressed desire that the private sphere would influence and change the public sphere.

Although there were male residents, Hull-House was clearly a woman's space. Never before had women been in such a position of power to burst the separation of public and private spheres. Most of the women were college educated, and many of them were not in relationships with men. Hull-House provided a sanctuary for women's independence and social separatism without the fetters of religious affiliation.

One reflection of Hull-House's women-centered orientation can be observed in the common description of the residents' work as "social housekeeping." This characterization of their work has the potential to marginalize their accomplishments given the historical devaluation of women's work within the cult of domesticity. Yet social housekeeping also reflects the moral demeanor of Hull-House as an inverted home. Addams and her colleagues did engage in public projects that were familiar to women in homemaking—caring for children and cleaning up the neighborhood—but they also applied moral dispositions from idealized homes to these social problems: listening, responding, and caring. Most commentators focus on the kind of work Hull-House residents undertook and overlook the ethical approach they took: socializing care. Addams, the resident public philosopher, explores the experiences in her books, such as *Democracy and Social Ethics*, where she takes stories of their social housekeeping and finds an emergent social theory.

Addams and her cohort applied the morality of a caring home, as they understood it, to the problems of the neighborhood (and later they applied them to the problems of the nation and the world). What are the phenomenal characteristics that mark an idealized notion of a caring home?

HULL-HOUSE AS A MODEL FOR SOCIALIZING CARE

Addams was a pragmatist. For those not familiar with American philosophy, pragmatism may elicit a number of connotations. For Addams, pragmatism was a philosophy and method of being in the world that was disinterested in truth or knowledge separate from its function and good in society. Accordingly, Addams was not an advocate of social settlements for their own sake, but she valued them for their function in society's well-being and growth. In "A Function of the Social Settlement" she describes social settlements as a crucial exercise in social epistemology: "It is an attempt to express the meaning of life in terms of life itself, in forms of activity . . . so the settlement, when it attempts to reveal and apply knowledge, deems its results practicable, when it has made knowledge available which before was abstract, when through use, it has made common the knowledge which was partial before, because it could only be apprehended by the intellect."[20] Hull-House was a community organization dedicated to collecting information for the purpose of transforming the vague and abstract into the real and tangible because authentic care requires a measure of tangibility. Accordingly, socializing care requires a degree of knowledge gathering. Institutions and organizations that are not reciprocal and cannot connect with their constituency to gain deeper understanding will have a difficult time being characterized as caring.

I suggest that at least six characteristics made up the socialized care that Hull-House employed to achieve so much success in local and later national reform. These characteristics include proximity, listening, respect for others, willingness to act, fallibility, and flexibility. These qualities resonate with Noddings's notion of an ideal caring home that in turn can be a model for social policy. The characteristics of the socializing care that Hull-House exhibited also map well onto Tronto's elements of an ethic of care: attentiveness, responsibility, competence, responsiveness, and integrity.[21]

Proximity

Vast physical distance does not extinguish care, but it can severely challenge the human capacity for the requisite connection. Physical distance truncates the character of transactions. For example, without contact it becomes easier to stereotype a member of a distant culture as foreign or alien. Geopolitical conflict often manifests such distrust for the distant and unfamiliar other. While family members often leave proximal relations over time without experiencing any diminished care, the relations were originally forged in proximity.

In "The Objective Value of a Social Settlement" Addams describes the intentionality of Hull-House's proximity to its neighbors and their social transactions: "The site for a settlement was selected in the first instance because of its diversity and the variety of activity for which it presented an opportunity. It has been the aim of the residents to respond to all sides of the neighborhood life."[22] The physical presence of the Hull-House residents provided numerous opportunities for intervention and support, but it also had epistemological implications. Proximity facilitates the gaining of affective knowledge—knowledge that goes beyond facts to a deeper personal understanding—that can spur caring that is not merely a personal emotional response of sympathy but, as Addams describes, can also have an impact on socializing care: "the residents of a social settlement have an opportunity of seeing institutions from the recipient's standpoint, of catching the sprit of the original impulse which founded them. This experience ought to have a certain value and ultimately find expression in institutional management."[23] Long before feminist standpoint theory was developed, Addams recognized that standpoint matters and it is important to bring knowledge of varied standpoints to the operation of social organizations. While close proximity does not guarantee understanding, it does facilitate better awareness of insider knowledge.

Hull-House demonstrated the significance of proximity for social programs and decision making. Addams and her cohort were literally neighbors, creating the opportunity for understanding, trust, and responsiveness not entirely possible from afar.

Listening

Hull-House began with little by way of plans. Although they made some mistakes, Addams and her cohort were master listeners who developed projects and plans based on the expressed needs of the neighborhood. Listening is perhaps the most important yet overlooked aspect of caring. It is difficult to imagine a caring relationship that does not involve authentic engagement and listening. Noddings refers to this as "engrossment," and Tronto addresses this as "attentiveness." Modern bureaucracies are perceived to be antithetical to the notion of listening.

The creation of the "Jane Club" was an example of the responsiveness and listening skills of Hull-House residents. At a meeting of working women from a local shoe factory attended by Addams, it became clear that these laborers lacked clout because they were incapable of amassing effective strike efforts. Single women were particularly vulnerable to intimidation because they would lose their apartments if they could not make their monthly rent payments. Addams helped start a living cooperative so that the single workers could assist with one another's rent and responsibilities during times of need. The cooperative was named the Jane Club, and it was organized as self-sufficient from the Hull-House operation. The Jane Club eventually grew to occupy an entire building. Addams and the other residents would not have imagined such an undertaking when they started Hull-House, but they listened and responded to a need that presented itself.[24]

Respect for Others

One of the early critiques of care ethics was a concern for the threat of paternalism, borne out of the metaphor of the parent-child dyads, that so commonly represents the care relationship. The early operation of Hull-House could be accused of paternalism as well, given the biases that the upper-middle class women brought to the project. However, those paternalistic ideas quickly faded as Addams and the Hull-House residents gained an appreciation for the diversity of cultures and the vitality that such pluralism brought. They fought through cultural and political stigma to see and respect the common humanity in everyone. For example, when Mexican immigrants moved into the neighborhood and conflicts arose with the more established Italian immigrants, Hull-House residents insured that the new immigrants had the adequate use of their facilities despite the opposition.[25] The respect for diversity extended to political standpoints. While socialists, anarchists, and labor leaders were routinely persecuted, they were given an opportunity to speak at Hull-House functions even when their views differed from those of the residents.[26]

While they did not always live up to their ideals, the Hull-House residents strove for a fundamental respect for humanity that transcended race, class, and gender prejudice as well as prejudice against those who make poor choices. Addams describes the philosophy: "It [social settlements] must be grounded in a philosophy whose foundation is on the solidarity of the human race, a philosophy which will not waver when the race happens to be represented by a drunken woman or an idiot boy."[27]

Willingness to Act

Most care theorists recognize that care lies within a continuum of commitment. Noddings's distinction between natural and ethical caring is one such acknowledgment that caring is not a monolithic response. Action is associated with deeper commitments to care. As Noddings describes, "Caring requires me to respond to the initial impulse with an act of commitment: I commit myself either to overt action on behalf of the cared-for . . . or I commit myself to thinking about what I might do."[28] The residents of Hull-House were always willing to respond to their neighbors with action. Addams linked ethical theory to performance: "action is indeed the sole medium of expression for ethics. We continually forget that the sphere of morals is the sphere of action, that speculation in regard to morality is but observation and must remain in the sphere of intellectual comment, that a situation does not really become moral until we are confronted with the question of what shall be done in a concrete case, and are obliged to act upon our theory."[29] Hull-House was a place where the imagination could take thought to action. If a need arose and there was no precedent for action, Addams and the other residents would not limit the possibilities.

An example of the organization's willingness to act came with the creation of a juvenile court—the first in the nation. Entering another new arena, jurisprudence, the residents of Hull-House helped advocate for, and ultimately staff, a court dedicated to juvenile offenders. Previously, youths who committed crimes were tried and sentenced as adults, resulting in prison sentences that often carried them deep into adulthood. More important, young people were imprisoned with adult criminals who could have nothing but a detrimental influence. This was purely a punitive model of justice. Listening to the families of immigrants fret over their teenage children and observing the plight of youth gangs motivated the Hull-House residents to take action. Recognizing the environmental factors in what was then referred to as delinquency, Hull-House residents, including Addams, Alinza Smith, Julia Lathrop, and Louise Bowen, helped pass an 1899 law creating the juvenile court.[30] Judges in this court had the freedom to respond to the situation of particular youths by allowing them to make young offenders wards of the state, assign probation, or send them to an appropriate correction facility rather than an adult prison. For our purposes, the point of this endeavor is that care on the part of the Hull-House residents was not limited to relationships with individual youths; it took on a more radical character in the form of changing social policy. They took action to socialize care.

Fallibility and Flexibility

Perhaps the one aspect of Hull-House that is most foreign to modern public discourse was its humility. Addams and her peers were quite willing to make and admit their mistakes, of which there were many. They viewed their errors as opportunities for learning and growing. There is something very human about fallibility. Mistakes made in an earnest attempt at caring are not only forgivable but can foster an even stronger bond if they are admitted to and dealt with in their proper context. Today, social institutions and public leaders seldom admit to error, which can lead to an atmosphere of distrust. In employing the metaphor of the ideal home, Noddings explicitly acknowledges, "I left room for mistakes and shortcomings—losses of temper, shared blame, acts of coercion not strictly necessary, doubts about the importance of inferred needs and the goods of expressed needs."[31] The goal of socializing care is not perfection or some unrealistic moral world. The aim of socializing care is to create policies and institutions that value care through their attentiveness and responsiveness in a fundamentally human manner—which will entail mistakes.

Addams's writings are replete with anecdotes from Halsted Street, and she readily includes failed undertakings. However, Addams is not merely writing memoirs. Her recounting of an experience is usually accompanied with the lessons learned. Addams is committed to education and growth that cannot afford to be deluded by fantasies of infallibility. For example, applying the latest information about nutrition and diet, Hull-House added a public kitchen and coffeehouse with all the latest culinary equipment to their campus. They hoped to assist the community by improving nutrition and economics by teaching about portion control as well as providing an alternative to the ever-present saloons where there were morally questionable activities taking place. As it turned out, the coffeehouse was initially unpopular because the cuisine was less than inspiring and the decor was off-putting for the neighbors. While they held admirable goals, Addams later realized how paternalistic they had been: "The experience of the coffee-house taught us not to hold to precon-ceived ideas of what the neighborhood ought to have, but to keep ourselves in readiness to modify and adapt our undertaking as we discovered those things which the neighborhood was ready to accept."[32] They did modify and adapt the coffeehouse, resulting in its eventual popularity as a useful part of the Hull-House complex. More important, Hull-House residents learned from their errors. After the early years, paternalistic decisions were less frequent and the neighborhood increasingly trusted Addams and her cohort. Addams viewed socializing care as a value that would grow and change with those who would be cared for: "the one thing to be dreaded in the Settlement is that it lose its flexibility, its power of quick adaptation, its readiness to change its methods as its environment may demand."[33]

IMPLICATIONS FOR THE TWENTY-FIRST CENTURY

While Jane Addams and the Hull-House community were products of the nineteenth and twentieth centuries, it appears to me that they have continuing lessons for socializing care in the twenty-first century. While I do not expect social settlements to reemerge any time soon, they had a commitment to so-cial improvement through responsiveness to community members sorely lacking in many modern institutions. To speak of "institutional care" seems oxymoronic, but Hull-House developed a communal culture of care that sought to employ sympathetic understanding to local issues. Fighting for garbage collection, establishing juvenile courts, creating playgrounds for children, and dispensing birth control information were all caring responses to the needs of the neighborhood and attempts to bring about what Addams called lateral progress—a form of social progress that encompasses the gen-eral populace and not merely the elite. Addams demonstrated how collective efforts could infuse care into a harsh city life and ultimately beyond.

Perhaps one might retort that such progress was possible because Hull-House was a relatively small neighborhood organization and thus more easily capable of exhibiting care. However, Hull-House's influence went far beyond Halsted

Street. In 1903 Hull-House residents, spearheaded by Florence Kelley, began a campaign to create a Federal Children's Bureau that would collect and provide information on the health and well-being of children and spearhead advocacy for reforms. After a massive effort by social reformers, the Children's Bureau became a reality in 1912, and former Hull-House resident and Addams's confidant, Julia Lathrop, became the first woman to head a federal agency. Lathrop explicitly modeled the Children's Bureau on what she had learned at Hull-House. Even through it was a federal agency, headquartered in Washington, D.C., it adopted the posture of listening, responsiveness, flexibility, and willingness to act that characterized Hull-House. As Robyn Muncy describes:

> Bureau workers . . . showed warm concern for the countless women who wrote letters to them. . . . Women wrote to the Bureau to confide beatings, ignorance about birth control, menstrual problems, and pregnancies outside of marriage . . . . Such letters revealed the Children's Bureau's reputation for responsiveness, which was a reputation well-deserved. Every plea for help elicited a personal reply from the Bureau's staff and often involved long hours attempting to ensure adequate care. Usually that care came from an appropriate local agency to which the Bureau referred the supplicant . . . . The Bureau contradicted latter-day preconceptions about bureaucracy: it was not simply an impersonal machine cranking out studies and forms according to standard operating procedures, but also a flexible institution, responding to problems outside its official ken.[34]

While the Social Security Act effectively put the Children's Bureau out of business, the socialized caring of the agency was not so easily replicated. The women of Hull-House had successfully brought the morality of their inverted home to the national scene.

Hull-House reveals that institutions and public policies can be caring if we have the political will to make them so. Such a commitment is not easy because it involves trusting in humanity and making room for ambiguity and mistakes.

NOTES

1. Joan Tronto, *Moral Boundaries: A Political Argument for an Ethic of Care* (New York: Routledge, 1993), 103.

2. Tronto, *Moral Boundaries*.

3. Tronto, *Moral Boundaries*, 125.

4. Tronto, *Moral Boundaries*, 126.

5. Ironically, the economic environment in the 1890s epitomized what many free-market conservatives aspire to today: few labor laws, virtually no environmental controls, cheap and abundant labor with no benefit costs. To see where free-market measures

can lead, one only has to look to the quality of life for most laborers at the turn of the last century.

6. Allen Davis, *Spearheads for Reform: The Social Settlements and the Progressive Movement 1890–1914* (New York, Oxford University Press, 1967), 12.

7. Jane Addams, *Twenty Years at Hull-House* (New York, Signet, 1960), 76.

8. William James, quoted in Deegan, *Jane Addams and the Men of the Chicago School 1892–1918* (New Brunswick: Transactions Books, 1990), 254.

9. Jane Addams, *Democracy and Social Ethics* (Urbana, Ill.: University of Illinois Press, 2002), 117.

10. Addams, *Democracy and Social Ethics*, 7.

11. Virginia Held. "I am coming to the view that care and its related considerations are the wider framework—or network—within which room should be made for justice, utility, and the virtues." "Liberalism and the Ethics of Care" in *On Feminist Ethics and Politics*, ed. Claudia Card (Lawrence: University Press of Kansas, 1999), 302.

12. Jane Addams, "Social Control," *Crisis: A Record of the Darker Races*, I (January 1911), 21–22.

13. Addams, *Twenty Years at Hull-House*, 100.

14. Nel Noddings, *Caring: A Feminine Approach to Ethics and Moral Education* (Berkeley: University of California Press, 1984), 47.

15. Jane Addams, "A Function of the Social Settlement," *Annals of the American Academy of Political and Social Science*, 13 (January–June 1889): 56.

16. Reinhold Niebuhr, *Moral Man and Immoral Society* (New York: Charles Scribner's Sons), xi.

17. Nel Noddings, *Starting at Home: Caring and Social Policy* (Berkeley: University of California Press, 2002), 1.

18. Beatrice Webb, "A Fabian Visits Hull-House," in *100 Years at Hull-House*, eds. Mary Lynn McCree Bryan and Allen F. Davis (Bloomington: Indiana University Press, 1990), 61.

19. James Weber Linn, *Jane Addams: A Biography* (Urbana: University of Illinois Press, 2000), 14.

20. Addams, "A Function of the Social Settlement," 326.

21. Tronto, *Moral Boundaries*, 127.

22. Jane Addams, "The Objective Value of A Social Settlement," in *The Jane Addams Reader*, ed. Jean Bethke Elshtain (New York: Basic Books, 2002), 32.

23. Addams, "The Objective Value of A Social Settlement," 39.

24. Addams, *Twenty Years at Hull-House*, 106–7.

25. Peggy Glowacki, "Bringing Art to Life: The Practice of Art at Hull-House," in *Pots of Promise*, eds. Cheryl R. Ganz and Margaret Strobel (Urbana: University of Illinois Press, 2004), 21–22.

26. Addams, *Twenty Years at Hull-House*, 139.

27. Addams, *Twenty Years at Hull-House*, 98.

28. Noddings, *Caring*, 81.

29. Addams, *Democracy and Social Ethics*, 119.

30. Jane Addams, "The 'Juvenile-Adult' Offender," *Ladies' Home Journal* 30, no. 10 (October 1913): 24.

31. Noddings, *Starting at Home*, 230.

32. Addams, *Twenty Years at Hull-House*, 103.

33. Addams, *Twenty Years at Hull-House*, 98.

34. Robyn Muncy, *Creating a Female Dominion in American Reform 1890–1935* (New York: Oxford University Press, 1991), 52–53.

Chapter Seven

From "Giving Care" to "Taking Care": Negotiating Care Work at Welfare's End

Deborah L. Little

"How are you going to support your kid in five years?" the teacher asked the welfare-reliant women in a welfare-to-work agency in 1997. She was expressing the reality of welfare's end in the United States. American welfare reform transformed care work. Globally, it was part of a larger neoliberal work enforcement project in Western welfare states, one which is transforming poor women into (male) breadwinners, a gendered family activity.[1]

In contrast to those who explore welfare's end primarily as work enforcement I examine it as a transformation in care work. Welfare's end was one facet of changes in the conditions under which care is given and received.[2] The cutbacks in welfare state commitments and spending represent a pulling back from efforts to socialize care. A discussion of care was absent from the national legislative debates as most policy makers considered the problem resolved with the provision of some monies for paid child care. However, in local welfare-to-work programs street-level workers implemented the new work demands by redefining the meaning and place of care in the lives of welfare-reliant mothers.[3]

Thus I examine welfare reform as a negotiation over the meaning of care. Using Joan Tronto's account of four "phases" of care I demonstrate the ways in which welfare-to-work staff challenged the primacy of direct caregiving for welfare-reliant mothers through discursive strategies that persuaded these mothers to shift from "giving care" to "taking care of," or from mothering to wage work.[4] These state representatives: 1) proposed a liberal feminist theory that women were trapped by domestic caregiving but could be fulfilled by wage work, 2) promoted a vision of caregiving in which children's needs were in conflict with the needs of their mothers, and 3) identified wage labor as the appropriate way for mothers to care for their children. Fully aware of the centrality of direct care for their clients, welfare-to-work staff redefined the meanings of "care" and "mother" as they pushed women off welfare and into wage work.

Any discussion of transformations in care necessarily implicates gender. Tronto's phases reflect the gendered division of labor in care work. Historically, women have been those who "give care" through direct caregiving, while men are the ones who "take care" by deciding how care needs should be met. Thus, in persuading women to change from "giving" to "taking" care, or from mothering to wage earning, the state persuaded women to adopt a more "masculine" form of care. I argue that these activities represented a crucial aspect of welfare reform.

In focusing on the implementation of welfare reform I join other ethnographers in demonstrating that state policy is both altered and given meaning primarily in the face-to-face relationships between street-level workers and their clients.[5] While these researchers focus on various aspects of welfare reform, all challenge understandings of identity derived only from the policy level of welfare state programs. Their work suggests that welfare state clients are constructed, shaped, and transformed not only by hegemonic policy discourses or their own social location but more particularly by their local interactions with state representatives.[6] I argue that welfare state representatives sought to produce a new social identity among their clients. They began with the premise that their clients had two dominant identities in their relationship with the state—a stigmatized identity of welfare recipient and a positive identity of mother. Rejecting a strategy that shamed recipients into wage work, staff focused instead on deconstructing the centrality of motherhood while promoting a dominant identity of worker. Thus, while some scholars have argued that American welfare reform represents an abandonment of care,[7] I argue that state representatives worked to transform the meaning of caregiving. One consequence of this transformation was that underlying structural inequalities in caregiving were obscured.

POLICY REGIMES

To organize my analysis I identify three policy regimes. The first, which I call the "welfare regime," existed from 1935 to 1988. The second regime, named the "welfare-to-work regime," existed from 1988 to 1996. The third regime, which I call the "workfare regime," began in 1996. Each regime began with national welfare legislation directed at single mothers.[8] I differentiate these regimes according to their support for full-time maternal caregiving and their demands for wage work by welfare-reliant women.

Welfare Regime: Supporting Direct Caregiving

The welfare regime began with the 1935 enactment of the Aid to Dependent Children program, later called the Aid to Families with Dependent Children

(AFDC) program. AFDC was created to enable the caregiving labor of (white) widowed mothers who otherwise might be forced out of their homes into wage work, putting children at risk of neglect and families at risk of separation. The hegemonic gender ideology of the period supported men and women in separate spheres with full-time mothering and full-time male breadwinning. Nonwhite women were considered employable and restricted in their use of welfare benefits until the 1950s and 1960s.[9] Nonetheless, over the course of the century many of the behavioral regulations were abolished. The benefits gave women some independence from individual men and some regular income to support caregiving. In addition, the program evolved from one serving primarily white widows to one serving a racially diverse population of divorced, separated, and never-married mothers. While some efforts to encourage wage work were made in the 1960s, especially with the Work Incentive Program of 1967, these efforts were limited by continuing ambivalence about requiring mothers to enter wage labor.[10] The state supported direct caregiving, albeit in racist, stingy, and controlling ways.

Welfare-to-Work Regime: Decentering Direct Caregiving

The welfare-to-work regime began with enactment of the 1988 federal Family Support Act. Policy makers saw welfare-reliant women as reluctant and/or unskilled workers in need of training, education, and encouragement. Therefore, ever-greater numbers of welfare-reliant mothers were required to participate in a range of training programs each year. However, the state remained ambivalent about forcing these mothers to forgo direct caregiving for wage work. Women were encouraged to move into wage work even as their eligibility for aid remained tied to their status as caregivers. Thus, this regime was a transitional one between the welfare regime that supported direct caregiving and the workfare regime that ignored it.

There are multiple conflicts inherent in care work, and welfare workers used these to construct new client identities. During the welfare-to-work regime, welfare staff focused on the conflict between caring for self and caring for others by trying to decenter direct caregiving. Staff maneuvered between the ongoing support for caregiving represented by continued eligibility for AFDC benefits and the evolving state demands that welfare-reliant women enter wage work by using a discourse that highlighted conflicts between women's own needs and those of their children.

Workfare Regime: Disregarding Direct Caregiving

By 1996 many single and married mothers were in the labor force, at least part time, and expectations regarding full-time mothering were in flux. Welfare reformers had justified their 1988 welfare-to-work demands by pointing to the numbers and changed behaviors of working mothers.[11] Political attitudes were affected as well by the ongoing perception that AFDC was a program that benefited undeserving, unwed, black teen mothers.[12] In the face of rising, rather than shrinking, caseloads in the welfare-to-work regime, policy makers enacted more draconian legislation.

The workfare regime began with the abolition of AFDC in 1996. Under the Personal Responsibility and Work Opportunities Reconciliation Act (PRA), welfare recipients are required to enter some form of work activity within two years and face a lifetime benefit limit of five years. The fact that these mothers are the sole caregivers for their children is essentially ignored, except insofar as women are expected to place their children in day care or after-school care. Many of the welfare-to-work regime training and education programs were limited or eliminated and states began pushing women into what is called "work first"—either job hunting or workfare in community public and private agencies. The workfare regime views all "parents" as breadwinners.[13]

The direct caregiving labor of AFDC-reliant mothers was ignored and devalued as legislators required single mothers to provide the means for care, rather than the care itself. Welfare-to-work staff responded to the new work requirements by essentially disregarding direct caregiving and focusing instead on wage work as the required form of care. No longer needing to maneuver between continued AFDC eligibility and increased work expectations, staff presented an alternative understanding of care in which mothers take care of children by breadwinning and being role models. Because it is impossible for most women in capitalist economies to both provide the means of care and provide direct care for their own children,[14] direct caregiving was to be provided by others. Of course, mothers remained bound to direct caregiving but now were expected to purchase care services while they performed wage work. Their own direct caregiving in a "second shift" remained invisible.[15] Overall, then, implementation of the workfare regime led state representatives to discursively reconstruct the meaning of care.

Thus the welfare regime viewed women as mothers and supported direct caregiving labor. The welfare-to-work regime viewed women as reluctant workers and focused on decentering caregiving. The workfare regime views women as unemployed breadwinners and disregards direct caregiving while demanding that women take care of their families as wage earners. My focus is on the latter stages of welfare reform, beginning with the FSA welfare-to-work programs that existed between 1988 and 1996 and concluding with the PRA workfare programs that began in 1996. I explore the discursive strategies employed by welfare workers during the last two regimes. These strategies reflected and responded to the existing structures and ideologies of welfare.

STUDYING WELFARE-TO-WORK IN TWO REGIMES

My research is based on two periods of participant observation in a New York City welfare-to-work program that provided adult basic education (pre–General Education Diploma) and work experience. I call this agency the Community Education Center (CEC). The CEC occupied a brick building in a low-income neighborhood filled with public housing, small retail stores, fast-food outlets, schools, and public agencies. I spent seven months at the CEC in 1993 when the agency ran a program under the welfare-to-work regime. I returned to the same program for another eight months in 1996–1997 after the workfare regime began. During both periods, I attended classes, assemblies, peer group meetings, and staff meetings for several days each week. I had innumerable unstructured discussions with students and staff. I supplemented this fieldwork with interviews of ten welfare-reliant women in 1993 and eight women in 1997.[16] In addition, I formally interviewed eight staff (of twenty-two), six of whom had worked at the agency from 1992 to 1997, and another two who left before 1996.[17]

During the welfare-to-work regime women were required to "work" or train for work twenty hours per week. Consistent with the assumptions of AFDC, the work training demands did not interfere with women's caregiving labor, allowing them to meet school buses and tend to children. During the workfare regime New York City required women to attend work programs thirty hours per week and put greater emphasis on finding jobs. Children's schedules were not taken into consideration except when welfare department workers pressured clients to find child care.

CARE WORK IN THE WELFARE STATE

While there is a large literature on women and states, it generally follows three separate trajectories. The most substantial literature examines women as clients of welfare states, charting the complicated ways in which states structure gender identities, channel women into wage or reproductive work, and affect gender equality.[18] Another body of work examines the implications for women of welfare state policies that enforce a gendered notion of citizenship.[19] Recently, feminist scholars have tried to integrate literature on women's work as caregivers with literature on welfare state retrenchment and reconstruction.[20] This literature examines the relationships between states, markets, and families and the ways in which these institutions shape the provision of care.

In contrast to the literature on women and the welfare state, much of the literature examining the material impact of welfare reform has ignored or sidelined the impact of retrenchment, especially welfare reform, on different aspects of care work.[21] Ethnographers have explored the discursive practices of street-level workers engaged in efforts to enforce wage work.[22] While they have focused on the gendered discourses operating in these programs, their emphasis has been on the production of wage earners rather than the transformation of care. Certainly the program I studied was involved in teaching skills and encouraging wage work. Their practices had implications for women's material well-being and willingness to forgo state support in exchange for wage work. However, this research asks a different question. From the outset, this agency focused on the fact that its clients were mothers. How, then, did this welfare-to-work agency encourage women to transform their mothering from care work to wage work?

In discussing care it is important to begin with definitions. Initially, feminist care researchers defined care as labor plus love.[23] Tronto agrees that caregiving is both a practice and a disposition, but defines the practice to include caring about, taking care of, caregiving, and care receiving. These phases are explained as follows: 1) "caring about" involves recognizing that a need exists and deciding to address it, 2) "taking care of" includes taking responsibility for the need and deciding how to respond, 3) "caregiving" entails actually meeting the need through one's own labor, and 4) "care receiving" recognizes the response of the care recipient to the first three phases.[24] Thus Tronto adds to direct caregiving labor the tasks of acknowledging the existence of a need and assuming some responsibility to meet the need.

The particular value of Tronto's understanding of care lies in its expansion of our notions of care to include, and therefore potentially value, types of care activity beyond direct caregiving. Of course, welfare-reliant women already performed the first three aspects of care insofar as they recognized their children's need for care, determined to take care of the need with the financial support of welfare, and performed direct caregiving. However, feminist scholars generally agree that the primary challenges confronting efforts to socialize care are the social devaluing of care and the gender division of labor around care. In other words, we will not achieve either gender equality or an effective socialization of care unless we are able to distribute all phases of care more equally among both genders. Tronto reminds us that the different tasks of care are presently divided by race, class, and gender so that whites, men, and the powerful generally perform only the first two aspects of care, while women, nonwhites, and the less powerful perform the physical work of direct caregiving. The first two aspects of care are more highly valued than the third.[25] It would seem an easy task, then, to induce poor nonwhite women to leave a less powerful status like caregiver to embrace the greater respect and authority associated with taking care of others through wage labor.

However, care as affect and practice has long been assigned to women. Research on welfare recipients has demonstrated that many women have defined themselves in terms of their roles and statuses as mothers.[26] Certainly the structure of welfare itself required that they self-identify as mothers. Welfare reform changed the rules for these mothers. This shift in expectations contains the possibility for conflict between the state and welfare recipients, yet overt conflict has been relatively minor. While some welfare rights groups asserted a demand for continued support for full-time caregiving, many more have struggled over the conditions of workfare and work. Did welfare-reliant mothers ultimately agree, then, with the state's demand that they be breadwinners? This research cannot generalize in such a way. But it suggests that the new worker identity required in the workfare regime had to be generated by street-level welfare workers. These processes involved negotiations over the ways in which mothers would care for their children.

NEGOTIATING CARE WORK

The CEC served an African American and Latina population drawn from one of the most impoverished congressional districts in the country. When the women spoke of their children, they spoke of labor as much as love. Good maternal practice was defined by a welfare-reliant mother at the CEC as follows: "Good mothers are the ones making sure that their kids don't run around all raggedy. They take care of their kids, make sure that they're home, went to school, and weren't out there robbing nobody."

This definition also reminds us that these mothers raised their children under conditions of severe oppression. Patricia Hill Collins wrote that African American motherhood included teaching self-reliance, socializing children for survival, and providing better chances for their children.[27] Mothering also had many personal costs, including coping with unwanted pregnancies and the stress of providing for one's children. Poverty, crime, educational failure, juvenile delinquency, violence, and poor health constituted the environment in which the mothers at the CEC tried to raise children. Interview data and fieldwork from both periods of research reveal that they placed value on their own caregiving because they protected their children from these social ills. Mothers spoke of juggling bills and of using food stamps wisely at the beginning of the month to ensure enough food for the whole month. Even so, some had to rely on food pantries. On a typical day, many women missed school because of caregiving obligations caused by the poor health of family members. While a few women lived near decent schools or had obtained scholarships for parochial schools, the majority struggled to get their children decent and safe educations in the public schools. Crime was a frequent companion for most mothers. They shared strategies for keeping children safe while doing laundry, while on the street, and while moving about in public housing.

How, then, did staff encourage the women to seek wage work, given the constrained and difficult caregiving world they faced? This is not the right question to ask. Most women, like recipients in other studies, expressed a desire to work.[28] In fact, most had worked or were working, in small, part-time, off-the-books jobs that did not conflict with their children's schedules. When trusted care providers like grandmothers were present, some women had worked full time. A more accurate question, then, is how did staff negotiate an understanding of care that placed wage work ahead of caregiving? Staff used different strategies under the two regimes. The strategies changed because the terms under which public assistance was given changed.

THE WELFARE-TO-WORK REGIME: DECENTERING DIRECT CAREGIVING

During the welfare-to-work regime, welfare-reliant women at the CEC identified mothering as both a primary role and as the basis for their entitlement to AFDC. CEC staff recognized the primacy of caregiving, even while national, state, and city policy makers tried to ignore it. One teacher said, "Parenting is the one clear thing these clients have. It's something that they can be proud of." The welfare-to-work regime, however, demanded that these mothers be trained for wage work. Staff's challenge was to encourage work and undermine the centrality of mothering, within the context of social policy that still provided benefits precisely because the clients were mothers. How did they do this?

These welfare workers pursued several interconnected discursive strategies as they complied with the mandates of the welfare-to-work regime. First, staff painted a liberal feminist portrait of wage work as a development of self and an escape from domesticity. As part of this portrayal, they redefined domestic labor as skills development, portraying mothering as a practice that taught marketable skills. Second, they emphasized the inherent conflict between developing yourself through wage work and devoting your labor to children in the home.

As I have elaborated in other work, some of the educational curriculum encouraged CEC students to conceptualize domestic work, from shopping to child care, as a set of skills they could list on their résumés.[29] Many women embraced this interpretation of their caregiving, correcting mothers who belittled themselves as lacking skills. For the most part, however, staff turned their energies to convincing women that wage work was the route to fulfilled womanhood. The word "career" was used to describe any job in which the student expressed interest—from home health aide to security guard. Teachers asked the mothers to identify their own interests, skills, and personality traits and then to match those with a job description. Students were taught to say, "I want to get a career," where "career" was defined as something you train for and want to do for a long period of time. The rewards were often portrayed in the gendered discourse of liberal feminism. Work would give you independence from eligibility workers and from men. Work would also help you to become more than a mother—you would develop your talents and skills. Staff thus told clients that welfare and men were obstacles to growth and development.

Caregiving was also presented as an obstacle to personal growth. This strategy reflected staff's genuine belief that caregiving was the primary reason that the women were limited to low education, low skills, and low-wage work or welfare. One staff member described a speaker who was coming to talk at the CEC as an "inspiration," because she obtained her GED *despite* ten years of "family stuff" getting in the way. Teachers often expressed concern about the narrow world the students lived in, saying, "They just go from home to CEC to the welfare office to the kids' school to the local store and back home." Staff described both education and wage work as doorways into the world. During a class discussion about employment, a teacher asked her students why they should go to work. "For the kids," the mothers replied. "But what about for *you*?" queried the teacher.

Given clients' assertions of caregiving demands in the face of welfare-to-work rules, CEC staff saw their task as reducing its importance to the women. The teachers stressed that mothering was for a limited period, asking students what they would do when the kids were gone. They praised women for their academic work, telling the clients that they should succeed for themselves and not just as role models for their children.

Welfare-reliant mothers readily accepted the discourse about men being obstacles in their lives. They complained that many men were unreliable, jealous, controlling, and belittling and that they let women do all the work, acted like babies while stressing their own importance, and failed to support their children. Some mothers spoke of domestic violence and of the substance abuse of former boyfriends or husbands. CEC staff had sympathy for these complaints. They used the women's allegations of standing up to men as examples of students overcoming barriers.

Congruent with the strategy of reconstructing clients as working women, staff suggested that children, as well as men, could be a hindrance. This was not a perfect analogy. Children were not portrayed as selfish or immature in the way that men sometimes were. However, staff told the mothers that the needs and demands of both men and children interfered with women's own needs. Putting caregiving first, staff suggested, led to the same consequences as catering to men.

Some program rules reflected the decentering of direct caregiving as well. The most obvious example was the requirement that recipients continue to attend welfare-to-work programs during the summer months. The mothers challenged this, asking why they had to attend programs when the kids were out of school. One teacher explained, "Because you don't get summers off when you're working." "But we don't HAVE jobs," the students responded logically. "Well," replied the teacher, "They want to get you in practice. . . . That's what work will be, that's what it means to be a working adult." This teacher inadvertently began to prepare the mothers for the workfare regime that would treat them as working adults not bound by school schedules and children's vacations.

Traustadottir theorized that care work is "a specific kind of labor that women perform that requires that women constantly organize and arrange their lives to meet the needs of others. . . . [It is] a life-defining phenomenon in women's existence and a medium through which women are accepted into and feel that they belong in the social world."[30] This role was one that welfare-reliant women in my study asserted in the face of welfare-to-work demands. When staff told women that they could no longer arrange their lives to meet their children's needs, they questioned the "one clear thing" that they knew their clients had faith in, the activity about which the mothers were proud.

Nonetheless, during this intermediate regime, staff always acknowledged the emotional component of caregiving, even as they struggled to reduce its importance to their clients. They never challenged their clients' assertions that children "come first." At times, they assisted women in obtaining deferments so that they could be home attending to their families. The welfare-to-work regime policies allowed some deferments to attend to family needs, and women always had the option of dropping out and risking benefit reductions or other sanctions. Given this structure, staff sometimes deferred to caregiving demands.

Welfare-to-work staff performed a crucial role in the changing welfare regime. They softened the demands for work by framing work in the most desirable terms, using liberal feminist discourse about women's fulfillment through wage work. They challenged the social construction of mothers by encouraging women to think of themselves in terms of work careers. However, this construction of "working women" was insufficient to achieve the work objectives of the regime. Thus staff had to directly confront caregiving by linking care with a disregard of self, by connecting inequality with maternal work, and by pointing out the conflicts between the needs of children and their mothers.

THE WORKFARE REGIME:
DISREGARDING DIRECT CAREGIVING

Under the new workfare regime, welfare-to-work staff no longer had to persuade women to choose wage work over caregiving. Policy makers viewed mothers and fathers as breadwinners who were responsible for the economic support of children. While staff had been enthusiastic partners in the state's efforts to persuade mothers to train for wage work under the welfare-to-work regime, they became reluctant enforcers of the work demands of the workfare regime. As New York City's welfare department made it clear that the rolls would be cut, CEC staff determined to push their clients into wage work quickly. They began to define wage work as the central task of care.

In marked contrast to their strategies during the welfare-to-work regime, CEC staff spent large amounts of time talking about immediate work rather than training for careers. Work readiness requirements that had been handled in a haphazard way during the welfare-to-work regime were now enforced. Teachers put pressure on students to complete cover letters, draft sample job applications, and prepare résumés, all to have at the ready should any job opportunities present themselves. The school implemented a dress code, arguing that the women needed to be available to go to an interview at a moment's notice.

When staff did speak of mothering, they usually promoted a breadwinner identity in the context of minimal choices. A teacher advised her students that they would not all be able to get their high school equivalency degrees before welfare ended but told them that there was work that they could do. "You only have five years. Then there won't be any welfare left for you. The state won't care that you still have a child. How are you going to *support your kid* in five years?" When students actively rejected another teacher's demands that they practice job interviewing skills, the teacher began to lecture them with the new regime demands. She reprimanded them, saying, "You're preparing here for life. The time limits from this welfare reform are dictating to you. This is *serious*—it's a serious business. You all are mothers. Mothers are the most serious people on earth. You have to do this for your family." This exhortation reflected the new type of care work demanded of mothers. Again and again staff emphasized the obligation to earn financial support for children. This labor was linked to caregiving because it was represented as the work of mothers. In addition, teachers told women that work would make them positive role models for their children. To work, then, was to fulfill the important moral and caring obligations of mothers.

In the face of pressures to get a job, the students themselves began to speak of the conflicts in direct caregiving. While the mothers at the CEC rarely expressed the feeling that their children were "unwanted," they began to point to children as a cause of their own welfare recipient status.[31] In one classroom the teacher asked women to recount employment stories. The women spoke of losing jobs because of pregnancies and loss of child care. The teacher translated their stories, saying, "See, you lost jobs because of a man!" There was instantaneous denial from the women. "NO!" they rebutted. "We lost our jobs because of a kid!"

Staff still acknowledged the conflict between caregiving and women's own needs, but they were much more cautious in their assertions than they had been during the welfare-to-work regime. For example, one teacher asked women to list their barriers to achieving work goals. The answers were fairly consistent: "No skills, no GED, my boyfriend, no babysitter, my kids, having a baby before I finished high school." The teacher replied, very carefully, "Kids are a big problem. I don't want to say that your kids are an obstacle, but they do keep you from doing things."

CEC staff no longer encouraged mothers to tend to family problems before welfare-to-work activities. One teacher went so far as to suggest to the mothers that they imagine themselves as truly separate from their kids. She said, "You need to look at yourself outside of your children. When you go home, try not to associate yourself with your children." This suggestion was greeted with derisive laughter. On occasion, the staff even told women to ask for care from their kids. One teacher explained a "Family Support Agreement" that was distributed at orientation. She told the students to take the form home to their children. "Tell them, 'I'm trying to make things better for you. So what will you do to support me?'"

These welfare-reliant mothers were fully aware that their direct caregiving no longer mattered. Women exchanged stories in outraged voices, telling each other about the new demands that they hire someone to stay with a sick child rather than miss a workfare activity. They complained that some workfare programs no longer allowed them to be absent on days that their children's schools were closed. However, while women continued to assert among themselves that their children came first, they rarely sought exemptions from program requirements. When other welfare clients were sweeping the streets in bright orange blazers, school was an attractive alternative.

While the conflicts between women and their children were a central focus of staff trying to persuade welfare-reliant women to enter wage work during the welfare-to-work regime, these conflicts became less important in the workfare regime. Here, the conflict between women and children was less important than the need to convince women that wage work was the best way to provide care.

Perhaps the most poignant expression of what has been lost in the new world of welfare reform came in a student-written play performed during the spring 1997 awards ceremony. Staff had told the mothers that the theme of the ceremony was to be family, but organized the ceremony as a series of speeches by employers. The students in one classroom, however, had seen a film of Lorraine Hansberry's play *A Raisin in the Sun* and decided to write their own family drama. They incorporated the real experiences of class members and created a complex female-headed family in which some children were successful while others struggled. The government was present in the story, in the form of a Child Protective Services (CPS) worker. While the mother received welfare, there was no mention of workfare or wage work in the play. Instead, this mother struggled with the practices of maternal love. The CPS worker entered as a threatening presence investigating the reported truancy of both high school children. In the end, however, she did not take the children, punish the mother, or demand that she become a breadwinner. Instead, she offered information and services in the form of a drug-treatment program for the addicted daughter and an art program for the talented son who had been toying with the idea of selling drugs to bring home extra money. The family chose to use those services. At play's end, the son sold a picture instead of drugs, the younger daughter finished junior high with honors, the addicted daughter came home drug free, and the oldest daughter returned from college for a weekend celebration.

This drama presented a remarkably defiant vision. While not ignoring the coercive power of the state represented by the ability to remove children from the family, this play stressed ways in which the state could support care. In some ways care was socialized as the family, the state, and community agencies worked together to foster the growth of children. The contrast between the series of employer speeches offered by staff and the welfare state vision represented in the play symbolized the profound losses in welfare's end. Without sentimentalizing or offering an unrealistic dream of self-sufficiency or career, the students portrayed a past in which the state threatened but also aided.

CONCLUSION

From the perspective of only one moment in time, CEC staff's emphasis on finding a job in the later period seems unremarkable. Welfare reformers enacted the workfare regime as a form of "tough love" designed to kick women out of the alleged comforts of state support and into the real world of working adulthood. A narrow focus on work appears completely consistent with the demands of the new regime. However, this emphasis is remarkable when viewed from the perspective of the two welfare reform regimes. Only by contrasting the two periods can one see the processes by which the meaning and task of care were transformed.

In the welfare-to-work regime, the CEC treated the caregiving labor of their clients as central. This perception reflected the structural context of the welfare-to-work regime and the history of public assistance, which had defined women as direct caregivers and provided some financial support for that labor. The task of CEC staff, then, was to sell wage work and to decenter the primacy of mothering. These state representatives suggested that the costs of direct caregiving (i.e., the daily physical labor of care) were too high for the women themselves.

In contrast, the direct caregiving of welfare-reliant women was essentially ignored in the workfare regime. Welfare-reliant mothers were forced to engage in a thirty-hour work week of workfare, job hunting, or wage work with only limited time and support for training and education. Mothering as caregiving was eliminated by fiat. In this new structural context there was no need to sell work or persuade women to choose wage work over caregiving. Women were defined as workers by the new welfare policies. In this new environment, staff struggled to push, cajole, or coerce clients into finding jobs as soon as possible. They rarely spoke of caregiving. This silence was deafening.

We cannot fully understand the implementation or impact of welfare reform without attending to these profound changes in caregiving expectations. Research that examines welfare's end only as a problem of work ethic or labor market skills misses this crucial element of reform. While policy makers have chosen to ignore the caregiving of welfare-reliant women, street-level bureaucrats have not been able to do so. Context matters. The welfare regime validated direct care, coming as it did from a period in which gender ideology espoused separate spheres for men and women. While the choices available to mothers had expanded over the sixty years of welfare's existence, women with constrained labor market opportunities used welfare to support their children. They justified welfare reliance by asserting the importance of caregiving in impoverished communities. This justification had to be dealt with by staff implementing the new welfare rules.

What lessons can we learn from the CEC's implementation of welfare reform as we contemplate the practical struggle to socialize care? Joan Tronto's conception of the phases of care offers a way out of a narrow understanding of the gender division of labor in care. Her phases of care incorporate the types of care performed by most members of society. However, Tronto acknowledges that our popular understanding of care is fragmented and bounded, because the empirical reality is that we divide the tasks of care by gender, race, and class. Welfare reform then becomes a cruel joke as implemented, because it tells women to shift their care task to one done by men and claims that this shift both preserves care and leads to greater status and economic well-being. The reality is that welfare-reliant mothers are being channeled into low-wage work,[32] sometimes doing direct caregiving for the children of strangers.

Tronto's vision of socializing care is not met in welfare reform, which instead privatizes, marketizes, and refamilializes care. Rather than enhancing the value of care, state representatives diminish the value of direct caregiving by constructing it as in direct conflict with the gender equality of mothers. This conflict is real, but the solution is not the abandonment of caregiving in favor of a masculinized version of taking care. Welfare reform takes us away from efforts to socialize care.

This is evident when we review the consequences of the workfare regime. While poor single mothers used to be able to turn to welfare benefits as form of paid family leave or unemployment benefit, leaving work or workfare when necessary to tend to children or parents, this option is no longer available. Even if women have jobs with employers mandated to provide twelve weeks of leave, that leave is generally unpaid (California is a recent exception). Insofar as these women also provided direct care for elderly and disabled parents while tending to children, their labor is no longer available, and replacement workers are not funded by the workfare regime (although some elderly may access home health aides through Medicare). While women are told to turn to the market for care workers, the benefits provided under the workfare regime are insufficient to fund decent child care for extended periods. Low-income women are turning to relatives to provide care, unable to afford the costs of center-based care.[33] While studies of the relationship between welfare reform and rises in foster care placement are preliminary, there is some evidence that benefit reductions, immediate work requirements, tough sanctions, and short lifetime benefit limits are associated with increases in out-of-home placement of children.[34]

The workfare regime began during an extended period of economic growth. It now enters the third year of increasing poverty. While scholars have studied the economic impact of replacing welfare benefits with wages, we know much less about the impact of replacing direct caregiving with wage earning. However, we do know that the caregiving previously performed by these mothers has not been replaced with a sufficient amount of quality child care.[35] Women scramble to cobble together child care in the context of inflexible employers, erratic hours, low wages, and unstable jobs. Finally, 20 percent of the workforce in the United States performs paid caregiving work, and the vast majority of these employees are women and minorities.[36] While some of this work is professional, much of it is low-wage work without benefits. Studies of welfare leavers indicate that the majority are entering sales and service occupations.[37] Thus, it appears that some formerly welfare-reliant women are merely transferring their direct caregiving labor from state-supported work in their own homes to market-based care work.

What would a welfare policy that truly socialized care look like? Basic aspects of such a regime are not hard to imagine. Many of these policies exist in other industrialized welfare states. If women need wage work to promote gender equality, as some argue, and if we need to replace their direct caregiving and support the caring that they still perform, then a welfare regime that socialized care would provide universal family allowances, state-supported day care, paid family leave, universal health care, an increased minimum wage, limitations on work hours, and more housing subsidies. Some of these benefits are indirectly provided to middle and upper class families in the United States. These families can access dependent care tax credits, quality group day care, employer-provided health insurance, above-minimum-wage jobs, and a mortgage interest deduction that subsidizes the costs of good housing. The United States provides few of these benefits for low-income working families, however. Most can only access child health insurance benefits, earned income tax credit additions to low wages, and insufficient subsidies for day care and housing.[38]

Some have pointed to other costs of this shift in the type of care performed by poor mothers. Increasingly parents, especially women, are being held responsible for the successes or failures of children in school and for criminal behavior by their children. Some face charges of neglect and abuse for failing to give enough direct care because they are juggling the demands of wage work.[39] These demands occur as states withdraw from supporting care.

In the context of these larger welfare state changes, the efforts of welfare-to-work staff to promote wage earning through a specific construction of caregiving appears cruel. The irony is that CEC staff really "cared" about their clients. They believed in the promise of wage work, they believed that caregiving was too costly for their clients, and they hoped that the welfare-reliant women would move on to better lives. However, the three discursive strategies used by staff generally helped the state withdraw support for care. These strategies muted client dissent, garnered women's consent to the new parental obligations, and shifted blame for women's continued personal and material difficulties from welfare state retrenchment to children's needs.

The lesson here is not merely about the ways in which a retrenchment in socializing care can by legitimated by street-level workers. The more profound implication is that the meaning of caregiving can be manipulated to reduce demands on the state. The issue in welfare reform is not whether poor women want to do wage work. It is the discursive transformation of wage work into a form of care. This transformation muted discussions of the social provision of care and the real needs of single mothers.

Many feminists point to two challenges in efforts to socialize care—the problem of valuing care and the problem of ending the gender division of labor around care work. Tronto's attention to a broader understanding of care offers the prospect of bringing men into all phases of care. However, this research reveals that relatively powerless women can be encouraged to leave direct care in order to "take care," as men do, without any comparable shift by men, and with a retrenchment in overall state support for care. Efforts to socialize care were set back by welfare reform, which relied upon an expanded notion of care to manipulate poor women rather than to increase support for caregiving.

NOTES

1. See the extended discussions of this gendered aspect of welfare reform in Gwendolyn Mink, *Welfare's End* (Ithaca, N.Y.: Cornell University Press, 1998). For arguments that welfare reform is part of a larger neoliberal work enforcement project, see Catherine Kingfisher, ed., *Western Welfare in Decline: Globalization and Women's Poverty* (Philadelphia: University of Pennsylvania Press, 2002), and Julia O'Connor, Ann Shola Orloff, and Sheila Shaver, *States, Markets, Families: Gender, Liberalism and Social Policy in Australia, Canada, Great Britain and the United States* (Cambridge: Cambridge University Press, 1999).

2. A number of scholars have addressed the care crisis facing Western welfare states. See, for example, Arlie R. Hochschild, "The Culture of Politics: Traditional, Post-modern, Cold-modern, and Warm-modern Ideals of Care," *Social Politics* 2, no. 3 (1995): 331–45; Madonna Harrington Meyer, ed., *Care Work: Gender, Labor, and the Welfare State* (New York: Routledge, 2000); Nancy J. Hirschman and Ulrike Liebert, ed., *Women and Welfare: Theory and Practice in the United States and Europe* (New Brunswick, N.J.: Rutgers University Press, 2000); Mary Daly and Jane Lewis, "The Concept of Social Care and the Analysis of Contemporary Welfare States," *British Journal of Sociology* 51, no. 2 (2000): 281–98; Claire Ungerson, "Social Politics and the Commodification of Care," *Social Politics* 3, no. 4 (1997): 362–82; Susan McDaniel, "Women's Changing Relations to the State and Citizenship: Caring and Intergenerational Relations in Globalizing Western Democracies," *The Canadian Review of Sociology and Anthropology* 39, no. 2 (2002): 125–50.

3. See Michael Lipsky, *Street-Level Bureaucracy: Dilemmas of the Individual in Public Services* (New York: Russell Sage Foundation, 1980) for an influential discussion of the ways in which "street-level bureaucrats," like welfare workers and the police, transform official policy as they perform their duties.

4. See Joan C. Tronto, *Moral Boundaries: A Political Argument for an Ethic of Care* (New York: Routledge, 1993). Joan Tronto and Berenice Fisher defined caring "as a species activity that includes everything that we do to maintain, continue, and repair our 'world.'" See Berenice Fisher and Joan C. Tronto, "Toward a Feminist Theory of Care," in *Circles of Care: Work and Identity in Women's Lives*, ed. Emily Abel and Margaret Nelson (Albany, N.Y.: State University of New York Press, 1991), 40, cited in Tronto, *Moral Boundaries*, 103. More particularly, their definition encompassed a range of activities from thinking about to receiving care. I use their term "direct caregiving" to describe the daily physical and emotional nurturance that welfare

recipients provided to children. Many care researchers use "caregiving" to describe this aspect of care and refer to breadwinning as "support for caregiving" (Francesca Cancian and Stacey J. Oliker, *Caring and Gender* [Thousand Oaks, Calif.: Pine Forge Press, 1999]). While this is the conventional view of these two tasks, I argue that welfare workers used the broader notion of care to encourage welfare-reliant women to turn direct caregiving over to others.

5. See, for example, Catherine Kingfisher, *Women in the American Welfare Trap* (Philadelphia: University of Philadelphia Press, 1996); Sharon Hays, *Flat Broke with Children: Women in the Age of Welfare Reform* (New York: Oxford University Press, 2003); Anna C. Korteweg, "Welfare Reform and the Subject of the Working Mother: 'Get a Job, a Better Job, Then a Career." *Theory and Society* 32, no. 4 (2003): 445–56; and Stephanie Limoncelli, "'Some of Us Are Excellent at Babies': Paid Work, Mothering, and the Construction of Need in a Welfare-to-Work Program," in *Work, Welfare and Politics: Confronting Poverty in the Wake of Welfare Reform*, ed. Frances Fox Piven, Joan Acker, Margaret Hallock, and Sandra Morgen (Eugene, Ore.: University of Oregon Press, 2002).

6. I define social identities as constructions of self created through interactions with existing social hierarchies. Identities are fluid and multiple following the cultural meanings attached to social locations within those hierarchies. Different social identities are salient in different social contexts and new identities are created not only by dominant ideologies but also in face-to-face relationships. Some identities serve hegemonic ends and are constructed in reference to legitimating ideologies that obscure an awareness of injustice. (For a longer discussion of identity construction, see Judith A. Howard, "Social Psychology of Identities," *Annual Review of Sociology* 26 (2000): 367–93.) At other times, identities are constructed in resistance to hegemonic ideologies.

7. See, for example, Eva Feder Kittay, *Love's Labor: Essays on Women, Equality, and Dependency* (New York: Routledge, 1998); Stacey J. Oliker, "Examining Care at Welfare's End," in *Care Work: Gender, Labor, and the Welfare State*, ed. Madonna Harrington Meyer (New York: Routledge, 2000): 167–85, and Dorothy Roberts, "Welfare's Ban on Poor Motherhood," in *Whose Welfare?*, ed. Gwendolyn Mink (Ithaca, N.Y.: Cornell University Press, 1999), 152–70.

8. The welfare regime offered single mothers a monthly means-tested cash benefit through the Aid to Dependent Children program. The welfare-to-work regime implemented the 1988 Family Support Act's requirements that states offer vocational training, adult basic education, high school equivalency or English as a second language classes, work experience, and community work programs. Unlike earlier work legislation, this act explicitly mandated employment training for welfare-reliant women. When these programs were unsuccessful in decreasing the welfare rolls, AFDC was abolished, and the workfare regime began. The 1996 Personal Responsibility Act required that welfare recipients enter some form of paid work or workfare within two years. Workfare programs require mothers to work for their checks, generally in some public or private agency where they clean or do clerical tasks. Each recipient faces a five-year lifetime limit on her receipt of aid. In this chapter I refer to each period by its regime name.

9. AFDC was the national successor to Mother's Pensions programs developed in most states in the 1910s and 1920s. While wage work outside the home was discour-

aged, most recipients had to perform some kind of work within their homes in order to adequately provide for their children. Many did laundry or sewing or took in boarders. For extensive discussions of the race, class, and gender aspects of this program see the following: Winifred Bell, *Aid to Dependent Children* (New York: Columbia University Press, 1965); Mimi Abramovitz, *Regulating the Lives of Women* (Boston: South End Press, 1996); Linda Gordon, *Pitied but Not Entitled: Single Mothers and the History of Welfare* (New York: Free Press, 1994); Gwendolyn Mink, *Wages of Motherhood: Inequality in the Welfare State, 1917–1942* (Ithaca, N.Y.: Cornell University Press, 1995).

10. Nancy E. Rose, *Workfare or Fair Work: Women, Welfare and Government Work Programs* (New Brunswick, N.J.: Rutgers University Press, 1995), and Jill Quadagno, *The Color of Welfare: How Racism Undermined the War on Poverty* (New York: Oxford University Press, 1994). The 1962 AFDC-Unemployed program required fathers to register for training and permitted mothers to remain home, and the 1962 Community Work and Training Programs focused on unemployed men. Not until the 1967 Work Incentive Program did the state formally require some poor mothers to enter training for wage work. WIN offered a "carrot" by allowing a welfare recipient to keep some of her grant after she began working. However, WIN did not slow rising welfare rolls. President Nixon's proposal for a Family Assistance Plan failed in 1973 in part because of continued ambivalence about working mothers. Mothers organized in the National Welfare Rights Organization fought Nixon's plan because they feared a loss of income for full-time mothering. Eileen Boris, "When Work Is Slavery," in *Whose Welfare?*, ed. Gwendolyn Mink (Ithaca, N.Y.: Cornell University Press, 1999), 36–55.

11. Nancy A. Naples, "The 'New Consensus' on the Gendered 'Social Contract': The 1987–1988 U.S. Congressional Hearings on Welfare Reform," *Signs* 22, no. 4 (1997): 907–45.

12. Nancy Fraser and Linda Gordon, "'Dependency' Demystified: Inscriptions of Power in a Keyword of the Welfare State," *Social Politics: International Studies in Gender, State, and Society* 1, no. 1 (1994): 4–31.

13. Some scholars argue that the transformation of mothers into breadwinners was part of ideological demands that all citizens, including all parents, support their families without reliance on the state. See Kingfisher, *Western Welfare*; Mink, *Welfare's End*; Nancy Fraser, *Justice Interruptus: Critical Reflections on the "Postsocialist" Condition* (London: Routledge, 1996). In reality all parents receive some state support; however, the level and type of support varies by class and marital status.

14. Kittay, *Love's Labor*, chapter 5.

15. Arlie R. Hochschild, *The Second Shift* (New York: Harper Collins Publishers, 1990).

16. Two-thirds of CEC students were Latino, especially Puerto Rican, in 1993 and 1997, one-third were African-American, and the others were Caucasian or East Asian. Almost 100 percent of the students were mothers.

17. The director of the CEC was female, as were 50 percent of the teachers and 80 percent of the counseling and advising specialists. There was one male and one female job developer. The staff was 20 percent Caucasian and 35 percent Latino, with the remainder being equally African American and Asian American.

18. For a comprehensive literature review, see Julia O'Connor, "From Women in the Welfare State to Gendering Welfare State Regimes," *Current Sociology* 44, no. 2 (1996): 1–124. See also Diane Sainsbury, *Gender, Equality and Welfare States* (Cambridge: Cambridge University Press, 1996); Diane Sainsbury, ed., *Gender and Welfare State Regimes* (London: Sage Publications, 1994); Ann Shola Orloff, "Gender and the Social Rights of Citizenship: The Comparative Analysis of Gender Relations and Welfare States," *American Sociological Review* 58 (1993): 303–28; and Jane Lewis, "Gender and the Development of Welfare Regimes," *Journal of European Social Policy* 2, no. 3 (1992): 159–73.

19. O'Connor et al., *States, Families*; Carole Pateman, *The Sexual Contract* (Stanford, Calif.: Stanford University Press, 1988).

20. See, for example, Hirschman and Liebert, *Women and Welfare*; Meyer, *Care Work*; Daly and Lewis, "The Concept of Social Care"; McDaniel, "Women's Changing Relations"; Kari Waerness, "Caring as Women's Work in the Welfare State," in *Patriarchy in a Welfare Society*, ed. Harriet Holter (Oslo: Universitetsforlaget, 1984), 67–87.

21. For example, see Mary Corcoran, Sandra K. Danziger, Ariel Kalil, and Kristin S. Seefeldt, "How Welfare Reform Is Affecting Women's Work," *Annual Review of Sociology* 26 (2000): 241–69; Maria Cancian, Robert Haveman, Thomas Kaplan, Daniel Meyer, and Barbara Wolfe, "Work, Earnings, and Well-Being after Welfare," in *Economic Conditions and Welfare Reform*, ed. Sheldon H. Danziger (Kalamazoo, Mich.: W.E. Upjohn Institute for Employment Research, 1999), 161–86; Frances Fox Piven, Joan Acker, Margaret Hallock, and Sandra Morgen, ed., *Work, Welfare and Politics: Confronting Poverty in the Wake of Welfare Reform* (Eugene, Ore.: University of Oregon Press, 2002).

22. Chad Broughton, "Reforming Poor Women: The Cultural Politics and Practices of Welfare Reform," *Qualitative Sociology* 26, no. 1 (2003): 35–52; Korteweg, "Welfare Reform"; Limoncelli, "Some of Us."

23. See Hilary Graham, "Caring: A Labour of Love," in *A Labour of Love: Women, Work and Caring*, ed. Janet Finch and Dulcie Groves (Boston: Routledge & Kegan Paul, 1983), 1–10. Influential work that has expanded this understanding of care includes Tronto, *Moral Boundaries*; Kittay, *Love's Labor*; Sara Ruddick, *Maternal Thinking: Toward a Politics of Peace* (New York: Ballantine Books, 1989). Other foundational work includes Carol Gilligan, *In a Different Voice: Psychological Theory and Women's Development* (Cambridge, Mass.: Harvard University Press, 1982) and Nel Noddings, *Caring: A Feminine Approach to Ethics and Moral Education* (Berkeley and Los Angeles: University of California Press, 1984). Many of these theorists emphasize the interconnectedness and interdependence in caring relationships.

24. Tronto, *Moral Boundaries*, 105–8. These phases were first identified by Berenice Fisher and Joan Tronto as they developed their definition of care.

25. Tronto, *Moral Boundaries*, 112–15.

26. See, for example, Ellen K. Scott, Kathryn Edin, Andrew London, and Joan Mazelis, "My Children Come First: Welfare-Reliant Women's Post-TANF Views of Work-Family Tradeoffs and Marriage," in *For Better and for Worse: Welfare Reform and the Well-Being of Children and Families*, ed. Greg J. Duncan and P. Lindsay

Chase-Lansdale (New York: Russell Sage Press, 2001), 132–53; Karen Seccombe, *"So You Think I Drive a Cadillac?"* (Boston: Allyn and Bacon, 1999); Stacey J. Oliker, "Work Commitment and Constraint among Mothers on Workfare," *Journal of Contemporary Ethnography* 24, no. 2 (1995): 165–94.

27. Patricia Hill Collins, *Black Feminist Thought: Knowledge, Consciousness, and the Politics of Empowerment* (New York: Routledge, 1990).

28. Kathryn Edin and Laura Lein, in *Making Ends Meet: How Single Mothers Survive Welfare and Low-Wage Work* (New York: Russell Sage Foundation, 1997), studied the choices low-income mothers make, noting that wage work alone exacted greater hardships than the combination of work and welfare.

29. Deborah L. Little, "Independent Workers, Dependable Mothers: Discourse, Resistance, and AFDC Workfare Programs," *Social Politics* 6, no. 2 (1999): 161–202.

30. Rannveig Traustadottir, "Disability Reform and Women's Caring Work," in *Care Work: Gender, Labor, and the Welfare State*, ed. Madonna Harrington Meyer (New York: Routledge, 2000), 249–69, 269.

31. Patricia Hill Collins discussed the costs of unwanted pregnancies in her work on the motherhood of oppressed nonwhite women. Collins, *Black Feminist Thought*, chapter 8.

32. In 2002 the median hourly wage of welfare leavers was $8.06, and only one-third of welfare leavers had employer-provided health insurance. Almost a quarter of former recipients had to return to welfare after leaving for a job, while about 14 percent had become "disconnected" from the welfare system, without apparent sources of support. Pamela Loprest, "Fewer Welfare Leavers Employed in Weak Economy," *The Urban Institute* 2003, www.urban.org/url.cfm?ID=310837 (1 May 2004).

33. Freya Sonenstein, Gary Gates, Stephanie Schmidt, and Natalya Boshun, "Primary Child Care Arrangements of Employed Parents: Findings from the National Survey of America's Families," *The Urban Institute* 2000, www.urban.org/url.cfm?ID=310487 (1 May 2004).

34. Bruce Fuller, Sharon Lynn Kagan, and Susanna Loeb, "New Lives for Poor Families? Mothers and Young Children Move through Welfare Reform," *Wave 2 Findings—The Growing Up in Poverty Project* (Berkeley: University of California Berkeley, 2002).

35. Sonenstein et al., "Primary Child Care."

36. Nancy Folbre and Julie Nelson, "For Love or Money or Both?" *Journal of Economic Perspectives* 14 (Fall 2000): 123–40.

37. Corcoran et al., "How Welfare Reform Is Affecting Women's Work."

38. See generally the chapters in Meyer, *Care Work*, for a discussion of race, class, and gender inequalities in care in the United States.

39. Christina Paxson and Jane Waldfogel, "Welfare Reforms, Family Resources, and Child Maltreatment," *Journal of Policy Analysis and Management* 22, no. 1 (Winter 2003): 85–113.

I would like to thank Michael Burawoy, Leslie Salzinger, Dan Weymouth, and the editors of this series for their insight and contributions to this work. All errors are, of course, my own.

Part II

CARE IN SOCIAL ACTION
AND CONTEXT

Chapter Eight

The Curious Case of Care and Restorative Justice in the U.S. Context

Margaret Urban Walker

"9 of 10 Nursing Homes in U.S. Lack Adequate Staff, a Government Study Finds" is the title of a recent article in the *New York Times*.[1] The reported study, ordered by the U.S. Congress in 1990 and prepared by the Department of Health and Human Services, concludes that 90 percent of U.S. nursing homes have too few workers to provide "minimally necessary" care and that nursing homes with a low ratio of nursing personnel were more likely to provide substandard care that endangers life and health of residents. Yet the report considers minimum staffing ratios "not currently feasible" because of costs. The Bush administration agrees, rejecting minimum staffing regulation in favor of publishing data on staffing levels so that an "informed public" can create the "market demand" for better nursing home staffing.

The report and coverage of it are unexceptional in exhibiting the stark absence in U.S. political culture of a discursive and moral framework of care. Even in a context where talk of "care" is descriptively unavoidable— providing for the sick and frail aged—talk of care as a value, obligation, or responsibility is absent. Instead, the report and the newspaper article repeatedly articulate the situation in terms of unacceptable cost, economic realism, and individual responses to market forces as a solution. Those elderly needing care are positioned as a costly social problem, and the *Times* inserts the alarming fact that the age eighty-five and older population will double by 2030. There is a pattern here. The "welfare to work" agenda of the 1990s in the United States acquiesced in framing the "welfare mother"—not poverty, inadequate social support, bad schools, lack of affordable and reliable child care, runaway male incarceration in nonwhite race groups—as a social problem that had become too expensive to tolerate. In recent years "education" has been retooled as a mainstream and cost-free political bandwagon implemented through standardized testing that ignores growing levels of child

145

poverty in the United States. So too inadequate nursing homes—another paradigmatic "care" problem—become a target for economic containment strategies rather than a trigger of moral shame.

And yet there is an area of activity, experiment, and activism in the United States that crosses public and private boundaries where not only are care values invoked but care discourse is also made central, and where these values and their discursive frame seem politically acceptable and even popularly digestible. The area is restorative justice as an ethical vision and a set of practical strategies for dealing with victims and offenders of crime and their communities. Restorative justice, even though marginal, seems to be rising in visibility and in persuasiveness even as incarceration in the United States has soared to unprecedented levels. It is entering mainstream thinking both from the bottom-up efforts of private organizations and advocates and from the top-down institution of state programs to deal with criminal offenders and victims of crime.

I will use this case to open a discussion of why an ethic of care seems to have achieved expression in such unexpected quarters even as it remains largely excluded from the U.S. public figuration of social and political problems that are seemingly more obvious sites for normative discussions of care—the needs of vulnerable children, the physically and mentally ill, the sick and frail elderly. Where these "care" problems are not represented largely in terms of economic calculation—that is to say, where they are represented in moral terms at all—they are most likely to be shaped by appeals to rights: the rights of children, rights to health care, rights to dignity in old age. Yet in the domain of spreading restorative justice practice one hears repeatedly about the *needs* of the victim, the offender, and harboring communities; the importance of empathy, attention, and the candid expression of feeling; and the importance of sustaining and repairing human relations in an environment where victims and offenders are supported by their communities of care.

I begin looking at some identifying commitments of care ethics, attempting not to elevate one particular version but to focus themes and language that reveal care thinking.[2] I then turn to a brief look at some of the theoretical and practical activity in the growing area of restorative justice as an approach to crime, exploring how the clearly moral language that legitimates restorative justice programs is, rather surprisingly, a language of care. Finally, I raise some questions about the complexities of how an ethical discourse of care is marginalized and deflated by its gendered associations in its most obvious sphere but is also eclipsed or captured by communitarian, therapeutic, and religious discourses that can deflect the potential of care ethics to assume its role as a public moral discourse.

In all this, I do not suggest that the perspective of care ethics enjoys more than a liminal existence in U.S. public life. In fact, my hypothesis is that the saturation of the restorative justice movement with care discourse is an exception that proves the rule, while helping to illuminate what the rule is. Care language can find public expression where it is not identified as such, nor identified with traditionally feminized arenas of care. Care discourse is excluded from those areas where it threatens to spill the "private" sphere into the public one just where the particular public/private boundary in question is one that has been historically, and continues largely to be, gendered. Where care language carries the load of the sentimental, feminine, servile, and domestic spheres, it is not serious discourse for public-policy debate in the United States. In the area of criminal justice policy, heavily gendered as masculine in its target population (male offenders), its personnel (criminal lawyers, judges, corrections official, prison personnel), and its public imagery (crime as a male domain and a hypermasculine behavior), care language is marginal but can be entertained as an "alternative philosophy." Even there, however, the philosophy in question is virtually never identified with "care ethics" but most commonly with a (loosely) communitarian and/or explicitly religious frame. In some instances, ideas and practices that embody care values are celebrated as a legacy of indigenous cultures, now a benefit of a multicultural society that can learn from people and lifeways it once attempted to exterminate.

THE "INFORMATION BASE" OF CARE ETHICS

Substantive affinities between an ethic of care and an ethic of capabilities have been noticed by political theorist of care Joan Tronto and philosopher of dependency work Eva Kittay.[3] Here I borrow a methodological rather than a substantive idea employed by economist and capabilities theorist Amartya Sen. In *Development as Freedom* Sen contrasts theories of justice by examining the "information base" that they select as decisive for addressing the problems that they would answer.[4] For example, utilitarians seek to answer questions of social policy by directing attention to subjective satisfaction or the fulfillment of preferences, while Rawlsian theory focuses on liberties, income, and self-respect as primary goods in addressing the justice of societies' basic institutions. Sen emphasizes that identifying the information base of moral theories—the considerations they make relevant and irrelevant in deciding moral issues—can be crucial in testing the scope and adequacy of theories in response to a question like "What is a just society?"

Identifying the information base of divergent theories is also, however, a useful way to reveal that theories that superficially appear to be answering the same question from different views of the same subject matter at hand are often in fact constructing different subject matters for our view. In the political deployment of moral discourses, this is especially important to notice. Often what is politically decisive is whether a certain kind of consideration or problem can be made visible as something to be concerned about before any substantive normative conclusions about it are reached, before political positions on it are hardened as "issues," or before decisions of policy about it are taken. The constitution of subject matters for moral and political concern, and the replacement or displacement of some subject matters by others, are a powerful process in sustaining what philosopher Cheshire Calhoun has called "ideologies of the moral life," those nonlogical implications of styles of theorizing or discussion that make some questions and considerations seem inevitable, important, or natural and make others seem exceptional, deviant, secondary, or unimportant.[5]

Using this lens, how might we characterize the information base of care ethics in addressing questions about a just and morally responsible society?

I suggest that care ethics can be seen (without adopting one particular formulation of it) in terms of three key facts and four central value commitments. Call the first fact the "fact of dependency" as an inevitable feature of the human cycle of life; all begin in radical and fragile dependency, all experience it in times of illness, weakness, and disability during life, and all who grow old enough are very likely to return to it as an ongoing way of living. Call the second fact the "fact of vulnerability" as an unavoidable feature of human beings' fragile bodies and feelings. Both of these are features that social arrangements can render more or less threatening or fearsome to human beings by providing forms of care and protection. Call the third the "fact of interdependence" as an ineliminable feature of human social existence. As we are dependent upon others for our very survival at the outset and at many times in our lives, we are dependent on many others throughout our lives for the necessities and amenities of a tolerable or a good life. Social divisions of labor and social ties and memberships make possible much of what any of us values beyond bare survival, while specific modes of social organization and cultural norms make only certain forms of interdependence visible and valued. These three facts encompass the primary information base of care ethics, which is tapped by this question: What do people need from each other to live well in the world?[6]

As a perspective on moral value, with directive force for individual choices and for social institutions and political policies, care ethics elevates four goods: responsiveness to human needs; responsibility and competence in meeting needs; valuing of connection and relationship itself; and valuing of caring labor and activities. In the face of dependency, vulnerability, and interdependence as our unalterable human condition, care ethics holds individuals and their societies responsible for attending to, assessing, and weighing responsibilities for human needs and for acknowledging our needs for each other. Care ethics affirms the dignity and profound importance of our efforts to meet human needs, most so those needs at stake in conditions of vulnerability that threaten survival or in relations of dependency on which survival and health depend. While these values need not be seen as comprising a complete ethics, care ethics sees these as values without which no ethical vision is adequate or, more strongly, humanly sane.[7]

This leads care ethics to identify as fundamental problems of justice the distribution of caring (who gets taken care of), the distribution of responsibilities to engage in caring labor (who gives care), and distributions of the social resources and protections available to caregivers and those needing care (on what terms of burden and reward people give and receive care). These problems have often, bizarrely, not been treated as moral issues at all, or have been bifurcated into "realms" or "spheres" which elevate the executive functions of organizing care delivery (as in the modern welfare state) to the status of issues of "public" justice, while demoting actual caregiving to the "private" sphere of unskilled, low-wage, or unpaid work that must get done but is not worth paying (much) for.[8] Care ethics, however, need not be restricted to those activities that are seen as "caregiving" in the most stereotypical sense. As Selma Sevenhuijsen says, "practically all human behaviour carries aspects or dimensions of care."[9] Rather, the vision of care ethics is one of "a *relational* ethics which places the highest value on the promotion, restoration, or creation of good social and personal relations and gives priority to the needs and concerns of 'concrete' [i.e., particular] . . . others," in Fiona Robinson's words.[10] Flexible attentiveness to the individual case, mindfulness of and responsiveness to needs of particular human beings, and valuing relations of interdependence and the activities of care that sustain them are marks of care values in all contexts.

AN UNEXPECTED ARENA FOR CARE ETHICS

Care language and values are largely absent in contemporary public, politically authoritative discussion in the United States in those contexts where one would naturally expect them to have some weight.[11] At the same time a restorative justice movement has emerged within and around the U.S. criminal justice system, and this movement, in both its governmental and nongovernmental forms, speaks a language that is in fact, whatever its origins, identical to the language of care. It is not the case that care ethics has been the chosen framework for the development of restorative justice ideas and ideals. Rather, the case of restorative justice is interesting to reflect on because it is an (increasingly) institutionally recognized and legitimate discourse with some significant practical impact that is organized around moral ideas indistinguishable from care thinking. A care-based approach achieves at least the legitimacy of a practical policy alternative in the U.S. criminal justice domain.

Although many became aware of the idea of "restorative justice" through worldwide interest in South Africa's Truth and Reconciliation Commission, the concept of restorative justice already had a history in criminal justice practice two decades before. Innovations in the form of victim-offender conferences seeking offender accountability and restoration of victim losses began in Canada and United States in the mid-1970s.[12] Once the concept was in play, it steered attention toward varied social practices in many cultures, some of them ancient, that fit the basic idea.[13] New Zealand's extensive family conferencing program was based explicitly on long-standing practice of Maori culture; sentencing circles in Canada and the United States embody First Nations practices in Canada and have been adopted in some African American communities; the Navajo Peacemaker Courts in Arizona continue or revive preconquest practices of communal deliberation under the direction of a respected individual.[14] Immarigeon and Daly helpfully survey multiple "streams" of thought and activism that have flowed into restorative justice practice, including victims' and prisoners' rights movements, feminist activism on rape and domestic violence, the ascendance of mediation and alternative dispute resolution, indigenous traditions, the peacemaking practices of religious communities, and popular sentiment. All sought more responsiveness to victims, or less incarceration and more genuine accountability in the case of (at least nonviolent) offenders, or more community representation, or more than one of these.[15]

Restorative justice is an international movement in theory and practice that is also thriving in the United States An extensive system of Reparative Probation Boards exists in Vermont, and websites for agencies of the states of New Jersey, Pennsylvania, Minnesota, and Michigan advertise their restorative justice ventures. The state of Arizona, with its deserved reputation for tough penal practices, has just revamped and renamed its Victims' Rights Program as the "Office of Restorative Justice" to emphasize policies that involve crime victims in the process of dealing with juvenile offenders. Academic conferences and training courses for restorative mediation can easily be found on the Internet, as can nongovernmental and religious organizations that advance restorative justice, like the Mennonite Central Council (an originator of U.S. victim-offender reconciliation programs), the Formation and Justice Ministries of the United Methodist Church in Missouri, or the Victim-Offender Mediation Association, a network of theorists, researchers, and practitioners.[16] Restorative justice is a banner for both inventing and adopting new programs for dealing with the aftermath of crime (as well as other community or school discord and violence) in ways other than, or in addition to, punitive measures. Restorative justice framing also gives a fresh face, and perhaps a slightly different meaning, to some existing programs, like community policing or victim-witness assistance.

Although there are differences of philosophy and practice within restorative justice networks and programs, the key ideas are quite uniform. A concise definition of restorative practice by Bazemore and Walgrave is as follows: "restorative justice is every action that is primarily oriented toward doing justice by repairing the harm that has been caused by a crime."[17] Crime is understood as a concrete harm to specific persons and to their communities, and restoration has material, emotional, and moral dimensions. The contrast, which is usually explicit and always implied, is with a retributive criminal system that gives the offender, at best, what is "deserved" in the way of punishment according to a system of precalibrated punishments for scaled offenses, and typically gives the victim nothing but the possible satisfaction of seeing the offender punished. Restorative justice is committed to putting the repair of harm done by crime in the hands of the "stakeholders," defined as the victims, the offender, and their "communities of care."

Restorative justice is typically done through court-administered or police-run programs where authorities linked to the criminal justice system orchestrate forms of conference between offenders, victims, and in some cases families or representatives of affected communities. The scene of restorative justice is a meeting or conference among these "stakeholders" in various combinations. Participation in restorative programs is ostensibly voluntary on the part of the principals, and the function of the meeting is to repair damage by doing at least some of the following: hearing the experience of victims (and communities) about the concrete harms of crime, allowing offenders to take responsibility for the offense, providing information, explanation, apology, and offers of reparative action, arriving at an agreement about the course of action to be taken to repair the harm.[18] The substantive values of restorative practice are repair and "healing." Restorative justice programs are most popular (and, one assumes, politically acceptable) for juveniles, but adult offenders of nonviolent crime may also be considered candidates for restorative intervention. Restorative justice programs are most popular (and one assumes, politically acceptable) for juveniles, but adult and (in some programs) violent offenders may also be considered candidates for restorative intervention.

What is striking is the language used consistently in both theoretical writing and practical contexts in discussing restorative justice practice. Restorative practice is focused on the needs created by the fact of a harm or crime and a corresponding obligation to respond by addressing those particular needs; the importance of direct, attentive (sometimes respectful or compassionate) listening and expression (ideally face to face) between parties to the harmful event; the opportunity for the offender to take responsibility and directly respond to the victim's anguish, anger, fear, and suffering; and the assumption that parties to the process will arrive at a solution that does justice in the particular case at hand without supposing that the resolution of a restorative intervention must conform to an antecedent rule or be replicated in like cases.[19]

Sullivan and Tifft describe restorative justice as a "needs-based conception of justice," and literature on such programs often speaks of balancing needs of victims, offenders, and communities.[20] It is also about human relations that individuals have the power to break and repair, rather than rules or laws, the transgression of which "belongs" to the state.[21] The process emphasis is on direct expression and acknowledgment of needs and feelings; the substantive emphasis is on accountability and a concrete response that addresses material, emotional, and moral needs, and in which victim and offender often literally address each other. In conferences that involve communities—often referred to as "communities of care"—communities are expected to provide support within a context that does not blur the roles of victim and offender but that allows the offender an opportunity to assert agency and competence by taking responsibility for making a meaningful reparative response to the victim. This often includes apology as well as some attempt at restitution or symbolic amends. The substantive value of "restoration" in restorative justice rests heavily on what victims, offenders, and communities see as repair, but the structure of restorative practices makes clear that connection among the parties, and, where possible, reconnection of people within their communities (sometimes called "reintegration" for offenders, following Braithwaite) is the ideal (if not always available) end of restorative justice practice. It thus sets itself in opposition to the alienating, distancing, and depersonalizing effects of an adversarial criminal process that treats crime as an offense against the state, that encourages offenders to deny responsibility, that exiles offenders through incarceration and stigmatization, and that excludes offenders from an active role in "setting things right," making them spectators to the harm they have done and even to some of its consequences for them.[22]

The keynote themes of care thinking are pervasive in restorative justice literature and practice. Restorative justice practice, of course, is a tiny patch on the huge and still swelling incarceration industry into which the U.S. criminal justice establishment has metastasized. Annual expenditures on prisons have increased more than 500 percent in the last two decades, and state prison budgets are growing in the United States while social services are being cut.[23] The United States currently incarcerates more people than any other country in the world, including mainland China. A large majority of those incarcerated are nonviolent offenders.[24] Racism is rampant in this "justice" system. It is estimated that by 1994 one of every three black males between 18 and 34 years old in the United States was under some form of correctional supervision.[25] No doubt one of the factors driving interest in alternative models of dealing with crime is precisely the frightening growth, expense, racism, and inhumanity of this system. But why has care ethical thinking managed to get a hearing, and more than that, a hold (even if experimental) in this field? What can we make of this?

SOME SPECULATIONS ABOUT
U.S. RESISTANCE TO CARE TALK

The case of restorative justice shows that the values and points of focus of care ethics can in fact become a legitimate and legitimating discourse in a significant area of public policy in the United States, even if its impact is relatively slight. This has not happened because these practices and rationales are labeled or promoted as "an ethic of care." Researchers on the origins of restorative justice theory and practice acknowledge some contribution of women's movements and feminism to restorative thinking, but no one considers this more than a slight, and perhaps indirect, contribution, and that contribution may well be through feminist uses of "rights" discourses, rather than care ethics.[26] It seems few researchers have explored this link or deployed care ethics as a main theoretical rationale.[27]

Restorative justice thinking has been fed by many streams, including community policing movements, victims' rights movements, religious organizations, and communitarian thinking. Restorative justice practice embodies a robust and consistent version of care ethics even though it rarely appears under that description. Its language of "community participation," of "needs of the victim," of the "competence" and "accountability" of the offender, of the goal of "restoring victims, offenders, and communities," can be heard in various registers, ideologically and practically, and perhaps this is important. There is no sense that the values are "feminist," where the latter term continues to arouse prickly, defensive, and derisive feelings in many quarters in the United States. One might then say that care ethics, in the U.S. context, works best by another name or in tandem with other perspectives that are more acceptable to a broad U.S. public. Certainly a broad U.S. public is responsive to talk based on ostensibly Christian values. Perhaps more important, Christian and communitarian perspectives embody values that do not seem threatening, suspect, or too "radical" in the U.S. social imaginary. Christian religious appeals and communitarian language generally are familiar to most Americans. At any rate, these frameworks appear politically viable to (still overwhelmingly) white male Christian middle class lawmakers, administrators, and bureaucrats. For this reason, these orientations are able to carry legitimacy, and their acceptance by those in power reinforces whatever legitimacy they possess in the first place.

In a different way, so does the idea of indigenous tradition carry some appeal. Of course, honoring or reviving indigenous traditions of peacemaking and communal harmony have independent importance as they embody respect for peoples and cultures long subjugated and actively threatened with extermination. Restorative justice programs rooted in local or traditional indigenous practice can thus be ways to affirm forms of self-determination and control for these populations.[28] Also, for a political and criminal justice establishment premised on Euro-American liberal individualist and modern statist culture, indigenous ideas and values that emphasize community and participation can be seen as refreshingly new and useful alternatives for the dominant culture. Perhaps these ideas derive some appeal when they are seen as benefits of "multiculturalism." The idea of multiculturalism has become at least familiar and has positive associations for many white Americans of European descent, even if these same citizens are not familiar or comfortable with the *people* whose cultures supply this diversity, much less with the idea that native peoples are minority nations, rather than a minority group.[29]

Compared to the Christian, communitarian, and even multicultural appeals of restorative thinking, my guess is that its feminist credentials are unimpressive or worse. A discourse that can be identified as feminist is still likely to evoke a defensive backlash in a U.S. context; at any rate it will be easily labeled as socially or politically "radical." It is important to clarify my point: I do *not* mean to say that what is "really" going on here is care ethics, not communitarianism, or the traditions of indigenous peoples, or the religious values of faith communities. Instead, what we see is a remarkable overlap among moral views that in various ways repudiate aspects of liberal individualist, formal universalist, and theoretical-juridical understandings of morality and society.[30] My point is not that restorative justice uniquely requires or exhibits a care ethics perspective but that it shows that values wholly consistent with and central to that perspective can get a hearing that they do not necessarily get when advanced as care ethics.

It need not be, of course, that restorative justice practices are being adopted because of the caring, or communitarian, or Christian, or indigenous values that support them. Practices gain currency and are seen as institutional options for many reasons, and perhaps for different reasons by different interested parties.[31] The question here, however, is not about the actual political conditions, social forces, and distributions of power that explain the adoption of restorative justice practices, although that is an important question, and one on which the success of institutionalizing restorative justice programs is likely to depend. The issue I am exploring is the relative acceptability and effectiveness of different discourses as legitimating ones in a public sphere, in this case the contemporary United States.

Whatever the actual reasons for the adoption of certain practices, some languages of value and justification are found acceptable and effective in presenting and justifying these practices to the public, or are offered as the terms in which policy options are to be understood by the public. The question I have been asking here is, Why do care language and values (under whatever banner) qualify as legitimating with respect to restorative justice practice, making their way onto websites and into state-manufactured pamphlets, but remain relatively ineffective and unlegitimating in their more obvious areas of application to the care of the young, the frail, the sick, or other dependent persons? There are really two questions here. One is: Why does care language get a successful grip in the case of restorative justice, when it does not seem to do so elsewhere, including in the more obvious realms of application? I have already suggested that the language and values of care used to couch rationales for restorative justice can be and are actually subsumed under politically safer or more acceptable evaluative outlooks that share care language and values. The second question is: Why is care language often ignored or spurned in those more obvious realms? Couldn't it achieve some stature there, if perhaps under different descriptions, as in the restorative justice case? In response to this, I focus on two linked factors. On the one hand, there is a special "contamination by the feminine" that is unavoidable for caring discourse in its more obvious realms of application, for these areas of needs for care and caring remain, in reality and perception, largely associated with women and (so) with the "private" sphere. At the same time, there is a real threat—social and economic—that care thinking represents to the gendered and raced division of labor that has allowed U.S. society to continue to "ride free," or at least artificially cheaply, on the strained and inadequate but private (that is, domestic or privately paid) provision of care in these most obvious spheres.

These two factors—a symbolic contamination and a real threat—might explain rejection and delegitimation in the U.S. public sphere of the discourse of care precisely when it is applied to still deeply feminized spheres. Care talk addresses the still conspicuously gendered sectors of what Eva Kittay calls "dependency work," paid and unpaid, which is also historically "raced and classed," in Joan Tronto's phrase.[32] That is, care talk is more alarming personally, socially, and institutionally when it threatens to breach the private/public boundary in its gendered (and also racial) form. The dynamics here are complicated, mixing practical, social, economic, and symbolic factors.

An ethic of care is threatening in the imagined U.S. public space of supposedly competent, self-sufficient, free individuals who are pictured as enjoying full reciprocity of obligation and entitlement. Care thinking instead demands attention to those who engage in unpaid and low-paid dependency work, and these are people — put curtly, women and minorities — whose labor has been and continues to be exploited within a system of socially restricted choices and opportunities in the United States. An ethic of care further demands attention to those who are dependent and so rely upon this work. Sociopolitical discourse in the United States struggles with inserting the "caregiver" and the "human being needing care" into the citizen role and inserting the continuous human needs for care into the picture of the independent, autonomously rights-wielding citizen as a culturally normative ideal. The culturally normative U.S. citizen is an adult, a classically rational actor, a "man" whose life cycle is not socially premised on childbearing and child care, a white person fitted for education that leads to more than menial work (which is suitably done by those of other races), a person with a life planned for security and self-sufficiency who enjoys the social and economic resources to make such plans realistic. The ethics of care can appear alienating and actually distressing to many Americans who want to be that citizen or want to believe they actually are and will continue to be that citizen. It is comforting to picture the dependent as the exception and the caregiver as someone else. Perhaps it is more alienating and distressing to men than to women given the (growing) gender gaps in polls and in elections where women in the United States are significantly more concerned with active government support for social welfare and health care. At least it would seem, put flatly, that while the public sphere of policy and legislation remains overwhelmingly dominated in the United States by higher-educated white men, it remains easier to see dependency and the caring labor it requires as someone else's problem so long as it is in fact someone else's problem.

Furthermore, when care ethics justifies increased demands on public resources, it collides with the discourse of "costly social problems." When the necessity of responding socially to human vulnerability and dependency is framed in this way, it expresses resistance to paying for what has been and usually still is free, and otherwise is cheaper than it would be under moderately fair conditions of occupational choice and compensation. Care of the dependent and vulnerable remains commonly done by women as an unpaid full-time job or an unpaid double or triple shift in the home in addition to paid labor, or is done as low-paid "unskilled" work performed by a disproportionately nonwhite labor force in the workplace (where that workplace is also sometimes someone else's home, in the case of home care attendants, babysitters, housecleaners).[33] These social needs are indeed costly to meet, but the issue is where the cost is to be placed. The discourse of "costly social problems" evinces resistance and resentment to paying a cost that really "should" not be a public "burden," and in which those who constitute the burden are a "problem." I suspect that the criminal justice sector is open to care talk and caring values because there it does not threaten to breach an economic, social, and political barrier that represents and is represented by the feminized and raced version of the "private" sector: unpaid or minimally paid dependency work that can be socially demanded from or socially assigned to women and people of color (who may also be noncitizens). Criminal justice has been a public concern solidly for at least the last century in the United States.[34] The kind of privatization that tempts a grotesquely overgrown and massively expensive U.S. corrections establishment is the economic lure of offloading corrections to private industries. The loaded associations of the gendered and raced sphere of "private" or "domestic" activity have no place here.[35]

Finally, if "crime" (in the popular imagination, violent crime) encourages us to be anxious about our vulnerability to predators, that vulnerability can be made to seem avoidable if we build enough prisons, pass enough draconian sentencing legislation, hire enough police, and give them enough coercive powers. This is perhaps why restorative justice has found uptake in the United States mostly in connection with juvenile offenders and with nonviolent adults, even as the incarcerations establishment swells. There remains an interest in keeping people believing that they are vulnerable to violent crime and that more incarceration is the way to limit that vulnerability. This interest is consistent with introducing alternatives for lawbreakers who are not "a menace to society," and perhaps serves even to reinforce that idea that people are in prison because they are dangerous (even as admissions to federal prison now are overwhelmingly for nonviolent violation of drug laws). In any case, this kind of "controllable" vulnerability—incessantly magnified by politicians' rhetoric and the popular press—is very different from the forms of vulnerability and dependency we all cannot avoid, no matter what we build or buy, or whom we bully.

The language of care in its most characteristic applications reminds people of a largely uncontrollable vulnerability, and its implications for dependency and interdependence, which are immensely less disturbing when vulnerability remains private in another sense, that is, when it remains not only less socially expensive but also out of sight and out of mind (until it strikes at home). The caring language of restorative justice escapes the charged resistance and the sense of threat carried by care ethics when it is identified as such—as care ethics—and applied in the most obvious places. This is, I have suggested, precisely because care ethics unavoidably brings unwelcome reminders that we are all both responsible for, and in need of, the massive work of caring on which all human societies rest. U.S. society, the only remaining industrial society without universal health care coverage and with negligible publicly supported provisions for parental or other child care, does not seem ready for a collective public acknowledgment of this truth and its political, social, and personal implications.[36]

NOTES

1. Robert Pear, "9 of 10 Nursing Homes in U.S. Lack Adequate Staff, a Government Study Finds," *New York Times*, 18 February 2002.

2. Some of the influential accounts of care ethics I take as paradigmatic are Joan Tronto, *Moral Boundaries: A Political Argument for an Ethic of Care* (New York: Routledge, 1993); Selma Sevenhuijsen, *Citizenship and the Ethics of Care: Feminist Considerations on Justice, Morality and Politics* (London: Routledge, 1998); Eva Kittay, *Love's Labor: Essays on Women, Equality, and Dependency* (New York: Routledge, 1999); Sara Ruddick, *Maternal Thinking: Toward a Politics of Peace* (New York: Ballantine Books, 1989); Virginia Held, *Feminist Morality: Transforming Culture, Society, and Politics* (Chicago: University of Chicago Press, 1993). The two founding accounts are Carol Gilligan, *In a Different Voice: Psychological Theory and Women's Development* (Cambridge, Mass.: Harvard University Press, 1982), and Nel Noddings, *Caring: A Feminine Approach to Ethics and Moral Education* (Berkeley: University of California Press, 1984). A useful set of readings is found in Virginia Held, ed., *Justice and Care: Essential Readings in Feminist Ethics* (Boulder, Colo.: Westview Press, 1995).

3. Tronto, *Moral Boundaries*, 140. Kittay, *Love's Labor*, 131–32.

4. Amartya Sen, *Development as Freedom* (New York: Anchor Books, 1999), 56–8.

5. Cheshire Calhoun, "Justice, Care, Gender Bias," *Journal of Philosophy* 85 (1988): 451–63.

6. See Joan Tronto's and Berenice Fisher's definition of care as a basis for an ethic of care: "On the most general level, we suggest that caring be viewed as a *species activity that includes everything that we do to maintain, continue, and repair our 'world' so that we can live in it as well as possible.* That world includes our bodies, our selves, and our environment, all of which we seek to interweave in a complex, life-sustaining web." From Berenice Fisher and Joan C. Tronto, "Toward a Feminist Theory of Care," in *Circles of Care: Work and Identity in Women's Lives*, ed. Emily Abel and Margaret Nelson (Albany, N.Y.: State University of New York Press, 1991), 40, cited in Tronto, *Moral Boundaries*, 103.

7. See, for example, Eva Kittay's argument for a third principle of justice, in addition to John Rawls's two principles, that acknowledges "our unequal vulnerability in

dependency . . . our moral power to respond to others in need, and . . . the primacy of human relations to happiness and well-being." Kittay, *Love's Labor*, 113.

8. See Tronto on this fragmentation of care that tracks lines of social privilege: those of higher status in gender, race, economic, and citizen hierarchies are associated with the public roles that "take care" of social problems, while the actual work of caregiving is the province of those less powerful in homes and in the workforce, in Tronto, *Moral Boundaries*, 112–17. See also Kittay, *Love's Labor*, chapters 3–5. On the ways in which discussion of needs has been institutionalized within modern welfare state contexts, and the tendency to shift questions of meeting human needs into questions of how needs satisfaction can be administered institutionally, see Nancy Fraser, "Talking About Needs: Interpretive Contests as Political Conflicts in Welfare-State Societies," *Ethics* 99 (1989): 291–313.

9. Sevenhuijsen, *Citizenship and the Ethics of Care*, 23.

10. Fiona Robinson, *Globalizing Care: Ethics, Feminist Theory, and International Relations* (Boulder, Colo.: Westview Press, 1999), 46.

11. Eva Kittay's analysis of contemporary discussions of 1990s "welfare reform" in the United States is instructive here. See "Policy and a Public Ethic of Care" in Kittay, *Love's Labor*.

12. For a clear account of the emergence of these programs and some evaluative research on them, see Mark S. Umbreit, Robert Coates, and Ann Warner Roberts, "Cross-National Impact of Restorative Justice through Mediation and Dialogue," *ICCA Journal on Community Corrections* 8 (1997): 46–50.

13. John Braithwaite, one of the founding figures in restorative justice thinking, gives an overview in the first chapter of his recent book *Restorative Justice and Responsive Regulation* (New York: Oxford University Press, 2002). See also Dennis Sullivan and Larry Tifft, *Restorative Justice: Healing the Foundations of Our Everyday Lives* (Monsey, N.Y.: Willow Tree Press, 2001).

14. See, for example, Dennis Sullivan, "Navajo Peacemaking History, Development, and Possibilities for Adjudication-Based Systems of Justice: An Interview with James Zion," *Contemporary Justice Review* 5 (2002): 167–88. For a philosophical reflection on Navajo practice, see Robert Yazzie, "'Life comes from it': Navajo Justice Concepts," *New Mexico Law Review* 24 (1994): 175–90.

15. Russ Immarigeon and Kathleen Daly, "Restorative Justice: Origins, Practices, Contexts, and Challenges," *ICCA Journal on Community Corrections* 8 (1997): 13–18.

16. www.stop.violence.com (23 April 2005) summarizes restorative justice legislation enacted in twenty-nine states, and www.pfm.org//AM/Template.cfm?Section=Justice_Fellowship1 (23 April 2005) lists over twenty kinds of programs with restorative purposes. See Howard Zehr, *Changing Lenses: A New Focus for Crime and Justice* (Scottsdale, Pa.: Herald Press, 1995) on the origins of Victim-Offender Reconciliation in an experimental program through the Mennonite Church.

17. Quoted in David Karp, "Harm and Repair: Observing Restorative Justice in Vermont," *Justice Quarterly* 18 (2001): 727–57.

18. David Karp, who has studied the Vermont system, notes that the "restoration" in question can be relatively "thin," involving any positive act directed to a crime victim or affected community (for example, apologies at a distance or community ser-

vice), or relatively "thick," when the procedure aims at addressing and repairing the specific harm done to victims or communities, which is typically material, psychological, and moral. "Harm and Repair," 730–31.

19. This last is the hot spot of restorative practices in the eyes of those who hold that the consistency of treating like cases alike is definitive of justice, and for those who fear that resolution of restorative practice can either be unjustly severe or unjustly slight. These are real problems, but they are not within the scope of my brief discussion here. John Braithwaite concedes that "There can be little doubt that courts provide superior formal guarantees of procedural fairness than conferences," and thinks the answer is on the one hand, constraint of restorative process by human rights guarantees and the right of appeal and to legal representation within restorative contexts, thus forging a "creative interplay between restorative forums and traditional Western courts." See Braithwaite, *Restorative Justice and Responsive Regulation*, 12–16 on human rights, and 164–66 on procedural worries.

20. Dennis Sullivan and Larry Tifft, "Court Interventions in Corrections," *Crime and Delinquency* 21 (July 1975), 213.

21. Howard Zehr gives nicely straightforward statements of the contrast between retributive and restorative modes. Retributive justice: "Crime is a violation of the state, defined by lawbreaking and guilt. Justice determines blame and administers pain in a contest between the offender and the state directed by systematic rules." Restorative justice: "Crime is a violation of people and relationships. It creates an obligation to make things right. Justice involves the victim, the offender, and the community in a search for solutions which promote repair, reconciliation, and reassurance." See Zehr, *Changing Lenses*, 181.

22. See Braithwaite, *Restorative Justice and Responsive Regulation*, 12, on process and values. See also Heather Strang and John Braithwaite, "Introduction," *Restorative Justice and Civil Society* (New York: Cambridge, 2001).

23. Katherine Beckett and Theodore Sasson, *The Politics of Injustice* (Thousand Oaks, Calif.: Pine Forge Press, 2000), 4. On the continuing growth in prison expenditures, see John M. Broder, "No Hard Time for Prison Budgets," *New York Times*, 19 January 2003, WK5.

24. Beckett and Sasson, *The Politics of Injustice*, 9.

25. Beckett and Sasson, *The Politics of Injustice*, 3. Extensive studies in 1999 and 2000 reported that minority youth, especially African American but also Hispanic and Latino, are many times more likely to be arrested, tried, imprisoned, or tried as adults when juveniles, than whites.

26. For a direct use of care ethics, see J. Pennell and G. Burford, "Widening the Circle: The Family Group Decision Making Project," *Journal of Child and Youth Care* 9 (1994): 1–12, and Charles Barton and Karen van den Broek, "Restorative Justice Conferencing and the Ethic of Care," http://ethics-justice.org/v2n2/conference.html (30 June 1999). Immarigeon and Daly, "Restorative Justice: Origins, Practices, Contexts, and Challenges," cite feminist movement against violence against women and feminist justice theory as contributions. See also Gordon Bazemore and Mara Schiff, *Restorative Community Justice: Repairing Harm and Transforming Communities* (Cincinnati: Anderson Publishing, 2001). Some feminist interventions include C. G. Bowman,

"The Arrest Experiments: A Feminist Critique," in *Taking Sides: Clashing Visions on Controversial Issues in Crime and Criminology*, ed. R. Monk (Gilford, Ct.: Dushkin Publishing, 1994); M. K. Harris, "Moving into the New Millennium: Towards a Feminist Vision of Justice," in *Criminology and Peace-Making*, ed. H. Pepinsky and R. Quinney (Bloomington: Indiana University Press, 1990); F. Heidensohn, "Models of Justice: Portia or Persephone? Some Thoughts on Equality, Fairness and Gender in the Field of Criminal Justice," *International Journal of the Sociology of Law* 14 (1986): 287–98. Kathleen Daly lists as one of several unhelpful "myths" about restorative justice that it is "a 'care' (or feminine) response to crime in comparison to a 'justice' (or masculine) response." My claim does not embody the falsely universalizing binary of care and justice as "feminine" or "masculine." I focus on care as a value theory that pulls from a certain information base; this interpretation does not load gendered meanings into an ethic of care and does not oppose care to justice. See Kathleen Daly, "Restorative Justice: The Real Story," in *A Restorative Justice Reader: Texts, Sources, and Context* (Portland, Ore.: Willan Publishing, 2003).

27. An online 1999 article by Charles Barton and Karen van den Broek, "Restorative Justice Conferencing and the Ethic of Care," http://ethics-justice.org/v2n2/conference.html (30 June 1999), aligns "justice" thinking that invokes "pre-established, universally applicable rules" applied dispassionately to eliminate bias and emotion in achieving consistent, and therefore fair, outcomes as the rationale of court-processing of crime, and care thinking that emphasizes particularity of actors, compassion and attentiveness, the importance of forming and restoring human connections, and openness to nongeneralizable outcomes with restorative justice conferencing practice. J. Pennell and G. Burford, "Widening the Circle: The Family Group Decision Making Project," *Journal of Child and Youth Care* 9 (1994): 1–12, use care ethics as the theoretical viewpoint for assessing a family group conference program that targeted domestic violence against women and children.

28. This was most unambiguously the case with New Zealand's comprehensive reform of its juvenile justice system to especially honor and implement Maori values. See Helen Bowen, "Restorative Justice in Aoteroal/New Zealand—Background and Training Issues," *ICCA Journal on Community Corrections* 8 (1997): 41–45, and Gabrielle Maxwell and Allison Morris, "Family Group Conferences and Restorative Justice." See also Sullivan, "Navajo Peacemaking . . ." and Yazzie, "'Life comes from it' . . . " above on Navajo Peacekeeper Courts. Sentencing circles are another case.

29. The most extensive and current study of the meanings of this distinction is Will Kymlicka, *Multicultural Citizenship* (Oxford: Clarendon Press, 1995).

30. On the "theoretical-juridical model" as the master template of twentieth-century academic moral theory, see my *Moral Understandings: A Feminist Study in Ethics* (New York: Routledge, 1998).

31. I thank Will Kymlicka for pointing this out.

32. The phrase is Joan Tronto's, *Moral Boundaries*, 112.

33. Nor is it any longer an entirely or largely national domestic division of labor that allots caring to women, people of color, or the economically disadvantaged. For the "gendered, raced, and classed" dimensions of caring labor in a global economy, see the introduction to Barbara Ehrenreich and Arlie Russell Hochschild, *Global*

Woman: Nannies, Maids, and Sex Workers in the New Economy (New York: Henry Holt and Company, 2002).

34. Restorative justice advocates like to point out that the "ownership" of crime by the state is a relatively recent development in modern industrial societies. See, for example, Zehr, *Changing Lenses*, chapter 7, "Community Justice: The Historical Alternative;" Braithwaite, *Restorative Justice and Responsive Regulation*, chapter 1, "The Fall and Rise of Restorative Justice"; and Nils Christie, "Conflicts as Property," in *A Restorative Justice Reader: Text, Sources, Contexts* (Portland, Ore.: Willan Publishing, 2003).

35. While it is common to read and hear of "the" private sphere, it is not obvious that there is one such sphere, and I am assuming here that there is not. Rather there are different lines of distinction along which affairs can be sorted into "public" and "private," and gender in U.S. society is one such constitutive dimension that both defines and is defined by a particular way of marking affairs as "private."

36. An earlier version of this chapter was originally prepared as an invited contribution to a Conference on Ethics and Public Policy sponsored by the Netherlands Organization for Scientific Research (NWO), held in Utrecht in May 2003. I thank the NWO for its sponsorship of the conference, and I thank those present at that presentation, including commentators Henk Manschot and Marian Verkerk, for their observations.

Chapter Nine

Ethical Globalization?
States, Corporations, and
the Ethics of Care

Fiona Robinson

INTRODUCTION

In a 2003 speech at the LSE, Mary Robinson, former president of Ireland and UN high commissioner for human rights, put forward the following claim:

> Essentially, my argument is that the binding human rights framework must become part of the rules of the road of globalization. These human rights commitments . . . must play a bigger role in shaping the decisions of governments in every policy arena, domestic or international. Only then will we be able to ensure a more values-led, ethical globalization.[1]

Robinson was speaking in her new role as executive director of the Ethical Globalization Initiative, whose mandate is to bring "key stakeholders together in new alliances to integrate concepts of human rights, gender sensitivity and enhanced accountability into efforts to address global challenges and governance shortcomings."[2] Taking an explicitly human rights–based approach, the Initiative is guided by the belief that globalization "could have many more positive aspects if it were more ethical"—especially if fundamental human rights were more widely recognized and exercised.[3]

Mary Robinson argues that the main driving forces of globalization are market forces—"increasingly pushing for open markets for trade, the trade in goods, services and capital"—and the "privatization of power," leading to a crisis of democratic accountability.[4] These forces, moreover, are creating, or exacerbating, a series of global crises: poverty—particularly for women; health care—especially HIV/AIDS; and environmental degradation. The challenge, therefore, is to recognize that globalization "exists"—in other words, that it is inevitable—and to work from a human rights–based approach to make it more "ethical," by ensuring that "the poor should not simply benefit from the charity of more resources, but must have legal and political space to claim their rights and take part in decision-making."[5]

This initiative must be recognized for its boldness, vision, and timeliness. Moreover, it is to be applauded for its attention to often-overlooked groups and issues, including and especially women, health care, and the natural environment. While I agree with the spirit of this important initiative, my aim in this chapter is to explore this idea of ethical globalization, but through a different lens—the feminist ethics of care. Specifically, I will interrogate the role of states and nonstate actors—particularly corporations—as moral agents and sites of potential resistance and transformation in the face of globalization. I will argue, in contrast with the rights focus of the Ethical Globalization Initiative, that a normative framework based on care ethics can contribute toward imagining, articulating, and implementing real alternatives to neoliberalism. In particular, the integration of the values and practices of care into social policy, as well as into the workings of private organizations, may be helpful in alleviating the deep gender and racial imbalances—in terms of access to wealth, resources, services, and power—caused, or at least exacerbated, by globalization. A care-based perspective shifts the focus from individual, autonomous rights holders to connected, interdependent families, households, and local communities. This enables us to see how the effects of globalization are distributed within and across these groups. Before we can answer the question of how globalization can be made more ethical, we must first ask questions about how globalization has transformed the gendered division of labor in both the North and the South. How has the relocation and reorganization of global production altered the nature of women's work? Who is responsible for the increased care work burdens that are created by neoliberal economic policies? Why is it that women, children, and the elderly are the most vulnerable groups in poverty-stricken countries?

The first part of this chapter will discuss the feminist ethics of care as a basis for moral and social transformation in an era of globalization. Care ethics will be understood here as both a "concrete activity, in the sense of caring about and for daily needs; and as a moral orientation—as an ethics or a set of values that can guide human agency in a variety of social fields."[6] This normative framework will then be used to build an argument for the importance of refocusing attention on the social responsibilities of states in both developed and developing countries. Here, I will argue that states must do more than respect rights and carry out obligations if they are seeking to repair the "social bond" that is currently at risk.[7]

Part two of the chapter will explore a relatively new phenomenon: the rise of corporate social responsibility. I will explore the role of corporations in constructing an "ethical globalization" using the lens of care. On this view, corporations—like states or any other institutional actors—are not seen as individualized moral agents with rights and obligations; rather, they are themselves social-moral communities with complex internal and external patterns of responsibility. Moreover, they exist not as autonomous actors but as part of a set of social-moral systems that make up the global arena.[8] Understanding states and corporations in this way makes it possible to highlight and address patterns of exclusion and oppression—including and perhaps especially gender bias—as well as possible sites of progressive transformation in a wide range of social, political, and economic areas.

STATES AND THE ETHICS OF CARE IN
AN ERA OF GLOBALIZATION

Feminist Ethics

The ethics of care is now widely known as a feminist critique of Kantian-liberal and rights-based approaches to ethics. Genealogies of feminist care ethics usually begin with the work of Nancy Chodorow, whose influential work *The Reproduction of Mothering* argued that male children need to differentiate themselves from their mothers and create a separate, oppositional entity. This early childhood psychology was said to account for the fact that the basic feminine sense of self is one of relatedness or connection to the world, while the basic masculine sense of self denies relation, or is "separate."[9] It was this book that was to have the greatest influence on the work of Carol Gilligan, whose 1982 book *In a Different Voice* is now regularly cited as the seminal work in the development of the ethics of care. Gilligan's empirical investigations of women's responses to a series of moral dilemmas led her to argue that women define themselves "in a context of human relationship" and judge themselves according to their ability to care.[10] Since Gilligan's early work, a number of scholars have widened the debate surrounding care to include analysis of the ways in which care can help us to explain, understand, and ultimately transform the nature not only of personal but also of political and social relations.[11] In what follows below, I want to focus on the work of two such theorists—Margaret Urban Walker and Selma Sevenhuijsen—in order to think about how care ethics could be used as a normative framework for rethinking the nature of the state, and the relationship between states and citizens, in an era of globalization.

In terms of the role and nature of feminist moral philosophy in the process of social and political transformation, perhaps the best place to begin is with

Margaret Urban Walker's "expressive-collaborative" ethics. Walker's understanding of ethics complements and augments traditional care reasoning by adding a critical, sociopolitical dimension to feminist ethics. Morality, argues Walker, is not theory but certain kinds of practices. The theory of morality, then, is an attempt to understand those practices. According to Walker, the role of theorizing moral practice is to "interrogate some of the most morally troubling aspects of human social life: domination, oppression, exclusion, coercion, and basic disregard of some people by others."[12]

This view of ethics is similar to care ethics insofar as it locates morality in practices of responsibility—specific moral claims on us arise from our contact or relationship with others whose interests are vulnerable to our actions and choices. It goes further, however, in making the claim that this kind of ethics requires a view of moral judgment with significant expressive, interpretive, and (where possible) collaborative features.[13] Moral thinking, on this view, has two tasks. The first is to identify what people need to know to live according to moral understandings that prevail in their communities or societies. Second, it must supply critical strategies for testing whether understandings about how to live that are the most credited in a community or society deserve their authority. It will steer attention toward the discourses, procedures, and relations of authority that make it possible for some understandings to prevail.[14]

This sort of feminist ethical thinking certainly involves the responsiveness to individual needs in small-scale situations that is the focus of traditional care ethics. Paradoxically, this aspect is crucial to its role as a global ethic in the contemporary era. While studies of cosmopolitan citizenship and democracy dominate the normative literature in international relations theory, attention to care ethics reminds us that people's lives remain heavily embedded in the particular contexts of real places.[15] In spite of, and perhaps also because of, globalization, the struggles that occur at the local level are of great significance for most of the world's peoples. This embeddedness, however, need not lead to parochialism or moral exclusion.

Walker's view of ethics modifies traditional care ethics so that it is no longer focused exclusively on individuals and their needs. Indeed, the expressive-collaborative model is explicitly understood as a socially embodied medium of understanding and adjustment, rather than an individual action–guiding system. In this way, it must reflect and act upon not only our responsibilities to particular others that arise out of our relations with them but also how social structures and institutions give rise to relations and practices of responsibility that privilege some groups over others and that may make caring difficult or unlikely between members of groups.[16]

While Walker does not refer specifically to globalization or, indeed, to international politics, her approach to morality suggests an ethical view that refuses to limit moral concern to those within specific territorial or identity communities. Here, morality is seen not as a set of preexisting moral rules but as an ongoing dialogue between an ever-changing set of participants. While many cosmopolitan theorists concentrate their efforts on fashioning post-Westphalian world orders or engineering the spread and transformation of democracy to the global level, a feminist approach to ethics would focus on more modest transformations in policy and practice. Rather than seeking to achieve world citizenship through the universal exercise of democratic and human rights, feminist ethics recognizes the increasing sociopolitical inter-twinement brought about through globalization. Indeed, it draws our attention to the ways in which care work—of children, the elderly, the chronically ill, and the permanently disabled—is now not only private and local but also transnational global, as (mostly women) workers migrate from South to North in search of opportunities for paid care work. This creates just one ex-ample of the many types of "care gaps" that exist in the world today, as glob-alization intensifies the need for care, while simultaneously directing the re-duction or even withdrawal of care services at the level of the state.

Care Ethics and the Transformation of the Welfare State

In this section, I argue that the feminist view of ethics described above may be related specifically to the changing role of the state in an era of globaliza-tion. Thus we might ask, What do the theory and practices of care have to contribute to the construction of an alternative role for the state in the twenty-first century? Conventional accounts of the nature of the Western liberal state tell the story of the social contract as the primary mechanism bonding the cit-izens to the sovereign. Moreover, twentieth-century histories of the rise of the welfare state are often seen as an extension of this story—wherein a primary state function was to tax within its boundaries in order to ensure the welfare of the community. Until very recently, however, the role of women, care ethics, and caring practices in this story was rarely discussed; even today, it is only slowly making its way into mainstream literature. As Joan Tronto neatly puts it, "Care may be ubiquitous in human life, but it has remained hid-den from the conceptual lenses of social and political thought."[17] Gradually, however, recognition is coming to the innovative research that demonstrates the part played by women and by social and political disputes about the meaning of sexual difference, in the founding and construction of welfare states, as well as in the professionalization of care and the organization of so-cial work. The idea that gender occupies a central place in modern welfare states is slowly gaining recognition, leading to new insights into the operation and effectiveness of central concepts in the policies of the welfare state, such as equality and individualization.[18]

Recognizing the role played by women, gender relations, and care ethics in contemporary welfare states provides us with a starting point for conceptualizing the political role of care ethics in an era of globalization. Indeed, the irony is that while care has been integral to the making of the modern welfare state, care ethics embodies a moral-political potential that transcends that particular historical configuration. Thus, the changing nature of the state—from "welfare" to "competition"—signals not the demise of care but an opportunity to bring the notion of care to the forefront of political thought as a basis for contestation. In particular, care offers us a framework for rethinking both democracy and citizenship in an era of globalization.

When considering the role of care ethics in developed states in an era of globalization, it is instructive to examine the work of Selma Sevenhuijsen on care and citizenship. As institutions of global governance begin to replace many state functions, the relationship between citizens and the states is being irrevocably altered by globalization. Sevenhuijsen develops a model of citizenship in which the ethics of care has a significant place; this is in contrast to the radical model of identity politics, where the public sphere is seen as a sphere in which everyone can be "themselves" and on the basis of this can assert claims with regard to others. As she astutely points out, this latter model is very much in accordance with what she calls the "neo-liberal spirit of the times"; the "claims" of which she speaks are most often articulated as "rights" claims, and boundaries are continually being drawn between "us" and "them." By contrast, her feminist vision of active citizenship sees the public sphere as a meeting ground where people shape identities through action and interaction, through the exchange of narratives and opinion, through deliberation and debate. Here, importantly, identity depends "more on what you do than on what you are." The ethics of care, she argues, has a central place in such a conception of citizenship—while care ethics is committed to the recognition of people's differences, it does not take these differences as absolute but judges them within specific contexts of action. The links between care and democratic citizenship are made very clear:

> If we integrate values derived from the ethics of care, such as attentiveness, responsiveness and responsibility . . . the concept of citizenship will be enriched and better able to cope with diversity and plurality, and care will be "de-romanticized," enabling us to consider its values as political virtues. In addition, politics can take into account the importance of care as a social practice and acknowledge the diversity of values it embodies.[19]

This politicized notion of care, in which the care ethic is divorced from its association with a maternal identity, overcomes one of the key problems associated with the application of care not only to the narrow sphere of moral psychology but to the sphere of politics as well. As Catherine Eschle has argued, one of the difficulties with care ethics is that it universalizes a specific mode of being as a political strategy appropriate to all contexts.[20] Sevenhuijsen's understanding of care uses a more fluid, open notion of identity, based on action—what you do—rather than some fixed, reified notion of being. This means that social action based on care need not be limited to a specific form of activism or to a particular range of issues. Moreover, the "traditional" focus of care ethics on relationships is understood here as more than just "caring for" or "caring about"; rather, the value of relationships translates into an understanding of the public sphere as a site of dialogue and interaction where diversity and expression are valued, and collaboration and dialogue are encouraged.

Sevenhuijsen has translated these ideas into more concrete prescriptions for policy in later papers. Specifically, she argues that we can think of care as a democratic practice in developed countries in an era of globalization. Instead of taking as our moral subjects autonomous, self-contained individuals, we should instead start from notions of "selves in networks of care and responsibility" and "working and caring citizens."[21] Seeing citizens in this way provides us with a truly alternative moral ontology that can challenge the legalistic notions of rights and obligations, which are common to both supporters and most opponents of globalization. Moreover, bringing care to the forefront of norm building and policy making at this time could even provide a starting point for repairing, or rebuilding, the withered "social bond" that is threatening the stability society in many developed nation-states.

> When a norm of equality of access to the giving and receiving of care in both public and private contexts is combined with democratic notions of equality of voice (and thus with values of attentiveness and responsiveness), we can imagine that these institutions would have the capacity of generating loyalty and commitment on the part of those who participate in them and thus could work as vessels for solidarity and social cohesion.[22]

While the deficits in democracy and a lack of social cohesion are also problems in developing countries, there are many other problems that, if not more serious, are at least more immediate. In many developing countries, the effects of globalization are painfully obvious: increased and worsening levels of poverty, especially for women, and devastating crises in the realms of health, education, and the environment.

Care Ethics in the Global South

Prescribing policy directions for nation-states in the South is hugely problematic: here, states often lack the capacity to follow chosen directions, hindered as they are by external pressures—especially by international financial institutions, but also by other states on which they are dependent for trade and/or aid. These nation-states are also constrained by internal pressures—pressures that also exist in developed countries, but that are often more acute in the South: corruption, environmental constraints, and deeply entrenched cultural norms and practices, including those that influence gender relations. Indeed, Toni Erskine has questioned whether developing countries, or "quasi-states," can be classified as "institutional moral agents" and thus whether they can coherently be ascribed moral responsibilities.[23] Ultimately, she argues, these states are moral agents, and they can and should be assigned responsibilities—both prospectively and retrospectively. She argues that:

> Addressing issues of prospective responsibility through a model of institutional moral agency that helps one to understand who, or what, can act in response to moral imperatives, and under what conditions such duties can be discharged, promises to contribute to more coherent policy-making and theorizing about ethics in international affairs.[24]

While such an analysis raises important questions about the usefulness of assigning social, political, and moral responsibilities to developing states, it also is in danger of obfuscating the complex and multilayered networks of responsibility that already exist within these states, and across state institutions and other groups. Thus I would suggest that the questions for normative theorists are not if these states can take responsibility for their peoples, or what agent can act when faced with a crisis, or even what agent should be assigned the responsibilities/duties to prevent a crisis; rather, they should be, How are existing responsibilities within a nation-state distributed, and how are these responsibilities accounted for or justified through norms and social practices?

Understood in this way, responsibility in world politics is not synonymous with "duty"; rather, it is part of everyday social relations. Along with the other core values of an ethic of care—attentiveness, competence, and responsiveness—responsibility cannot be seen only as something that can be assigned after ethical deliberation; rather, it is central to what morality always already *is*.[25] This is in contrast to the view of responsibility often taken in the study of ethics in international politics; this view sees institutional moral agents as bearers of rights and duties, assigned by some rather nebulous authority—such as the "international community" or the normative theorist.

Thinking about responsibility in this way helps us to consider the role of the state in developing countries in an era of globalization. It means that we will ask not who or what is responsible for poor working conditions in the global South or the AIDS crisis in Africa, but rather how patterns of responsibility and practices of care are distributed and accounted for in particular so-cieties—and here we can think of nation-states and institutions as "societies," rather than "agents"—and how and in what ways those distributions are ei-ther enabling or exploitative for individuals and groups. Thus specific ques-tions might include, Who actually does the caring work required by people with AIDS in Africa? Where do the resources for this care work come from? How does this care work affect gender relations within households and com-munities? This type of analysis allows us to highlight the nature of gender re-lations—relations that are particularly important when considering how to improve the lives of all people in developing countries.

Neoliberal economic policies of contemporary globalization have meant that many developing countries have had to endure serious cutbacks in social services provided by the state, often mandated by powerful international fi-nancial institutions. These cutbacks are particularly disadvantageous for women, who are the major recipients and providers of such services. More-over, where state-run care services or support for care work has been reduced, women have found their burden of care increased. Finally, in many develop-ing countries, the reorganization of global production has led to the "femi-nization" of the labor work, where more and more women are taking up waged labor in manufacturing, especially in the South, where multinational corporations have relocated their production processes. This has created "gaps in caregiving," as more and more women are working in factories.[26] Thus while globalization has brought increased opportunities for women's paid employment, it has also brought more unpaid care work and dependency work for women in the domestic sector.[27] Globalization has, in effect, altered the "gender contract," shifting activities from the public sector to the house-hold or domestic sphere; in so doing, it has placed an increased burden of car-ing as well as additional community-related activities on family members.[28]

In light of this, I would argue that an understanding of global inequality is based on much more than simply the unfair advantage in power and knowl-edge that the rich countries of the North have over the poor countries of the South. Specifically, the multilayered structure of inequality in the global economy must be understood through the lens of gender and care. As Marc-hand points out, only a gender perspective can bring to the fore how profound a transformation globalization entails in terms of the day-to-day lived reali-ties of people.[29] For example, Dickinson and Schaeffer argue that the under-paid labor and unpaid work done by most women have made it possible for the structure of global inequality to remain intact. Although women comprise 50 percent of the population, they do over two-thirds of the world's work, most of it low-paid or unpaid. Moreover, because women still do almost all of the household work in addition to their wage labor and informal work, they often work between sixteen and eighteen hours a day.[30] Certainly, wage work in the periphery has helped intensify global production. That said, wages in the periphery usually do not even cover the cost of maintaining one household member. When we add to this the fact that state benefits in the South have declined, it is not surprising that more than half of the income of households in the South is generated by "self-organized" work. To make sense of this, it is important to appreciate that the public and private spheres are inextricably joined.

The impact of this burden on women, moreover, cannot be underestimated. According to the UNIFEM 2000 report on the progress of women worldwide, the double burden of paid work and unpaid care work is putting pressure on the health of poor women and children, as well as on the education of daughters who may have to drop out of school to substitute for their mothers. As the report points out, the domestic sector, managed globally by women, cannot be treated as a "bottomless well," able to provide the care needed regardless of the resources it gets from other sectors.[31]

As the analysis above demonstrates, a care-based approach to questions of development and the state in the global South would eschew a narrowly economistic focus, and instead would examine how the economy is contextually embedded in political and social institutions.[32] Furthermore, there is a need to begin from a relational ontology in thinking about women's and men's places within the networks of societies. Certainly, this does not mean idealizing women's relationships, or their "naturally cooperative nature" to guide policy—such as the focus on women for microcredit schemes. While moves such as this certainly assist women in many ways, it is important to remember that any kind of social relationship or network could be, or at least has the potential to be exploitative, or to contribute to social hierarchies and ethnic and class differences among women.[33] Because social norms and networks can sometimes justify inequality, there is a need to "analyze the dialectical relationship between the economic and cultural aspects of social life" in developing states.[34]

I have suggested that the feminist ethics of care can provide us with a starting point for rethinking the disintegration of the welfare state and the "social bond" in many developed nation-states as a result of globalization. Moreover, by bringing care ethics into development policies, we are able to rethink the concept of responsibility in world politics, as well as the role and nature of social networks and relationships in defining gender relations in the context of a developing economy. In the final section below, I will explore the relatively new idea that corporations—particularly transnational corporations—could and indeed should act as socially responsible actors for the promotion of ethical globalization. While I am optimistic about the potential role of corporations, there is a need for caution when advocating any move which could take responsibility for social provision away from states and place it on private actors.

CORPORATIONS AND GLOBAL RESPONSIBILITIES

While nongovernmental organizations (NGOs) and global social movements are most widely recognized as the source of resistance to globalization, attention has recently turned to corporations as a potential site of ethical transformation and even democratization. While we still live in a world of states, the role of corporations in the contemporary global political economy can hardly be overstated. Corporations are the "leading form of economic organization in the modern world," and their size and influence are staggering. By the mid-1990s, "fifty-one of the hundred largest economies in the world were corporations, not nation-states."[35] Increasingly, many corporations are becoming truly transnational in almost all aspects of their business; state boundaries have become less important, as companies are locating their operations in various parts of the world, employing local workers, and often marketing and selling worldwide. Perhaps the most visible symbols of globalization, transnational corporations wield tremendous economic power on a global scale, and they are "cosmopolitan" in the sense that they are not limited by national or state borders. That said, they are often also recognized as having done little to promote a fairer, more ethical globalization.

This is hardly surprising, given the near consensus that firms or transnational corporations are, along with states and international financial institutions, the main driving forces behind globalization. Even more explicitly than states, firms are motivated by improving their competitiveness and expanding their reach in terms of market share.[36] Recently, however, there has been a small but significant movement toward change. Although it can hardly be contested that the "prime responsibility of a company is generating profits," it is also the case that an increasing number of corporations are "promoting their corporate social responsibility strategies as a response to a variety of social, environmental and economic pressures."[37] Currently, we are witnessing corporations, not states, making "policy" that "leads to the development of . . . new spheres for existing relationships . . . regarding social dialogue, skills acquisition, equal opportunities . . . with reference to the reinforcement of economic and social cohesion."[38] In this section, I will argue that the ethic of care can be used as a "lens" to undertake a normative analysis and evaluation of the idea of corporate social responsibility, and that it can also provide a normative framework for the building of ideas and policy addressing the future direction of corporations.[39]

While there is no single, authoritative definition of the term "corporate social responsibility," it is generally understood to describe instances in which companies respond to interests in addition to those of their shareholders. The use of the word "responsibility" in the term is not incidental; indeed, it is essential to the meaning and purposes of the idea.

> Corporate social responsibility is essentially a concept whereby companies decide voluntarily to contribute to a better society and a cleaner environment. . . . an increasing number of European companies recognize their social responsibility more and more clearly and consider it as part of their identity. This responsibility is expressed toward employees and more generally toward all the stakeholders affected by business and which in turn can influence its success.[40]

Increasingly, there is recognition that the accountability of corporations must exceed simply the existing legal obligations to shareholders; "stakeholders" are defined as "constituencies affected (favorably and unfavorably) by the corporation's actions, including employees, customers, local communities and society at large."[41] Thus it is accepted that the effects of the activities of large corporations are widespread and that these powerful actors can no longer afford to turn a blind eye to the social, environmental, economic, and political effects of their decisions and actions.

Corporate social responsibility (CSR) may include, but is not necessarily limited to, what is known as "corporate citizenship." This concept is associated with what is sometimes known as "corporate philanthropy," including corporate charitable donations, support for community-building activities, and corporate volunteerism.[42] While this is one kind of CSR, there should be no confusion about the nature or extent of this charity. There is no suggestion that corporations will put their social responsibilities before the goal of profit. Indeed, in taking on these responsibilities, companies are understood to be "investing in their future," and may expect that the "voluntary commitment they adopt will help to increase their profitability."[43] Moreover, in one Canadian report on CSR, it was made clear that although there are those who question the very legitimacy of corporations, the proponents of the corporate social responsibility position accept that corporations exist to generate profits, but believe that they also have responsibilities that extend beyond the maximization of shareholder returns.[44] Thus CSR cannot be understood solely as "charity" or "altruism." Rather, as I will elucidate below, "responsibility" must be recognized as a complex moral notion that moves beyond the strict categorization of agents as "moral" or "immoral," but rather regards actors in the global economy as existing within webs of social relationships, characterized by the uneven distribution of different types of entitlements and responsibilities.

In order to understand the current discourse and make prescriptions for the future, it is necessary to "read" corporate social responsibility through the framework of care ethics. First, it is important to accept that corporate social responsibility is not simply an economic or even a political issue. Thinking about the responsibilities of corporations within the context of the social relationships in which they are immersed, and indeed which they create, highlights why consideration of the behavior of corporations must be understood, at least in part, from the perspective of ethics. CSR forces us to see beyond the institutional mask of corporations and to recognize that, ultimately, corporations are made up of people who are making decisions that have economic, social, and moral consequences beyond the institution itself. Those people, moreover, cannot be understood as atomized, individual agents any more than a corporation can be "personified" in this way. The individuals and groups of individuals involved in corporations can only make sense in the context of patterns and webs of relationships, both within and beyond the institution itself. Moreover, those individual and group actors are themselves acted upon by social structures, some of which may be external to them, and some of which they themselves may help to create.

Second, regardless of the extent to which it is being practiced, or indeed whether it is being practiced at all, the very idea of corporate social responsibility calls into question the values, discourses, and practices that are taken for granted by many actors in the contemporary global economy. In Walker's words, it "steers attention towards the discourses, procedures and relations of authority that make it possible for some understandings to prevail."[45] Thus thinking about and institutionalizing corporate social responsibility is a critical ethical practice that questions assumptions about politics and the global economy that we may take for granted: that a global capitalist economy must function in a certain way to sustain itself and that private corporations can only concern themselves with profit maximization if they are to thrive. There is a clear recognition in the various reports and papers on this issue that CSR must be addressed in the light of the "employment and social consequences of economic and market integration and in adapting working conditions to the new economy."[46]

Third, thinking about corporate social responsibility from the perspective of care ethics forces us to consider the importance of moral responses that are neither rights-based nor rule-based. While human rights are often mentioned in the same breath as CSR, I would argue that human rights are merely one example of that to which corporations are beginning to respond and for which they are beginning to take responsibility. Like the natural environment, individual human rights cannot be ignored or abused by responsible corporations. But responsiveness and responsibility, and the social/relational nature of responsibility, act as the actual moral engine behind CSR. As in Walker's argument, morality is located in practices of responsibility: "Specific moral claims arise from our contact or relationships with others whose interests are vulnerable to our actions and choices. We are *obligated to respond* to particular others when circumstance or ongoing relationships render them especially, conspicuously, or peculiarly dependent on us."[47] This is not to say, however, that corporate social responsibility can be a substitute for regulation or legislation concerning social rights or environmental standards. As a European report insists,

> In countries where such regulations do not exist, efforts should focus on putting the proper regulatory or legislative framework in place in order to define a level playing field on the basis of which socially responsible practices can be developed.[48]

Thus it is essential to recognize that rights—of workers, consumers, and human beings in general—are crucial if we seek to create a more inclusive, more just global political economy. But it is only once we situate rights in relationships that they actually make sense in this context. While legal rights and rule-based ethics have their place in the corporate world, the idea of corporate social responsibility forces us to see beyond a world of adversarial individuals (or individualized agents) pitted against one another in a constant struggle to secure rights against one another.

Fourth, we shouldn't imagine CSR as corporations suddenly deciding to "care about" the various constituents who are affected by their decisions—employees, local citizens, consumers, etc. Care is not simply something we wish others would do more (i.e., "if only governments/corporations cared more about people"), but rather as something that is ever-present within all kinds of social relationships, and upon which people are, at some point, dependent. If corporations can recognize care as the fundamental cornerstone of human life, it would naturally take a higher priority in the development of their socially responsible policies. Policies such as abolishing mandatory overtime for employees and facilitating child care—through day care centers, accessible schooling, maternity leave, and health insurance—will help women working in global production address their combined productive and reproductive roles.[49]

There is an inherent danger, however, in relying too heavily on corporations as socially responsible actors. The ethical significance of the shift in corporations toward taking greater social responsibility should not be overestimated; currently, the corporations participating in this kind of practice represent only a small minority. Moreover, it should not be assumed that the taking on of new "responsibilities" will eclipse those corporations' primary motivation: profit. Indeed, to a certain extent, many companies are accepting these responsibilities because they are aware of the pressures, largely by consumers, to do so, and of the long-term profitability of these changes. It is important to be cognizant of, and indeed wary of, the trend towards placing state responsibilities on non-state actors as part of the new global governance.

That said, the practices of CSR may indeed signal a shift in what has heretofore been taken for granted about the nature of the contemporary global economy. As Walker has argued, sometimes some of us can challenge the moral terms and assumptions that are already in place by appealing to other moral terms or by inventing new ones. Applications of moral concepts to familiar practices may be shifted, and applications to new or newly visible social practices may change understandings of what those concepts mean.[50] These changes are not merely semantic; rather, they are the first step in a gradual transformation of moral understandings. But as Walker also points out, there are certain social conditions that must be present for this kind of criticism to emerge: "Some coming apart of authority or authorities, or of the fit between ways of judging and practices, opens critical space: Moral understandings may then be questioned that could otherwise go on as before."[51]

The whole idea of corporate social responsibility has been prompted by a recognition of the need to address the "employment and social consequences of economic and market integration and in adapting working conditions to the new economy."[52] Indeed, the so-called Post-Washington Consensus is characterized by the development of an understanding among the international institutional policy community of the need for a stronger "governance dimension" to the international economic order.[53] This change has been brought about by, among other things, the protests against globalization and the general recognition that global liberalization brings with it increased inequality. This "coming apart of authority," however slight, opens critical space for the initiation of change. While the term "corporate social responsibility" is a new one, it is a term that may become more familiar to a wider audience in time, and may ultimately carry sufficient moral authority to make it the norm, rather than the exception.

CONCLUSION

This chapter has sought to explore the possibilities for achieving "ethical globalization" from the perspective of an ethic of care. This is in contrast to the newly emerging analyses of this issue that are firmly and centrally grounded in a human rights–based approach.[54] While human rights may have achieved universal recognition as a moral and political idea, there are many groups, including and perhaps especially women, who argue that dominant understandings of rights fail to address their needs and protect them from certain kinds of harm.[55] Moreover, rights-based ethics are intimately tied—in early modern and contemporary political theory—to the ethics and values that currently drive globalization.

An ethic of care, by contrast, offers an approach to ethics which is a genuine alternative to neoliberalism. Unlike neoliberalism, care is not an ideology; rather, it is a set of values, practices, and responsibilities that exist in societies but that lack the attention and recognition they deserve. An ethical approach to globalization would seek to uncover those responsibilities—especially, I have argued, for paid and unpaid caring work—and to interrogate how they are distributed and accounted for in particular societies and institutions. Moreover, it would aim to bring the core values of care—attentiveness, responsibility, competence, and responsiveness—into state policy making, in both developed and developing countries.[56] Finally, I have suggested that, while the task of relieving women of their heavy and often unmanageable caring burden must be focused on states and state institutions, the idea that corporations can be socially responsible in the face of globalization deserves some attention. Understanding both states and private institutions—such as corporations—not as atomized moral agents but as "social-moral communities" immersed in networks of relationships both within and outside their own borders, provides a new starting point for thinking about moral responsibility, and the possibilities for transformation, in an era of globalization.

NOTES

1. Mary Robinson, "From Rhetoric to Reality: Making Human Rights Work," speech delivered at the London School of Economics and Political Science, 23 October 2003, www.eginitiative.org/documents.

2. The Ethical Globalization Initiative, www.eginitiative.org.

3. Mary Robinson, "A Discussion on Ethical Globalization," *YaleGlobal* Online, 15 January 2003. http://yaleglobal.yale.edu, 2.

4. Robinson, "A Discussion," 2.

5. Mary Robinson, "Shaping Globalization: The Role of Human Rights," Fifth Annual Grotius Lecture, American Society of International Law, 97th Annual Meeting, Washington, D.C., 2 April 2003.

6. Selma Sevenhuijsen, "Caring in the Third Way: The Relation Between Obligation, Responsibility and Care in Third Way Discourse," *Critical Social Policy* 20, no. 1 (2000): 6.

7. Richard Devetak and Richard Higgott, "Justice Unbound? Globalization, States and the Transformation of the Social Bond," *International Affairs* 75, no. 3 (1999): 487.

8. The term "social-moral systems" comes from Margaret Urban Walker, *Moral Understandings: A Feminist Study in Ethics* (New York: Routledge, 1998).

9. Nancy Chodorow, *The Reproduction of Mothering: Psychoanalysis and the Sociology of Gender* (Berkeley: University of California Press, 1978): 169.

10. Carol Gilligan, *In a Different Voice* (Cambridge: Harvard University Press, 1982): 8.

11. See especially Joan Tronto, *Moral Boundaries: A Political Argument for an Ethic of Care* (New York: Routledge, 1993); Selma Sevenhuijsen, *Citizenship and the Ethics of Care* (New York: Routledge, 1998); Virginia Held, *Feminist Morality: Transforming Culture, Society and Politics* (Chicago: University of Chicago Press, 1993); Kimberley Hutchings, "Towards a Feminist International Ethics," *Review of International Studies*, vol. 25, Special Issue (December 2000); Olena Hankivsky, *Social Policy and the Ethic of Care* (Toronto: University of British Columbia Press, 2004).

12. Walker, *Moral Understandings*, 15.

13. Walker, *Moral Understandings*, 107.

14. Walker, *Moral Understandings*, 60.

15. See especially David Held, *Democracy and Global Order: From the Modern State to Cosmopolitan Governance* (Cambridge: Polity Press, 1995), and Andrew Linklater, *The Transformation of Political Community* (Cambridge: Polity Press, 1998).

16. Alison Jaggar, "Care as a Feminist Practice of Moral Reason" in *Justice and Care: Essential Readings in Feminist Ethics*, ed. Virginia Held (Boulder: Westview Press, 1995): 196–97.

17. Joan Tronto, "Care as a Basis for Radical Political Judgment," *Hypatia* 10, no. 2 (Spring, 1995): 142.

18. Selma Sevenhuijsen, *Citizenship and the Ethics of Care: Feminist Considerations on Justice, Morality and Politics* (London: Routledge, 1998), 69.

19. Sevenhuijsen, *Citizenship*, 14–15.

20. Catherine Eschele, *Global Democracy, Social Movements and Feminism* (Boulder: Westview Press, 2000), 106. Eschele uses the term "maternalism" rather than "care ethics."

21. Sevenhuijsen, "Caring in the Third Way," 29.

22. Sevenhuijsen, "Caring in the Third Way," 30.

23. Toni Erskine, "Assigning Responsibilities to Institutional Moral Agents: The Case of States and Quasi-States" in *Can Institutions Have Responsibilities? Collective Moral Agency and International Relations*, ed. Toni Erskine (London: Palgrave, 2001). The term "quasi-states" comes from Robert Jackson, *Quasi-States: Sovereignty, International Relations and the Third World* (Cambridge: Cambridge University Press, 1990).

24. Erskine, "Assigning Responsibilities," 37.

25. The conceptualization of an ethic of care as consisting of these four core values comes from Berenice Fisher and Joan Tronto, "Toward a Feminist Theory of Caring," in *Circles of Care: Work and Identity in Women's Lives*, ed. E. Abel and M. Nelson (Albany: State University of New York Press, 1990).

26. World Health Organization, *Ethical Choices in Long-Term Care: What Does Justice Require?* (Geneva: World Health Organization, 2002), x.

27. Ofelia Schutte, "Dependency Work, Women and the Global Economy," in *The Subject of Care: Feminist Perspectives on Dependency*, ed. Eva Feder Kittay and Ellen K. Feder (Lanham, Md.: Rowman and Littlefield, 2002), 151.

28. Marianne Marchand, "Challenging Globalization: Toward a Feminist Understanding of Resistance," *Review of International Studies* 29, Special Issue (2003): 148.

29. Marchand, "Challenging Globalization," 148.

30. Torry D. Dickinson and Robert K. Schaeffer, *Fast Forward: Work, Gender and Protest in a Changing World* (Lanham, Md.: Rowman and Littlefield, 2001), 15.

31. UNIFEM, *Biennial Report, Progress of the World's Women 2000* (New York: United Nations Development Fund for Women, 2000), 29.

32. Suzanne Bergeron, "The Post-Washington Consensus and Economic Representations of Women in Development at the World Bank," *International Feminist Journal of Politics* 5, no. 3 (November 2003): 407.

33. Bergeron, "The Post-Washington Consensus," 413.

34. Bergeron, "The Post-Washington Consensus," 414.

35. Canadian Democracy and Corporate Accountability Commission, "The New Balance Sheet: Corporate Profits and Responsibility in the 21st Century," Final Report (January 2002), 2.

36. Marianne Marchand and Anne Sisson Runyan, *Gender and Global Restructuring: Sightings, Sites and Resistances* (London: Routledge, 2000), 5.

37. Commission of the European Communities, Green Paper, "Promoting a European Framework for Corporate Social Responsibility," Brussels (July 2001), 3.

38. "Promoting a European Framework," 3.

39. Here I mean specifically the Green Paper from the European Commission and the Report from the Commission on Canadian Democracy and Corporate Accountability.

40. "Promoting a European Framework," 4.

41. "The New Balance Sheet," 5.

42. "The New Balance Sheet," 5.

43. "Promoting a European Framework," 3.

44. "The New Balance Sheet," 2.

45. Walker, *Moral Understandings*, 60.

46. "Promoting a European Framework," 5.

47. Walker, *Moral Understandings*, 107.

48. "Promoting a European Framework," 7.

49. Stephanie Barrientos and Naila Kabeer, "Enhancing Female Employment in Global Production: Policy Implications," *Global Social Policy* 4, no. 2: 153–54.

50. Walker, *Moral Understandings*, 72.

51. Walker, *Moral Understandings*, 72.

52. "Promoting a European Framework," 5.

53. Richard Higgott, "Contested Globalization: The Changing Context and Normative Challenges," *Review of International Studies* 26, Special Issue (December 2000): 137.

54. See, for example, the Ethical Globalization Initiative—www.eginitiative.org; the International Council on Human Rights Policy—www.ichrp.org; and the World

Commission on the Social Dimension on Globalization—www.ilo.org/public/english/wcsdg/index.htm.

55. See Fiona Robinson, "Human Rights and the Global Politics of Resistance: Feminist Perspectives," *Review of International Studies* 29, Special Issue (December 2003): 161–80. Also see Brooke A. Ackerly, "Women's Human Rights Activists as Cross-Cultural Theorists," *International Feminist Journal of Politics* 3, no. 3 (Autumn 2001): 311–46.

56. See note 26, above.

Chapter Ten

Care as a Cause: Framing the Twenty-First-Century Mothers' Movement

Judith Stadtman Tucker

The trick is to imagine a social world in which citizens' lives integrate wage-earning, caregiving, community activism, political participation, and involvement in the associational life of civil society—while also leaving some time for fun. This world is not likely to come into being in the immediate future. But it is the only imaginable postindustrial world that promises true gender equality. And unless we are guided by this vision now, we will never get any closer to achieving it.

—Nancy Fraser, 1996

Between the mid-1970s and late 1990s, mothers of young children entered the U.S. labor force in unprecedented numbers.[1] As America settles into the twenty-first century, considerable public attention and scholarship remain focused on the consequences of women's changing roles. In the media, cultural apprehension about mothers' employment is reflected in news reports and commentary highlighting negative fallout from nonparental child care and high-profile coverage of the so-called "mommy wars."[2] In academia, an interdisciplinary field of work-family study has produced a steady stream of authoritative works on the causes and repercussions of women's work-life strain. Backed by the findings of these studies, social analysts are attempting to shift the public discourse on motherhood and work by underscoring the connection between the gendered distribution of caring labor and the social and economic inequality of women.[3]

Today's mothers—whether their attachment to the labor market is motivated by financial need or personal aspiration, or when they forgo paid work to care for their families at home—are caught in an unforgiving double bind. The feminist ideal of equal parenting has proved to be elusive as a sustainable practice—although men's contribution to domestic work has increased over the last twenty-five years, mothers in dual-earner couples typically shoulder two-thirds of all child-rearing and household labor, even when husbands and wives have similar earnings.[4] Employers routinely reserve the best jobs and best pay for workers with the ability to provide unlimited work on demand, making it difficult, if not impossible, for employees with normal caregiving obligations to advance into prime occupations.[5] Mothers and others who try to "balance" paid work and family by working part-time receive less than proportional pay, few or no paid benefits, and limited opportunities for advancement—even when they have the same level of skill and experience as full-time workers in equivalent jobs.[6] Those who leave the paid workforce based on personal preference—or when they are squeezed out of jobs by rigid employment practices—are forced to contend with stereotyping of full-time homemakers as incompetent nobodies, social isolation in communities fractured by the postmodern lifestyle, popular depictions of baby tending as fabulous fun and child rearing as a leisure activity, and financial dependency on a partner's earnings.[7]

These factors—combined with inadequate public policies to support working families in the United States; scarcity of affordable, quality child care; garden-variety gender discrimination in and outside the workplace; the wage gap; tax penalties on secondary earners in married couples; and the failure to recognize or measure caregiving as socially productive and economically necessary work—disadvantage mothers in negotiations for fair sharing in domestic partnerships, limit their employment opportunities, and increase the likelihood they will experience economic hardship over the course of a lifetime.[8]

While married, middle class mothers struggle with professional and economic setbacks, the combination of workplace inflexibility and resistance to enacting family-friendly social policies has a devastating effect on low-income and single mothers.[9] Lone mothers are three times more likely to live in poverty than other nonelderly women in the United States, and are nearly twice as likely to lack health insurance as married mothers.[10] The United States has the highest rate of infant mortality among wealthy nations and has higher rates of maternal mortality than all but five OECD countries; poor mothers and mothers of color are disproportionately affected.[11] In 2002, over half of all children in households headed by single-parent women were living at or below the poverty line, and two out of every three of these children lived in families with incomes under $30,000 a year—less than the baseline living wage for a family of three in many U.S. communities.[12]

Out of a refreshed awareness of motherhood as a liability to women's economic security and quality of life, several organizations dedicated to providing support and education for mothers coping with workforce transitions and parenting issues are now endorsing advocacy and political action on behalf of mothers.[13] The spectrum of proposed reforms falling under the rubric of "mothers' issues" ranges from paid leave policies to revising the tax code, but the signature demand of mothers' advocates is for cultural recognition of the social and economic value of unpaid caregiving work.

This chapter discusses the political and ideological grounding of the emerging "mothers' movement" and examines the potential for predominant influences on the movement's formation—liberal feminism and maternalism—to result in political strategies that will neither eliminate the social and economic marginalization of mothers nor equalize the distribution of caring work within families or society as a whole. I will suggest that a third alternative—an ideological and rhetorical framework grounded in a feminist ethic of care—might be the best approach to satisfying the diverse and sometimes paradoxical demands of the new mothers' movement while advancing the status of women.

EXPERIENCE, IDEOLOGY, AND THE MOTHERHOOD PROBLEM

Numerous feminist critiques have exposed motherhood as an institution of patriarchy and the instrument of women's oppression, but an overwhelming majority of women—including many who identify with feminist ideals—continue to want and have babies.[14] A woman's desire to become a mother, and her expectations about how motherhood will alter her self-concept and life experience, are informed by an explicit cultural model that defines how normal mothers think, feel, and act.[15] According to this normative model—which is an outgrowth of the dominant ideology of motherhood—a specific quality and quantity of maternal devotion are essential for the optimal growth and development of children. External conditions and other relational ties are viewed as largely peripheral to children's welfare, and undesirable outcomes are predicted for those whose mothers fail to live up to prescribed standards of mothering. Finally, the dominant ideology of motherhood dictates that mothers, and only mothers, "know best" what children need to thrive, and that this knowledge is sex-based and instinctual rather than a learned response.

These tenets assure that individuals other than mothers are free from any fundamental accountability for the care and protection of the next generation—which, of course, is a tremendous boon for those who would rather not compromise their power and privilege by attending to dependency.[16] While mainstream feminism retains some ambivalence about what sort of personal and social meaning mothering might acquire for emancipated women, its fatal flaw has been a tendency to underestimate robust cultural resistance to liberating mothers from the constraints of idealized motherhood and the magnitude of social change that will be necessary to do so.

Sharon Hays describes the contemporary model of ideal motherhood as the ideology of intensive mothering. According to Hays, the mandates of intensive mothering tell us that "[child] rearing should be carried out primarily by individual mothers and that it should be centered on children's needs, with methods that are informed by experts, labor intensive and costly. This, we are told, is the best model, largely because it is what children need and deserve."[17] Mothers operate under ideological variations that account for the realities of their particular social and material situations, but all mothers and would-be mothers in United States are subject to the ideology of intensive motherhood.[18]

Even though the influx of highly qualified female workers into male-dominated fields has failed to substantially rehabilitate ingrained cultural attitudes about gender and care, the feminist strategy of promoting women's economic independence by removing barriers to their educational and occupational advancement has been moderately successful in securing a place for women—including women who mother—in the professional and skilled labor force. Since current economic conditions compel most parents to work for pay, Hays notes, contemporary mothers have absorbed ideological elements that conflict with the ideal of intensive mothering in order to self-identify as rational economic actors in the wider world. They have also assimilated egalitarian ideals that situate women as fully entitled individuals with the right to due respect, fair treatment, gainful employment, and self-expression outside the domestic role. As a result, the new generation of mothers is in a better position to view employment outside the home as simply one more aspect of conventional motherhood, but remains insufficiently insulated from the powerful sway of ideology that constitutes motherhood as the best and most important thing a woman can do with her life. No matter how adroitly a mother negotiates the conflicting demands of paid work and family, the cultural contradictions of motherhood ensure that she can never really get mothering "right."[19]

In *The Impossibility of Motherhood*, Patrice DiQuinzio argues that the dominant ideology of motherhood (which valorizes care, attachment, and altruism) dovetails with the ideology of liberal individualism (which prizes individual autonomy, self-determination, and rational choice) to form an integrated ideological system capable of supporting the institutions and distribution of power characteristic of a capitalist economy. Together, these complementary ideologies define the boundaries of public and private life and inform us "what exists, what is good and what is possible" in each domain.[20] Yet the aspects of self-expression segregated by this ideological fusion—care and attachment, self-interest and instrumentality—can be assumed to exemplify the dimensions of any well-actualized life. The contradictory ideologies of maternal altruism and rational individualism bifurcate the whole of human activity so arbitrarily that it's impossible for any one person—male or female—to live fully in both worlds.

Contemporary mothers encounter the dissonance between ideology and experience at every turn: in the home, where they routinely shoulder more of the domestic burden than they consider "fair" in a partnership of equals; in the workplace, where they face criticism from supervisors and coworkers who hold more conservative views about women, work, and family or who expect them to perform as "ideal," unencumbered workers; through exposure to news reports accentuating the dangers of nonparental care or dramatizing the role of maternal behavior in any tragedy involving the death or disappearance of a child; in advertising and media images depicting women (but usually not men) and children together "in the house, the yard, or the car;"[21] and as the chosen audience for a deluge of expert advice reinforcing the intensive mothering model but generally exempting fathers and other caregivers from the high-commitment child-rearing plan. The transitional patchwork of conventional and liberating ideologies gives mothers a foothold in each of the separate spheres but authority in neither, and this is the root of the twenty-first-century motherhood problem.

THE POLITICAL GROUNDING OF THE NEW MOTHERS' MOVEMENT

The new breed of mother advocates are very clear about their objectives: They want mothers to have better lives with less role strain and better options for combining work and family. They want respect and recognition for the social and economic value of mothers' work—both paid employment and the unpaid care work mothers do at home. They want more flexibility in the workplace, and they want equal pay for equal work. They want public policies that respond to the needs of dual-earner couples and single-parent women, they want reasonable protection from economic hardships mothers may incur due to their maternal status, and they want men to take a more active role in child rearing and domestic life in general. They would like these things as soon as possible, and they concur that an organized social movement—a broad-based grassroots uprising—will be crucial to achieving this kind of sweeping change. There is less agreement among advocates about why change is necessary. Is it necessary to improve the lives of women? Or is it necessary to improve the lives of children?

Several strands of political philosophy float through the logic and rhetoric of the emerging mothers' movement. The key variables are whether these different frameworks support or contest the dominant ideology of motherhood and whether they serve as a useful basis for developing advocacy positions that will advance, rather than obstruct, gender equality. Frameworks that challenge the dominant ideology of motherhood are attractive due to a growing awareness in popular culture that the idealization of intensive motherhood detracts from the personal experience of mothering, isolates fathers from the center of family life, and limits mothers' freedom of choice.[22] Frameworks that align with the dominant ideology of motherhood are politically appealing because they support the plea for better treatment of mothers without posing a serious threat to the status quo. Activists and authors currently involved in the articulation of "mothers' issues" tend to sample from both conforming and nonconforming frameworks to legitimize their demands for reform. There are any number of philosophies and political theories that feed into the new thinking on motherhood as a social issue, but the three predominant influences are liberal feminism, maternalism, and feminist care theory.

Liberal feminism is nonconforming to the dominant ideology of motherhood and offers a vocabulary of rights, responsibilities, justice, equity, empowerment, and identity. This framework is essential to the interpretation of mothers as persons with individual and social rights, and is fundamental to the articulation of mothers' entitlement to self-expression within and beyond the bounds of the maternal role—including self-expression through paid employment or civic engagement, but not excluding a high degree of involvement in child rearing.[23] Liberal feminism qualifies mothers as equal citizens in an ideally egalitarian society, and justifies perception of the negative economic and occupational consequences of motherhood as disproportionate and discriminatory. It also provides a context for the strategic separation of the needs and interests of women who mother from those of their children. The mothers' movement has been referred to as the "unfinished business" of feminism.[24]

Maternalism conforms to the dominant ideology of motherhood and emphasizes the importance of maternal well-being to the health and safety of children. Maternalism introduces the language of morality and compassion and provides a framework for championing mothers' care work as a precious resource that must be supported, honored, and accommodated by private entities and the state. It contrasts the humane values of "the mother world" with the impersonal values of "the money world" and idealizes the power of maternal love to transform the future of children and society.[25] Maternalism overlaps with what has been called "difference feminism"—particularly the idea that females are inherently more empathic, less exploitive, and more sensitive to relational ambience than males.[26] Given that maternalist activism has historically concentrated on improving the world for children and concerned itself only incidentally with the status of women, the claim that it should be construed as a true form of feminism remains open to debate. What is undisputed is that between 1890 and 1920, the spirit of maternalism prompted millions of middle class women to organize for progressive social reform. The remarkable historical record of maternalist activism is one of the rationales behind recent campaigns for its revival.

A third—and I will argue, particularly salient—framework for conceptualizing the mothers' movement is feminist care theory. Feminist care theory is nonconforming to the ideology of intensive motherhood, nor does it conform to the ideology of individualism. This framework introduces the language of care as a public good and supports the definition of care as labor—labor that makes an essential and measurable contribution to social and economic growth. Feminist care theory describes caring as a deliberate practice rather than an irresistible impulse, and suggests that the cultural understanding of obligation could be reconfigured so that caring for children is allocated as a social responsibility rather than an exclusively maternal one.[27] The care frame also classifies the need to be "cared for" as a normal, healthy, predictable, and ongoing aspect of every human life, rather than a transitory condition affecting only the unusually vulnerable or unnecessarily dependent, and broadens the definition of care so the activity of caregiving becomes something more than what women do for men, children, and each other out of the spontaneous goodness of their hearts.

The declarations of intent from four groups presently associated with the mothers' movement—the Mothers & More *POWER Plan*; the Mothers Ought To Have Equal Rights (MOTHERS) *Economic Empowerment Agenda*; the Motherhood Project's *A Call to a Motherhood Movement*; and the Family and Home Network's *Principles of Wholehearted Family Policy*—illustrate how these three frameworks blend and mingle in the political construction of mothers' issues. These examples also reveal critical points of divergence in the articulation of the movement's agenda.[28]

The Mothers & More *POWER Plan*

Mothers & More (formerly F.E.M.A.L.E.: Formerly Employed Mothers At the Leading Edge) was founded in 1987 as a national support group for "women taking time out from full time paid employment in order to raise their children at home."[29] Although the organization's mission has always included advocacy for members' choices in combining parenting and other

work, in 2002 leaders of Mothers & More decided to position the organization at the forefront of a social movement to "improve the lives of mothers."
The group's current mission statement clarifies an intention to "address the
needs of mothers as individuals and members of society, and promote the
value of all the work they do."[30] Here, liberal feminism comes into play in
recognizing mothers as "individuals" and "members of society," while a
claim for the value of "all the work" mothers do—implying both paid employment and unpaid caregiving work—relies on the framework of feminist
care theory.

The Mothers & More *POWER Plan* elaborates on how and why mothers'
work should be valued: "Work needs to be redefined so that there is a broad
acceptance that the work of caring for others is valuable and vital work that
is essential to our families, communities, economy and society as a whole"
and "All the work mothers do—whether paid or unpaid—has social and
economic value."[31] Care theory is an obvious influence in the conceptualization of "caring for others" as an expansive public good with "social and
economic value," as opposed to a maternalist model that locates the primary
value of mothers' work in enhancing the lives of children. In other examples from the Mothers & More *POWER Plan*, the language of individual
rights prevails: "Mothers have the *right* to fulfill their caregiving responsibilities without incurring social and economic penalties" and "All women
deserve recognition for their *right* to choose if and how to combine parenting and paid employment" (emphasis added). And the title of the agenda—
POWER Plan—is a direct reflection of the feminist quest for women's empowerment.

Overall, the Mothers & More *POWER Plan* is a moderate, feminist-
informed agenda that supports solutions intended to minimize the economic
risks faced by mothers who reduce their work schedules or leave the workforce entirely. While the *Plan* recommends a full palette of educational and
consciousness-raising activities, it endorses only two action items: "to create
a plan for using and publicizing" data from the American Time Use Survey[32]
and "encouraging policy makers to make effective use" of that data, and "to
support legislation at state and federal levels" to ensure part-time parity. The
concerns of mothers who work full time, including the high proportion of
single-parent women who work full time, are not deliberately excluded from
the Mothers & More *POWER Plan*, but neither are they directly addressed. In
this regard, the plan lies somewhere between the liberal feminist and maternalist ends of the continuum. While the articulation of the *POWER Plan* is
relatively gender-neutral and includes an objective to "reshape our paid workplaces in ways that acknowledge that mothers, fathers and others who need to
care for their families and work for pay hold down two jobs, both equally important to our economy and society," it does not explicitly call for a greater

investment in caregiving by individuals other than mothers or society as a whole.

The MOTHERS *Economic Empowerment Agenda*

MOTHERS (Mothers Ought To Have Equal Rights) was founded in 2002 as an initiative of the National Association of Mothers' Centers, a thirty-year-old organization which facilitates peer-led support groups for new and seasoned mothers. Spearheaded by popular authors Ann Crittenden (*The Price of Motherhood*, 2001) and Naomi Wolf (*Misconceptions: Truth, Lies and the Unexpected on the Journey to Motherhood*, 2001), MOTHERS endorses an assertive agenda for grassroots activism to "correct the economic disadvantages facing caregivers." Of the unaffiliated groups associated with the birth of the mothers' movement, MOTHERS is the most politically proactive. The long list of policy and social reforms recognized by the *Economic Empowerment Agenda* includes paid parental leave, a refundable child tax credit, adding unpaid caregiving labor to the gross domestic product, guaranteed flextime and shorter workweeks for "either or both parents of infants and toddlers," Social Security credits for at-home mothers, part-time parity, elimination of the marriage tax penalty, assured child support for all children of divorce, federal guidelines to ensure equity in divorce, universal preschool, and living wages and professional training for paid caregivers. According to a supplement to the *Economic Empowerment Agenda*, "These initiatives, if enacted, would enable mothers and fathers to spend more time with their infants and children. They would increase family income, particularly the income of the family's primary caregiver. They would reduce the economic insecurity still plaguing women, particularly in old age. And they would acknowledge that ours is a civilized society that values the work of those who care for others, as much as it values other endeavors."[33]

The political framework of the MOTHERS *Economic Empowerment Agenda* leans strongly toward liberal feminism, especially through use of the language of rights and the claim that mothers' well-being hinges on economic empowerment. The organizational structure of MOTHERS—which eschews any form of centralized leadership—also seeks to re-create the style of political activism epitomized by the heady days of the early second wave. Even with this distinctively feminist approach, elements of maternalism surface in the MOTHERS rhetorical strategy. An introduction to the *Economic Empowerment Agenda* reads as follows: "America loves its moms and kids. So why shouldn't American mothers and children have the same economic support that moms and kids do in Britain, Canada, France, Belgium, Holland, Scandinavia? The answer is—THEY SHOULD!" Well yes, they should. But this logic seems to overlook the fact that the moms America "loves"—the ones deemed as worthy of veneration as the emblematic apple pie—are mothers who conform to the ideology of intensive motherhood. While a feminist standpoint is used to rationalize a demand for justice in the *Economic Empowerment Agenda*, the maternalist perspective is used to persuade.

The Motherhood Project's *A Call to A Motherhood Movement*

A Call to A Motherhood Movement—a maternal manifesto issued by the Mothers' Council, an informal collaboration of social activists and scholars associated with the Motherhood Project of the Institute for American Values—invokes all mothers to embrace "a new dedication to advocacy and activism to value motherhood and childhood, and, most especially, children." The *Call*, which was officially released at a "Symposium on Maternal Feminism" at Barnard College in October 2002, is a fervent and meticulous document upholding the values of mothering—"the essential ethics of care and nurturance"—as the moral medicine for a society overrun by rampant individualism and the hard-hearted values of commerce. "We, women who nurture and care for children, we who mother, call all mothers to a renewed sense of purpose, passion and power in the work of mothering," reads the opening statement. "We call for a motherhood movement to ensure the dignity and well-being of children."

While the *Call to A Motherhood Movement* does not entirely discard the pursuit of gender equity—the Mothers' Council takes no position on the best way to combine child rearing and employment and seeks "to build a movement focused on principles of equal dignity, regard and responsibility between men and women"—it situates the "motherhood movement" as parallel to, rather than part of, the ongoing struggle for women's equality. The goal of such a movement would be a "search for innovative political, economic and cultural strategies that honor and support mothers and enable mothers—and fathers—to spend more time on the vital work of nurturing children." The transparency of designating care as labor that results in an extended public good—as seen in the Mothers & More *POWER Plan* and the MOTHERS *Economic Empowerment Agenda*—is replaced in the *Call to A Motherhood Movement* by the fuzzier ideal of maternal "nurturing" and "nurturance" as the essential ingredient for tending and mending our broken world.

The underlying agenda of the "Motherhood Movement" is, in every way, classically maternalist. Rather than acknowledging that the dominant ideology of motherhood is used to justify withholding of public and private resources that would allow mothers—and their children—to lead more stable, dignified lives, the *Call to A Motherhood Movement* aspires to gather collective support for the institution of intensive mothering.

It is noteworthy that the maternalist framework of the *Call* attacks free-market capitalism for sanctioning the devaluation of women's caregiving work. Liberal feminism, which borrows heavily from the ideals of rational individualism, is not as well suited to this task.[34] However, undercurrents of the *Call to A Motherhood Movement* suggest that the war of values assailing American culture can only be won by abandoning, once and for all, the ideal of full social and economic equality for women who mother.

Family and Home Network's *Principles of Wholehearted Family Policy*

The Family and Home Network (FAHN), founded in 1984 to support and advocate for parents who "forgo or cut back on paid employment to nurture their children," stands out as a staunch defender of the ideal of intensive motherhood. Formerly the publishers of *Welcome Home*, a periodical "for the mother and father who have actively chosen to devote their time and talents to nurturing their family," FAHN remains an influential voice in the national debate surrounding maternal employment. Like other organizations discussed in this section, the Family and Home Network (formerly "Mothers At Home") reworked its image shortly after the turn of the century to incorporate a new focus on political advocacy. In a nod to the reality that both parents in most couples with children must work for pay, the organization expanded its self-definition and language to include fathers as primary caregivers.

FAHN positions itself in active opposition to the "child-care movement"—that is, efforts to legislate state-funded child care—and bolsters its arguments against nonparental care by citing studies and experts that find day care hazardous to children's health and development. FAHN's *Principles of Wholehearted Family Policy* demands equal time—and equal public resources—for parents who use their "initiative and ingenuity" to balance work and family without outsourcing child care. The *Principles* call on policy makers to acknowledge that "meeting children's needs for consistent nurturing care must be the basis of all family support policies," and insists that "tax policies should not favor paid child care over parental care of children." The FAHN advocacy agenda charges government agencies to rethink their priorities based on the "fact" that "parents are best suited to meet their children's needs," demands that income and assets be divided equitably when couples divorce, and warns that U.S. Department of Labor statistics on maternal employment do not "accurately reflect how parents care for their children and should not be used in policy debates, media discussions, or public discussions about the care of children."

Some of the positions spelled out in FAHN's *Principles of Wholehearted Family Policy* are not unreasonable; for example, equitable public policies that recognize caregiving as an extended public good must recognize and support all the ways care is provided—both within and outside of families—and all the people who provide it. Valuing care work equally with income-earning work when couples divorce mirrors policy positions endorsed by liberal feminist advocates. The inclusion of fathers as primary caregivers in the FAHN agenda seems downright progressive. However, the needs and interests of women who mother—beyond the desire to "nurture" their children—are not addressed by the *Principles of Wholehearted Family Policy*, and the pursuit of women's equality is far beyond its scope.

SOLVING FOR MOTHERHOOD AND EQUALITY

As the previous examples demonstrate, the mothers' movement is still in the early stages of formation and, at this time, there is no clear unifying cause. The organizations taking a stand on mothers' issues propose a wide range of solutions they believe will help mothers and their families lead better lives. Some of these approaches are more compatible with the egalitarian ideal than others, but all might reduce the well-being of women who mother by reinforcing conditions that marginalize them.

In a thought-provoking analysis of gender equality and the welfare state, Nancy Fraser develops an experimental matrix for forecasting which ideological framework for the distribution of labor in postindustrial America is most likely to improve women's social and economic standing. She then compares the potential of two idealized models to solve for gender equality.[35] The "universal breadwinner" model—"the vision implicit in the current political practice of most U.S. feminists and liberals"—aims to foster gender equity by promoting women's full employment. The goal of the "caregiver parity" model is to promote gender equity by enabling "women with significant domestic responsibilities to support themselves either through care-work alone or through care-work plus part-time employment." While Fraser's universal breadwinner model looks something like the product of an uncompromising expression of liberal feminism, her caregiver parity model is the near twin of the paradigm resulting from the blending and weaving of liberal feminist ideals of economic empowerment with the gendered morality of maternalism. That is to say, Fraser's caregiver parity model fits the political ambitions outlined by proponents of the nascent mothers' movement very well.

Fraser ranks her universal breadwinner and caregiver parity models against seven criteria: Does the ideal model do a good, fair, or poor job of combating women's poverty? Does it prevent exploitation of women and other vulnerable people? Does it promote equality of income; leisure time; and respect?

Does it prevent the marginalization of women in public life? Does it challenge assumptions that the male life course is the normative model, or is it intended to help women assimilate into social institutions and workplaces fashioned on the male norm?

Fraser concludes that a welfare state favoring women's full employment—which would require public provision of employment-enabling services such as child and elder care and strengthening regulations to assure equal opportunity in the workplace—would do a good job of decreasing women's poverty and preventing exploitation, but only a fair to poor job of solving for equality of income, leisure time, and respect, and only a fair job of preventing women's marginalization. By failing to challenge the legitimacy of workplace practices structured on male norms, the universal breadwinner model also rates poorly for breaking down the androcentrism dominating American culture. Fraser remarks that the universal breadwinner model—if it were fully supported by the political culture and social structure of the United States, which it is not—would do a much better job of improving the status of women than the existing welfare state, even though it would not solve for women's equality.

According to Fraser, the caregiver parity model would be characteristic of a society that elevates the work of "child bearing, child-rearing and informal domestic labor" to a level on par with formal paid labor. This is very much in alignment with the demands of present-day mothers' advocates for the reorganization of work "so that public policy, private practices and cultural attitudes reflect [a] definition of unpaid caregiving work as equal in value to paid work."[36] Public provision of caregiver benefits, such as paid parental leave and/or stipends for stay-at-home parents, and workplace reforms that "facilitate the possibility of combining supported care-work with part-time employment and of making the transition between different life-states," would be necessary to support Fraser's ideal model of caregiver parity. Workplace flexibility would be key. In this regard, Fraser's construction of the caregiver parity model is eerily predictive of the problem-solving model imagined by early proponents of the emerging mothers' movement.

Fraser determines that the caregiver parity model also comes up short in solving for gender equity. While it would potentially decrease women's poverty and protect women from exploitation by providing a regular source of income other than wages or a spouse's wages, caregiver parity does only a fair to poor job of meeting other baseline requirements for equality. By establishing a separate employment track with highly flexible part-time positions for women with caregiving responsibilities, caregiver parity is unlikely to produce income equality. Unless men substantially decrease their workforce participation and take on a much larger domestic role, caregiver parity is likely to institutionalize caregiving and domestic work as the province of women; thus, the parity model would only do a fair job of promoting leisure time equality and equality of respect. If it reinforces the gendered division of labor, caregiver parity is likely to exacerbate the marginalization of women. Fraser does note that the caregiver parity model—if it were fully supported by the political culture and social structure of the United States, which it is not—would do a far better job of improving the status of women than the existing welfare state, even though it doesn't promote equality for women.

Fraser's caregiver parity model of social organization would indeed be better than what we have now. It would "improve the lives of mothers" (Mothers & More) and "correct the economic disadvantages facing caregivers" (MOTHERS); it would "yield ample room for the values of the mother world" (Motherhood Project) and "not favor paid child care over the parental care of children" (Family and Home Network).[37] But the potential for reinforcing the gendered division of caring and paid labor and institutionalizing the marginalization of mothers in public life is high. Furthermore, the caregiver parity model is unlikely to do much damage to the dominant ideology of motherhood and the inequitable distribution of power it protects. Social change to rectify unacceptable conditions under which women mother in the United States is imperative, but organizations and individuals engaged in the new mothers' movement might pause to consider whether or not there is a long-range advantage to seeking relief now and worrying about women's equality later.

Fraser offers a tantalizing possibility for reorganizing society to provide good care and promote gender equity: not by making women "more like men are now," or "leaving men and women pretty much unchanged" and making the difference costless to women, but by inducing "men to become more like most women are now—namely people who do primary care-work." This third model, which Fraser calls the "universal caregiver" model, is completely consistent with the feminist ethic of care. To lay the groundwork for such a radical transformation of the social order, it will be necessary to infuse mainstream culture with the idea that normal women, including women who mother, need and want to do more than mothering, and normal men, including men who are fathers, need and want to do more than work and play. A broad-based grassroots mothers' movement—if envisioned within a framework of care—would be in an excellent position to deliver this message to the masses.

THE CARE FRAME

Joan Tronto writes, "Those who care do understand correctly the value of what they do. That care-givers value care is neither false consciousness nor romantic but a proper reflection of the value of human life."[38] If this is indeed the case, women who mother are uniquely situated to rally behind care as a cause. Even in its most conservative expression, the central issue of the emerging mothers' movement is *care*—not only the way mothers care for and about their children but also the way we care for people as a society. The mothers' movement is about recognizing, respecting, and responding to the needs of people who care for children and other dependents and how the distribution of caring work in our society keeps some people down and sustains the privilege and power of others. It's about the painful disconnect of living in a nation that generates enormous wealth but fails to provide adequate care for all its citizens. If there is a common sentiment among the new mothers' advocates, it's that care matters. The critical points of dissent are why care matters, and what to do about it.

A political framework based on a feminist ethic of care will permit the new mothers' movement to rise beyond the factionalism already developing within it. This is not to suggest that all groups currently involved in mothers' advocacy will be content to relinquish the maternalist point of view for more expansive definitions of care and motherhood. However, a framework of care could resolve some of the underlying conflicts in the movement as it is presently articulated. The care frame favors gender equity by promoting the status of care without valorizing maternal caregiving. It positions the need for care as a normal, healthy, predictable, and ongoing aspect of every human life, and represents women's caregiving experience as broadly normative rather than peripheral to the social order. A framework of care undermines the dominant ideology of motherhood by relocating responsibility for all kinds of care—including attending to the needs of children—to the whole of society and all the people in it, and challenges the myth of individualism and the legitimacy of the "ideal worker" model by questioning whether idealized conditions of autonomy and self-determination are desirable, or even possible, in a habitable society. Care theory ties the devaluation of care to the social and economic marginalization of mothers and other caregivers, but avoids maternalist logic; it provides a new focal point for explaining who wins and who loses in our society, and why. A framework of care holds out the hope of something better than parity for women in the public and private spaces of social life.

The mothers' movement could play an important role in instilling this enlightened vision of care and care work in the public mind. While theorists such as Nel Noddings and Sara Ruddick have used the mother-child dyad to illustrate exemplary forms of care,[39] Tronto's definition is especially adaptable for neutralizing cultural presumptions about the gendered nature of caring work. By defining care as an activity that "includes everything we do to maintain, continue and repair our world so that we can live in it as well as possible," Tronto acknowledges that care work involves not just the intentions and actions of men and women who are moved to care for other humans; it includes caring for the things that surround us.[40] Caring for children and other family members becomes part of a deliberate practice of maintaining and continuing "our world" rather than a contained private act ending with the individual who is cared for. The inclusion of activities such as doing laundry, sweeping the floor, and changing a flat tire in the definition of "care" accentuates just how much caring goes into keeping our world in working order. Most important for proponents of the mothers' movement, Tronto's definition of care counters the predominant ideological construction of caregiving as an intuitive feminine, or maternal, response.

The principal dilemma of adopting a framework of care for the mothers' movement is the danger of alienating mothers who are not yet willing to exchange the ideology of intensive motherhood—or the moral veneration they receive for doing "the most important job in the world"—for a genderless ethic of care that leaves the social and emotional roles of women who mother less distinct. But in order to relocate care as the central concern of human life, it will first be necessary to emancipate caregiving from its secondary status as women's work. To this end, the fundamental project of a mothers' movement based on a framework of care will be the deliberate reinvention of motherhood.

Considering how well fortified the dominant ideology of motherhood is against intrusion from incompatible ideals, this seems like an impossible task. Yet this formidable work is already under way. Mothers are presently laboring under considerable ideological strain, and many ascribe a portion of their distress to the fair share of caregiving work left undone by men. Today, new authors and activists encourage women to recognize and reject idealized representations of mothers and mothering and urge mothers to experience their discontent as the product of systemic, rather than personal, failure.[41]

To reach the tipping point, a mothers' movement will need to initiate an open discourse about the new future of motherhood—what will the lives of men, women, and children look like when tending and mending the world for others is no longer the particular duty of mothers? Central to this consciousness-raising effort will be reaffirming that socializing care is not intended to relegate women and their children to a loveless world where care is managed and delivered exclusively by the state. However, it's quite possible that "mother love" will acquire a different meaning in the lives of women who mother—perhaps a more fluid and authentic meaning—in a society governed by an ethic of care. A mothers' movement guided by a framework of care will invite women to search beyond the dominant ideology of motherhood and imagine what their lives might look and feel like in a more equitable and caring society.

If informed by a framework of care, the twenty-first-century mothers' movement might shift its advocacy focus from economic parity and caregiver entitlements to agitating for a shorter workweek with significant penalties for employers who require overtime hours. Mothers' advocates might expand their policy positions to include public funding of high-quality child care centers so that when loved ones have other responsibilities, children—and their paid caregivers—will be cared for as well as possible. Agitating for paid parental leave, paid sick leave, and flexible work schedules for all employees would remain a priority, along with ensuring these policies and practices are well regulated and protected so that both men and women can and will utilize them equally. Demanding equal pay and equity in divorce would be a given, as would supporting efforts to raise the minimum wage to a living wage. Mothers' advocates might also launch a campaign to detach protective social insurance, such as health care and old age and disability benefits, from employment status and earnings so that all workers have the bargaining power to negotiate adequate time for caring, education, civic engagement, and fun, and parents and other caregivers who take extended time out of the workforce will not lose essential coverage.

If driven by a framework of care, a mothers' movement could be instrumental in a profound cultural transition. Mothers would no longer be considered the ideal caregivers of children, although the unique relational bond a mother shares with her child would be respected and valued as a special and irreplaceable part of human life. The same relational quality would be valued in the father-child bond, and men would expect to play a much different role in domestic life and child rearing than they do now. More of the responsibility for providing care would transfer to the greater society, and the role of the state would be to make sure that all citizens, not just mothers and fathers, have equal opportunities to earn wages and care for the world as well as they possibly can. People unable to either work or care because of age, infirmity, disability, or dire circumstance would be well cared for and live with dignity in the mainstream of society. Wealth and political clout would not be the only hallmarks of personal achievement, or possibly the most important ones. Men and women, mothers and fathers, would be found working and caring in equal numbers in all sectors of society. In short, a mothers' movement could be revolutionary.

As the epigraph to this article suggests, it's unlikely we'll be living in this utopian world anytime soon, or perhaps ever, but it may be the only vision worth fighting for.[42] If we want our children—or our children's children—to live in a caring and just society, the mindful remaking of motherhood as we know it is the immediate task at hand.

NOTES

1. In 1975, 37 percent of married mothers with children under age six worked for pay in the United States; in 2001, 62 percent of these mothers were employed (U.S. Census Bureau, *Statistical Abstract of the United States 2002*, table no. 571). In 2002, 69 percent of American children under age fifteen lived with two parents, and 62 percent of those children lived in households where both parents worked (U.S. Census Bureau, *Current Population Reports, Children's Living Arrangements and Characteristics: March 2002*, issued June 2003, 9–10.)

2. Susan J. Douglas and Meredith W. Michaels, *The Mommy Myth: The Idealization of Motherhood and How It Has Undermined Women* (New York: Free Press, 2004), 85–109; Miriam Peskowitz, *The Truth behind the Mommy Wars: Who Decides What Makes a Good Mother* (Emeryville, Calif: Seal Press, 2005), 20–44.

3. See, for example, Mona Harrington, *Care and Equality: Inventing a New Family Politics* (New York: Routledge, 2000); Jody S. Heymann, *The Widening Gap: Why America's Working Families Are in Jeopardy—And What Can Be Done about It* (New York: Basic Books, 2000); Joan C. Williams, *Unbending Gender: Why Family and Work Conflict and What To Do about It* (New York: Oxford University Press, 2000); Ann Crittenden, *The Price of Motherhood: Why the Most Important Job in the World Is the Least Valued* (New York: Metropolitan Books, 2001); and Nancy Folbre, *The Invisible Heart: Economics and Family Values* (New York: The New Press, 2001).

4. Diane Ehrensaft, "When Men and Women Mother," in *Mothering: Essays in Feminist Theory*, ed. Joyce Treblicot (Totowa, N.J.: Rowman and Allanheld, 1983), 41–61; Scott Coltrane and Jusitn Galt, "The History of Men's Caring: Evaluating Precedents for Fathers' Family Involvement," in *Care Work: Gender, Labor and the Welfare State*, ed. Madonna Herrington Meyer (New York: Routledge, 2000), 15–36; W. Jean Yeung and John F. Sandberg, "Children's Time with Fathers in Intact Families," *Journal of Marriage and Family* 63, no. 1 (February 2001): 136–55; James T. Bond and Cynthia Thompson, *Highlights from the 2002 National Study of the Changing Workforce* (The Families and Work Institute, 2003), 16–20.

5. Williams, *Unbending Gender*, 63–113.

6. Bond and Thompson, *National Study of the Changing Workforce*, 8–13.

7. Susan T. Fiske and Amy J. C. Cuddy, "A Model of (Often Mixed) Stereotype Content," *Journal of Personality and Social Psychology* vol. 82, no. 6 (June 2002): 879–902. Deirdre D. Johnston and Debra H. Swanson, "Invisible Mothers: A Content Analysis of Motherhood Ideologies and Myths in Magazines," *Sex Roles* 49, no. 1–2 (July 2003): 21–33; Douglas and Michaels, *The Mommy Myth*, 110–39.

8. Crittenden, *The Price of Motherhood*, 87–130; Williams, *Unbending Gender*, 13–39; Rhona Mahony, *Kidding Ourselves: Breadwinning, Babies and Bargaining Power* (New York: Basic Books, 1995), 9–36, 37–64.

9. Heymann, *The Widening Gap*, 91–111; 139–59.

10. Karen Christopher and Paula England, "Women's Poverty Relative to Men's in Affluent Nations: Single Motherhood and the State," *Research Summaries* vol. 1, no.1 (Joint Center for Poverty Research, 2000); Women's Health Insurance Coverage, Henry J. Kaiser Family Foundation, July 2001.

11. OECD Health Data, 2004, *Infant Mortality, Deaths per 1000 Live Births*; *Millennium Indicators: Maternal Mortality Ratio per 100,000 Live Births*, World Health Organization, UNICEF, 2003. Of OECD nations only France, Korea, Luxembourg, Mexico, and Turkey had maternal mortality rates as high as or higher than those in the United States.

12. U.S. Census Bureau, *Current Population Reports, Children's Living Arrangements and Characteristics: March 2002*, issued June 2003; Jared Bernstein, Chauna Brocht, and Maggie Spade-Aguilar, *How Much Is Enough? Basic Family Budgets for Working Families* (Washington, D.C.: Economic Policy Institute, 2000), figure 2a.

13. Sarah Glazer, "The Mothers' Movement: Should Moms Be Reimbursed for Staying at Home?" *Congressional Quarterly Researcher* (April 2003) 13–13.

14. In 2002, 82 percent of U.S. women between the ages of 15 and 44 had given birth at least once (U.S. Census Bureau, *Current Population Reports, The Fertility of American Women*: June 2002, October 2003).

15. Angela Hattery, *Women, Work and Family: Balancing and Weaving* (Thousand Oaks, Calif.: Sage Publications, 2001), 18–40.

16. Eva Feder Kittay, *Love's Labor: Essays on Women, Equality and Dependency* (New York: Routledge, 1999), 23–48. Kittay defines caregiving as "dependency work" and argues that in a society where autonomy is highly rewarded, dependency and dependency workers are consistently devalued and marginalized.

17. Sharon Hays, *The Cultural Contradictions of Motherhood* (New Haven, Conn.: Yale University Press, 1996), 21.

18. Evelyn Nakano Glenn, "Social Constructions of Mothering: A Thematic Overview," *Mothering: Ideology, Experience and Agency*, ed. Evelyn Nakano Glenn and Grace Chang (New York: Routledge, 1994), 1–26; Sharon Hays, *Flat Broke with Children: Women in the Age of Welfare Reform* (New York: Oxford University Press, 2003), 1–31; Patrice DiQuinzio, *The Impossibility of Motherhood, Feminism, Individualism and the Problem of Mothering* (New York: Routledge, 1999), 1–29; Hattery, *Women, Work and Family*, 39–40.

19. Hays, *The Cultural Contradictions of Motherhood*, 131–51.

20. DiQuinzio, *The Impossibility of Motherhood*, 1–29; Hattery, *Women, Work and Family*, 20, 165–87.

21. Judith Stadtman Tucker, "The Mother and the Magazine: Sociologists Deirdre Johnston and Debra Swanson Discuss Their Recent Research on the Representation of Mothers in Popular Magazines," *The Mothers Movement Online*, August 2003, www.mothersmovement.org/features/mother_magazine.htm (27 May 2005).

22. See, for example, Andrea Buchanan, *Mother Shock: Loving Every (Other) Minute of It* (Emeryville, Calif.: Seal Press, 2003); Faulkner Fox, *Dispatches from a Not-So-Perfect Life, or How I Learned to Love the House, the Man, the Child* (New York: Harmony Books, 2003); Susan Maushart, *The Mask of Motherhood: How Becoming a Mother Changes Our Lives and Why We Never Talk about It* (New York: Penguin Books, 1999); and Douglas and Michaels, *The Mommy Myth*, 2004.

23. Sonya Michel, "Claiming the Right to Care," in *Care Work: Gender, Labor and the Welfare State*, ed. Madonna Herrington Meyer (New York: Routledge, 2000), 37–44.

24. "Some see this movement as the unfinished business of feminism, which in their eyes focused on getting women into the workplace but ignored the needs of moms." Vanessa E. Jones, "Parental Guidance," *Boston Globe*, 8 July 2004, www .boston.com/news/globe/living/articles/2004/07/08/parental_guidance/ (7 September 2005).

.   25. The Mothers' Council of the Motherhood Project (Institute for American Values), *A Call To A Motherhood Movement*, 29 October 2002, www.watchoutforchildren.org/html/call_to_a_motherhood_movement.html (25 May 2005); Jacqueline Honor Plumez, *Mother Power: Discover the Difference That Women Have Made All Over the World* (Naperville, Ill.: Sourcebooks, 2002), 1–21.

26. Carol Tavris, *The Mismeasure of Woman: Why Women Are Not the Better Sex, the Inferior Sex or the Opposite Sex* (New York: Touchstone Books, 1992), 57–92.

27. Joan C. Tronto, *Moral Boundaries: A Political Argument for an Ethic of Care* (New York: Routledge, 1994), 101–24; Nel Noddings, *Starting at Home: Caring and Social Policy* (Berkeley, Calif.: University of California Press, 2002), 230–47; Folbre, *The Invisible Heart*, 22–52.

28. Consult the following: Mothers & More, *The Mothers & More POWER Plan*, 2003, www.mothersandmore.org/downloads/POWERPlan2003.pdf (25 May 2005); MOTHERS (Mothers Ought To Have Equal Rights), *Economic Empowerment Agenda*, 2002, www.mothersoughttohaveequalrights.org/cando/meea.html (25 May 2005); Family and Home Network, *Principles of Wholehearted Family Policy*, October 2003, www.familyandhome.org/media/pr_nov2003.htm (25 May 2005); Mothers' Council, the Motherhood Project, *A Call To A Motherhood Movement*, October 29, 2002, www.watchoutforchildren.org/html/call_to_a_motherhood_movement.html (25 May 2005).

29. Mission statement as it appeared in the F.E.M.A.L.E. Forum, May 1998.

30. Mothers & More, July 2002. The full statement reads: "Mothers & More is a non-profit organization dedicated to improving the lives of mothers through support, education and advocacy. We address mothers' needs as individuals and members of society, and promote the value of all the work mothers do."

31. In the interest of full disclosure, the author of this chapter drafted an earlier declaration of intention for the Mothers & More Advocacy Department, and sections of the *POWER Plan*—including phrases that appear in several of the passages quoted in this discussion—were taken verbatim from that earlier document.

32. U.S. Department of Labor, Bureau of Labor Statistics, *The American Time Use Survey: Summary*, 14 September 2004, www.bls.gov/news.release/atus.nr0.htm (28 May 2005). The ATUS was the first large scale study of Americans' use of work and nonwork time.

33. "Mothers Ought To Have Equal Rights," www.mothersoughttohaveequalrights .org/about/ (25 May 2005).

34. DiQuinzio, *The Impossibility of Motherhood*, 30–60.

35. Nancy Fraser, "Gender Equity and the Welfare State: A Postindustrial Thought Experiment," in *Democracy and Difference: Contesting the Boundaries of the Political*, ed. Seyla Benhabib (Princeton, N.J.: Princeton University Press, 1996), 218–36.

36. Mothers & More, *POWER Plan*, 2003.

37. Mothers & More, *POWER Plan*; MOTHERS, *Economic Empowerment Agenda*; The Mothers Council, *A Call to a Motherhood Movement*; Family and Home Network, *Principles of Wholehearted Family Policy*.

38. Tronto, *Moral Boundaries*, 117.

39. Sara Ruddick, "Maternal Thinking," in *Mothering: Essays in Feminist Theory*, ed. Joyce Treblicot (Totowa, N.J.: Rowman and Allanheld, 1983), 212–30; Nel Noddings, "Caring" (1984), in *Justice and Care: Essential Readings in Feminist Ethics*, ed. Virginia Held (Boulder, Colo.: Westview Press, 1995), 7–29.

40. Tronto, *Moral Boundaries*, 103.

41. See, for example, Peskowitz, *The Truth Behind the Mommy Wars*; Douglas and Michaels, *The Mommy Myth*; Fox, *Dispatches from a Not So Perfect Life*; Buchanan, *Mother Shock*.

42. Fraser, "Gender Equity and the Welfare State," 235–36.

Chapter Eleven

A Public Ethic of Care: Implications for Long-Term Care

Cheryl Brandsen

The protections afforded the elderly in the United States through Social Security and Medicare are compromised when older adults become disabled
and need long-term care. Instead of receiving care through a coherent system, our frail elders must negotiate multiple and fragmented programs, each
with their own funding streams and eligibility requirements. Despite public
resources for long-term care, many frail elders cannot pay for services, go
without needed services, or receive services they neither need nor want as
a result of their attempts to patch together a plan of care. When the elderly
do receive care services, they are often of poor quality. Caregivers, both
paid and unpaid, bear heavy emotional and financial burdens that threaten
to overwhelm them as they carry out their commitments to loved ones.
These problems with long-term care are complex and deeply rooted in cultural norms that reduce the need for care to a commodity or a private trouble, construct old age as a medical problem, hold out self-determining independence as the norm for adults, and perceive women as natural
caregivers.

This chapter argues that a public ethic of care is a potential antidote to the
complex problems inherent in long-term care policy for frail elders. The argument is developed by considering the following large questions: 1) What
are the constitutive elements of a public ethic of care? 2) How does current
long-term care policy fare when evaluated through the lens of a public ethic
of care? 3) What would long-term care policy look like if care were a central
moral focus in our reasoning and judgments?

CONSTITUTIVE ELEMENTS OF A PUBLIC ETHIC OF CARE

Defining Care

Contrary to common understandings of care, "care is not just about changing nappies, cleaning the house and looking after the elderly; it is an activity in which the understanding of needs is central."[1] Fisher and Tronto define care as follows:

> On the most general level, we suggest that caring be viewed as a species activity that includes everything that we do to maintain, continue, and repair "our world" so that we can live in it as well as possible. That world includes our bodies, our selves, and our environment, all of which we seek to interweave in a complex, life-sustaining web.[2]

For the purposes of this paper, it is particularly important to note that how humans care for each other is not restricted to dyadic and intimate relationships of the family but permeates a variety of social, economic, and political institutions. It takes as its starting point the needs of others.

Fisher and Tronto further develop their definition of care by exploring four analytically separate but interconnected phases of caring, each with attending moral elements. The first phase, "caring about," recognizes that a need for caring exists and that caring is necessary. This phase recognizes that needs and responses to needs are culturally and individually shaped, and thus an accurate assessment of perceived needs must occur. While caring often assumes highly individualized care, it is also possible, says Tronto, to "describe caring about on a social and political level," and consider society's approach to health care, for example, in caring terms.[3] The ethical aspect that attaches to the phase of "caring about" is attentiveness. Attentiveness is required to recognize that there is a need about which to be concerned.

In the second phase of caring, "taking care of," someone or some group assumes some responsibility for the need that has been identified and determines how best to respond to it. This phase involves notions of agency and responsibility in the caring process; that is, if one believes that a problem exists about which something can be done, then one begins to think about and respond to needs. Resources of time, money, and skill are needed in "taking care of." This phase makes responsibility into a central moral category. Tronto understands responsibility as embedded in cultural practices rather than in formal rules or contractual promises.

The third phase of caring, "caregiving," is the concrete meeting of needs by individuals and organizations. Typically this is the physical, "hands-on" work of care, and usually involves direct contact with care receivers. The "caregiving" dimension gives rise to the importance of competence as a moral action. To demonstrate that one cares, caring work needs to be performed competently.

The fourth phase, "care receiving," involves the response of the individual, group, or thing that has received care. The responses of care receivers provide a means whereby caregivers can assess whether needs have been accurately identified and met in a way acceptable to both caregivers and care receivers. The moral aspect of caring that attaches to the phase of "care receiving" is responsiveness. Because care is concerned with experiences of vulnerability and inequality, responsiveness "requires that caregivers remain alert to the possibilities for abuse that arise with vulnerability."[4]

The first two phases of Tronto's framework are the explicit focus of this chapter. These phases focus on larger-scale social and political processes, processes where it is not always clear how an ethic of care can shape and inform what happens. The last two phases of Tronto's model are more concrete, addressing actual interactions and practices of care. Public and organizational policy certainly shape what occurs at this more micro level, and this is an important theme to develop; however, this task is beyond the intent of this chapter.

Defining a Public Ethic of Care

Tronto argues it is both morally important and theoretically possible to transform a private ethic of care into a public, political ethic of care. Exactly what a public ethic of care is, however, needs more careful attention. In some respects it is easier to identify what a public ethic of care is not rather than what it is. As used here, a public ethic of care is not intended to stir up a recovery of traditional family values with its attachments to the naturalness of heterosexual two-parent family structures and a willingness on the part of women to sacrifice for their families.[5] Conservative "family values" ideology is, in fact, antithetical to a public ethic of care. Within such an ideology, families are expected to take care of their own and avoid being a burden to others. At the policy level, public policies that flow from this ideology focus on the individual or the family as the problem, and individualistic strategies are identified to intervene. The burden of care continues to be invisible.

Nor is a public ethic of care simply a large aggregate of caring individuals or volunteers who work tirelessly on valued community projects. Such an understanding of a public ethic of care is, in fact, dangerous, as it romanticizes the potential of volunteers to address large-scale social problems and "legitimates minimal public activity in the private sphere of the family."[6] Rhetoric that encourages communities to take care of their own, while appealing in terms of the potential for delivering responsive care to particular individuals at the local level, is particularly dangerous to poor communities. Because 85 to 90 percent of charitable donations are raised and spent locally, communities most in need often are not able to generate the needed funds.[7] The result is a myopic sort of community caring, where those communities already advantaged by resources of time and finances are able to care for their own but unable or unwilling to extend their resources to those distant from themselves.

The notion of a public ethic of care, then, is not captured by equating caring sectors of community life or traditional thinking of family values with a public ethic of care. How then to understand a public ethic of care? As a moral value, a public ethic of care seeks to assure good care to all members of society. Such an ethic requires us "to recognize care as a national social value rightfully calling on Americans for meaningful support as a matter of high priority . . . as a primary principle of our common life, along with the assurance of liberty, equality, and justice."[8] As such, "it is not a parochial concern of women, a type of secondary moral question, or the work of the least well off in society . . . but a central concern of human life."[9] As a moral value, Sevenhuijsen reminds that a public ethic of care suggests that our political judgments are tempered by attentiveness, compassion, and empathy just as they are already tempered by the language of rights, duties, and decisions about obligations made impartially.

While the moral value of a public ethic of care constitutes an important starting point, this alone is not sufficient to support a public ethic of care. Tronto argues that a political context is needed to support an ethic of care; otherwise care remains gendered and private. In fact, it is only by understanding an ethic of care as a political idea that care can take on the transformative power that Tronto attaches to it. Recalling the four ethical aspects of the phases of care, attentiveness, for instance, recognizes that some groups are marginalized because of lack of access to needed resources. Discussions of responsibility for groups distant from the majority (in terms of either physical distance or privilege) can be brought to the foreground. Public or organizational policies that result in incompetent care practices can be challenged. The responses of those at the receiving end of care become essential for developing and evaluating policies that affect them.

Benchmarks of a Public Ethic of Care

A public ethic of care affirms care as a central moral value in the public square alongside equality and liberty and grounds care in a political context. As such, it suggests a number of benchmarks for public and organizational policy. These evaluative criteria recognize that care, or lack of it, is expressed in social and institutional contexts, and that if we wish to reflect the value that care is a central concern of human life, then we must change the structures and institutions through which care is reflected. These benchmarks, mentioned next, are developed later using long-term care as an exemplar.

The policies that flow from a public ethic of care will begin with a public discussion of needs, grounded in the experiences and perceptions of those giving and receiving care. With respect to the first two phases of Tronto's framework, it is important to consider the process for determining what counts as a need. We should be wary of decisions made by those some distance from concrete caregiving situations, usually elites, who, no matter how well-intentioned, cannot represent the life experiences of persons with little money or little power. Policy development must include the people whose lives are affected by the outcomes, and the inclusion of the ideas of these participants must be the raw material for whatever emerges formally.

The policies that flow from a public ethic of care will also allow for a contextual approach to caregiving and care receiving. Those closest to the practice of care—caregivers and care receivers—must be able to work together in such a way that responsive and competent care is realized. Implicit in this is the idea that caregivers and care receivers must be able to define what kinds of care they most value. Organizations must have institutionalized practices that foster effective care. They must have mechanisms through which caregivers' and care receivers' expertise can be heard, and procedures in which adaptations for care practice based on these expert recommendations can be made quickly. At the level of public policy, sufficient latitude must be offered to organizations to deliver care in ways that best reflect the needs of all citizens. Funding cycles should follow stringent outcome evaluations of care based upon caregiver and care receiver assessment, in the context of a democratic discussion of needs. In short, flexible policies and programs will be created so that different notions of what constitutes good care can flourish.

Third, the policies that flow from a public ethic of care will affirm a social conception of the self. As Tronto argues: "A society that took caring seriously would engage in a discussion of the issues of public life from a vision not of autonomous, equal, rational actors each pursing separate ends, but from a vision of interdependent actors, each of whom needs and provides care in a variety of ways and each of whom has other interests and pursuits that exist outside the realm of care."[10] If we focus on relationships between individuals, we must think carefully about how policies shape and define relationships. We might ask, for instance, whether a particular policy promotes care for citizens as citizens, or whether it stigmatizes and further divides people by their neediness. Relatedly, policies that affirm a social conception of the self would consider carefully how public and organizational policies shape and define the problem of care. Is the provision of good care considered an individual or family problem, and policies are designed to intervene at this individual level within the private life of the family, or is the provision of good care understood as a societal responsibility? A public ethic of care requires collective responsibility for protecting the welfare of vulnerable groups, including those who do the work of care. This collective responsibility should be apparent in how we intervene with caregivers and care receivers. A public ethic of care requires structural change such that a stronger public or governmental presence ensures a comprehensive range of social, economic, work-related, and medical services to support, rather than exploit, care work.

Finally, following Tronto, policies regarding care that flow from a public ethic of care must be firmly grounded in a liberal, democratic, pluralistic society and be connected to a theory of justice. The recognition that all of us need care at various points in our lives can move the discussion out of the marketplace, where such needs become commodities that only a few can afford to meet, and out of means-tested welfare programs, where those with care needs are stigmatized, into the public square. Here open negotiations can occur about precisely what care needs exist over the course of lifetimes and how best to allocate resources. Because care work is often cashed out along the lines of gender, ethnicity, and class, just care must also consider whether and how caregiving might be more equitably distributed and reimbursed.

EVALUATING LONG-TERM CARE BY
A PUBLIC ETHIC OF CARE

A public ethic of care, then, will be evident in public and organizational policy to the extent that such policies are grounded in a public discussion of needs in which the experiences and perceptions of those giving and receiving care are taken seriously, to the extent that they allow for a contextual approach to caregiving and care receiving, to the extent that they affirm a social conception of the self, and to the extent that care needs are connected to a theory of justice and are democratic in nature.

Long-term care for frail elders is used here as an exemplar through which to consider a public ethic of care. Continuing to use the first two phases of Tronto's framework, concerns about long-term care through the analytic lens of a public ethic is briefly addressed, followed by a consideration of how a commitment to a public ethic of care might shape public long-term care policy and the programs and services that develop from these.

Caring About: Evaluating Long-Term Care from an Ethic of Care

"Caring about" requires becoming aware of and paying attention to the need for caring. When we look attentively at the needs of frail elders, what becomes clear is that no coherent system of long-term care exists in the United States, nor are there any settled notions about how such a system should look. A brief look at the historical development of key long-term care policies in the United States clarifies this.[11]

Both home care and nursing home care evolved as responses to other issues, some legitimate of course, but nevertheless, not grounded in an intentional desire to meet the needs of frail elders. Holstein and Cole argue that long-term care developed "haphazardly," without benefit of sustained discussions among key stakeholders, particularly those in need of such care.[12] Instead, long-term care policies emerged to address other concerns: public perceptions of hospitals as places where people go to die, overcrowding and high costs of acute care hospitals, poverty, and so forth. The policies, most pointedly Medicare and Medicaid, that emerged were "an afterthought, a side effect of decisions directed at other problems."[13] These were developed in piecemeal fashion with little coordination or attention to consequences, and not guided by an overall vision of what needed to happen to meet frail elders' needs. Medicare, both in 1965 and now, responds to health care problems faced by elderly persons who worked during their adult lives (the "worthy" elderly); Medicaid is a means-tested health care insurance program for the poor, regardless of age. The language of cost savings in the context of medical care is the predominant discourse; left out of this picture are chronically ill frail elders whose needs for care cannot be easily categorized into acute versus custodial care.

Similarly, post-1965 policy initiatives, particularly the Prospective Payment System (PPS) and Diagnostic Related Groups (DRGs) of the 1980s, and the 1997 Balanced Budget Act (BBA), continue to shape the provision of long-term care, although explicit attention to the needs of frail elders is lost in the concerns of rising health care costs and containment strategies. Following the implementation of the PPS and DRGs, radical organizational restructuring of nursing home facilities occurred, care became increasingly medicalized, and the burdens of providing care shifted from formal to informal (i.e., family or friends) providers. Paid workers, such as nursing home staff, experienced intensified work loads to increase productivity.[14] With the BBA of 1997, similar cost-cutting and cost-containment strategies occurred in home care.

The PPS and the BBA of 1997 are credited with being among the most significant pieces of health care legislation since the enactment of Medicare and Medicaid in 1995.[15] Certainly the needs of a frail elderly population are met at some level; heath care is, after all, a valued social good, and beyond health care, many states did develop and fund non-medically oriented programs for frail elders. At the level of federal policy, however, long-term care is constructed to be medically oriented, preempting other legitimate social and personal needs, driven by and responsive to vendor systems between providers and the state, and cost conscious. While the economics of long-term care is not irrelevant, it is not the starting point for long-term care from a public ethic of care.[16] The starting point for caring about a frail elderly population is grounded in attentive discernment of their needs as they articulate them.

Taking Care Of: Evaluation of Long-Term Care from an Ethic of Care

The "taking care of" phase with its attendant moral emphasis on responsibility requires that someone or some group assume responsibility for the need that has been identified. Tronto understands responsibility not as formal obligations to which autonomous people freely commit within a larger context of distributive models of justice; rather she works with responsibility as embedded in cultural practices and political processes, and addresses questions about the responsibilities we owe each other and society.

Here it is useful to briefly consider what it is about responsibility as formal obligations in distributive models of justice that fall short in considering a public ethic of care. In distributive models of justice, the idea of responsibility as formal obligations sets forth two depictions, one of persons, and one of the goods to be distributed.[17] Persons here are viewed as unconstrained, self-assertive, and self-directive autonomous beings who make rational choices based on assessments of what is best for them and who are free to construct career selves for themselves.[18] The goods to be distributed are primarily commodities that can be parceled out fairly and equitably according to some set of principles.

With respect to long-term care, such a model falls short.[19] Frail elders in need of long-term care do not fit the picture of autonomous people who freely commit to obligations based on rational choice. The notion of a career self as a self who is socially and economically productive, if it fits for anyone, certainly is not an apt metaphor for someone nearing the end of life and dependent on others in very concrete ways for survival. Neither is the notion of a career self necessarily fitting for those who do the work of care. Oftentimes, decisions to care are not grounded in social and economic interests but emerge out of complex and often conflicting motives. And in terms of the goods to be distributed, some long-term commodities, such as nursing home beds and services and therapies delivered by home health care workers, are clearly issues of distributive justice. They are, however, mediated by social structures and embedded in a web of family, social, and institutional practices, practices that are invisible in justice-based conceptions of long-term care but nevertheless shape distributive patterns.[20] A few examples highlight the inadequacy of such a model when viewed through the lens of a public ethic of care.

First, under Social Security, citizens are constructed as wage-earners, and benefits are tied to employment. The self-made, socially and economically productive career self thoughtfully plans for retirement, and in return, the state's obligation to citizens is understood as some sort of economic security as such workers move into later life. Missing from this legislation are benefits to those unable to participate in the formal labor market. In other words, public policy here renders largely invisible those who spend their lives caring for wage earners (so that wage earners can be productive), and those who spend their lives informally caring for those with temporary or permanent dependency needs. Benefits are provided to career selves as they bring to a close their economic and socially productive lives. Persons unable to participate in the formal labor market do not fit easily into traditional models of distributive justice.

Second, with respect to the goods of long-term care, the level of responsibility for the health care of older adults assumed by the federal government (and to a lesser extent, state governments) increased with the passing of Medicare and Medicaid in 1965. As discussed earlier, however, neither enactment was intentional in its commitment to care about or for frail elders in need of long-term care; in fact, discussions surrounding the inclusion of home care benefits into Medicare and Medicaid were intentional in locking out benefits for persons with long-term care needs.[21] While acute health care was recognized as a valued social good, provision for this and lack of provision for long-term care sends a peculiar message: If there is hope of returning one to the status of a productive and self-determining person, federal and state assistance is available; if continued functional decline is expected, one is on one's own to secure assistance, or, if destitute, depend on stigmatized welfare programs. Persons unable to pull their own weight do not fit easily into traditional models of distributive justice.

Third, the market became a more intentional player in caring for frail elders in the 1950s and continues today.[22] The 1997 Balanced Budget Act opened the door for further Medicare collaboration with private health maintenance and managed care organizations. Enthoven's claim in 1980 that managed competition is "the only practical solution" to health care costs in the United States is re-echoed by Scully's claim in 1995 that "only by eventually moving all seniors to privately managed systems operating under a defined federal contribution can the federal government truly restrain growth and drive efficiency into the system."[23] Collaborations between the state and the market in the form of tax incentives and tax deductions for long-term care present intriguing yet morally problematic mergers. Although these proposals target different dimensions of long-term care, both use the tax code to address financing problems in long-term care and in doing so, reinforce individualistic strategies for long-term care planning.[24] Persons unable to participate in these market initiatives do not fit easily into traditional models of distributive justice.

CURRENT PRACTICES AND A PUBLIC ETHIC OF CARE

In short, no sustained and public discussion about what long-term care should be, who should care, and how best to understand responsibilities has occurred in the United States. The state continues to abdicate increasing responsibility for long-term care to the market. Families become the invisible default mechanism through which long-term care is delivered, serving as increasingly bigger and thinner safety nets.

This invisible way of assuming responsibility for frail elders is problematic from the perspective of an ethic of care for several reasons. First, this way of assuming responsibility keeps care out of sight as a central category of analysis. Caring for frail elders is largely assigned to the family, historically the private sphere and the domain of women's work, and thus it is both devalued and contained by "self-made figures" who "find it difficult to admit the degree to which care has made their lives possible" and for whom such an admission "would undermine the legitimacy of the inequitable distribution of power, resources, and privilege of which they are the beneficiaries."[25] Confinement of care to the private sphere also takes an enormous psychological and physical toll on those who provide care, yet by confining the provision of care to the private sphere, caregivers who buckle under their burdens are seen as being individually deficient, and their troubles are understood as private troubles. Because of the devaluation of care work, caregivers, care receivers, and the private sphere, it is difficult to catapult these troubles out of the private realm into the public realm for critical scrutiny. When care needs cannot be managed by the family, families turn to the market if they have resources, and they turn to the state. Even while providing nearly universal health care coverage for acute care needs through Medicare and in spite of Medicaid's uneven distribution of resources to the elderly, the state does not recognize the interdependent need for holistic care that most will need as they age; rather the state focuses primarily on the narrow dimension of acute care provision.

The distance of the state from the work of care is also problematic for a public ethic of care. Logically, in order to accept responsibility for a problem, there must first be recognition of the problem. As noted earlier, discussions regarding long-term care have focused primarily on economic issues and not on how frail elders and their families define long-term care needs. Consequently, while huge public expenditures are made on behalf of the elderly, these are not always accurately targeted toward attentive meeting of needs. Thus we have those who give and receive care who find that basic needs cannot be attended to in this expensive system, and we have policy makers and budget managers who disparage the disproportionate amount of resources already directed to the elderly. Furthermore, those who make state and federal policy about caring for frail elders are generally people of privilege in terms of economic and educational status who perceive that they have effectively met their responsibilities by allocating resources. They are not, generally, the ones who do the actual work of care, nor are they generally receivers of care as disabled persons, and in fact they might not even be aware of their need for care given their relative ease in purchasing care services. This, in tandem with the absence of a public discussion about attentively caring for frail elders responsibly, suggests that those who take care of frail elders may well be ignorant of precisely what is needed.[26] The distance of the market from the work of care is similarly problematic for a public ethic of care. Increasingly, federal and state governments hand over their responsibilities to the market. Besdine points out that "the operation of the free market has, in many instances, resulted in substantial distance between the recipients of the capitation dollars and the providers of care."[27]

REVISIONING LONG-TERM CARE INFORMED BY A PUBLIC ETHIC OF CARE

Our current system of long-term care falls short in terms of conceptualizing and delivering long-term care congruent with a public ethic of care. How might an intentional commitment to a public ethic of care shape long-term care policy and the programs and services which develop from these? First, long-term care would be grounded in meeting the needs of frail elders; the system would not be designed primarily around the economics of providing long-term care. Second, intentional lines of responsibility that are congruent with the assumptions undergirding a public ethic of care in caring for frail elders would be addressed; these practices will be the result of understanding responsibilities to care as embedded in cultural and democratic participatory processes.[28]

Meeting the Needs of Frail Elders

To say that a system of long-term care should be designed to meet the needs of frail elders requires that we consider what counts as a legitimate need. This is a very difficult task for several reasons. First, it presumes we have a shared view of what old age ought to be about, and more concretely, presumes we share a common understanding of the goals of health and social care for frail elders.

For neither frail elders nor their families are these presumptions accurate. We know, for instance, in terms of health care, that while some frail elders advocate improving the quality of life over the extension of days in old age, not all agree.[29] Neither is there strong consensus on where frail elders prefer to receive care. In spite of the common perception that frail elders prefer care at home, this preference is mediated by health care status (terminally ill or likely to recover), and anticipated extent of disability and subsequent need for care.[30]

Determining what counts is also difficult because our needs for caring are limitless, infinitely expansive, and constantly shifting. Callahan observes that with the exception of birth control pills, each of the medical technologies developed since 1950 have had the most significant impact on people over the age of 50.[31] New technological advances, while having only a modest effect on expenditures initially, are refined and more heavily utilized over time, particularly among the elderly.[32]

Finally, determining what counts as a legitimate need is difficult because needs are historically and culturally constructed and shaped. Walzer notes, for instance, that in medieval times, health care was not a need because it was mostly ineffectual. What was perceived as needed then was salvation of one's soul. Consequently, churches with regular worship services were in every parish, and communion was compulsory. The "cure of souls was public," and every effort was taken to ensure that each person had an equal chance for salvation and eternal life.[33]

Even if we were to have some consensus about what constitutes a legitimate need, meeting such needs is difficult because not all legitimate needs can be met with public funds. Health and long-term care for the elderly are recognized as the "black hole" of state budgets, and Medicare and Medicaid expenditures continue to rise. Difficult decisions regarding cost containment and allocation must be made, but in the absence of any public discussion of how best to care about and for frail elders, the family by default continues to assume great responsibility, and the market continues to define care as a commodity available for purchase rather than a moral responsibility in which we are called to consider how best to care for each other.

Caring For: Determining and Assuming Responsibility for Meeting Needs

Intentional lines of responsibility congruent with the assumptions undergirding a public ethic of care must also be considered. Margaret Walker's understanding of responsibility can do practical work for a public ethic of care with respect to articulating responsibilities.[34] According to Walker, morality consists of practices that arise and occur between people from which people learn that they are responsible to others and for things. In her account, selves are bearers of particular identities shaped by interactions and understandings that arise between and among people, not preformed identities that stand outside of time and history. Knowledge and practices of care, for instance, rise out of specific contexts in which it is recognized that moral understandings of our responsibilities are constructed by social understandings and social structure that are open to critical analysis and transparent reflection. This stands in sharp contrast to notions of formal obligations to which autonomous people freely commit, and to underlying assumptions of distributive models of justice.

DELIBERATIVE DEMOCRACY: A CONTEXT IN WHICH TO SORT OUT NEEDS AND RESPONSIBILITIES

Given that a public ethic of care requires that long-term care policies must be grounded in the needs of care receivers and caregivers and that these policies must be firmly grounded in a liberal, democratic, pluralistic society where moral responsibilities owed to each other can be determined, the resources of democratic deliberation are essential to a public ethic of care. Young argues that "under ideal conditions of inclusive political equality and public reasonableness, democratic processes serve as the means of discovering and validating the most just policies."[35] Democratic process is also essential to discovering and validating policies that reflect an ethic of care that are integral to expanding care beyond the private sector.

Young's framework of deliberative democracy is particularly helpful for understanding how democratic processes can shape and inform a public ethic of care. Young conceives of deliberative democracy as a form of public reason. As such,

> participants in the democratic process offer proposals for how best to solve problems or meet legitimate needs, and so on, and they present arguments through which they aim to persuade others to accept their proposals. . . . Participants arrive

at a decision not by determining what preferences have greatest numerical support, but by determining which proposals the collective agrees are supported by the best reasons.[36]

Young also holds out hope that the deliberative process is transformational, that is, the preferences and beliefs one hold might be changed after listening carefully to others who are situated differently.

Young's deliberative process is undergirded by several normative principles that shape and direct the relationships between deliberating parties. The principle of inclusion argues that decisions are legitimate "only if all those affected by it are included in the process of discussion and decision-making."[37] The principle of political equality requires that those included in the deliberations be included on equal terms; as nondominated persons they "ought to have an equal right and effective opportunity to express interests and concerns."[38] The principles of reasonableness require that those included in the deliberations have a set of dispositions that incline them to listen to others' ideas and be willing to work toward agreement, have an open mind, and are willing to change one's opinion based on what one hears. Finally, the principle of publicity requires that participants express themselves in ways that are acceptable to those who listen.

It is to the principle of inclusion that Young devotes much attention. Inclusion is concerned with the way in which people "lack effective opportunity to influence the thinking of others even when they have access to and procedures of decision-making."[39] Exclusion occurs when only limited forms of political communication are allowed. Argument, with its emphases upon being articulate, dispassionate, and orderly in public debate, is the primary exclusionary mechanism. To counter this, Young argues that additional accounts of political communication are needed, not only to counter exclusion, but to also produce trust and respect and move across structural and cultural differences.

More complete accounts of political communication include greetings or public acknowledgment, affirmative uses of rhetoric, and narrative and situated knowledge. Greeting or public acknowledgment requires that participants listen respectfully to those in the deliberations. Affirmative uses of rhetoric suggest that deliberators attend to, and not bracket, diverse forms of rhetoric. Deliberation based only on argument "actually carries the rhetorical nuances of particular situated social positions and relations."[40] Attending to rhetoric suggests paying attention to the emotional tone of what is said, the use of figures of speech, the forms of making a point beyond the use of speech (such as placards, demonstrations, or street theater), and paying attention to the particularities of one's audience. The use of narrative and situated knowledge is crucial in situations where shared understandings are lacking.

Such knowledge can help those who speak and those who listen name a group's suffering, for instance, and give an account of why this kind of experience is an injustice. Furthermore, narrative facilitates the kind of local public where people can come together on the basis of some affinity, raise consciousness, and help others understand particular experiences of individuals in particular situations.[41]

DELIBERATIVE DEMOCRACY AND LONG-TERM CARE

With Young's model of deliberative democracy as a framework, we can begin to envision how the deliberative process can be useful to building a system of long-term care grounded in meeting the needs of frail elders and attention to practicing responsibility.[42]

Young's normative principle of inclusion requires that those who will be affected by the outcomes of the decision be included in the process of deliberation and decision making. Most immediately this includes current Medicare and elderly Medicaid beneficiaries and those serving or likely to serve as informal caregivers. It might well include future cohorts of elders who might need long-term care, as well as those who set elder care policy, direct health and social agencies, and a variety of professionals and paraprofessionals who perform various tasks related to long-term care. Young's norm of political equality requires that this large group of deliberators do their work as nondominated persons who have equal opportunities to be heard. Consequently, the same kind of careful attention given to what a state legislator presents must also be given to the cognitively intact, frail, eighty-five-year-old African American woman receiving Medicaid. Young's norm of reasonableness means that deliberators enter the discussion as both givers and hearers of reasons, that they express a willingness to work toward agreement and are willing to be influenced by what they hear. Differences, which are to be expected, are not bracketed but rather used to understand a full range of visions and concerns.

Young's norm of publicity requires that deliberations occur in an assortment of venues, all of which are open and transparent in their dealings. Public hearings, town hall meetings, government legislatures, and courts, for instance, are familiar places for such work to be done. Deliberations should also occur, however, in nursing homes, where the arrangements of physical space and attending sights and smells of medically modeled institutions cannot be ignored, in homes where medical appliances have overwhelmed common living spaces; in senior centers and adult day care centers; with homebound elders receiving "meals-on-wheels"; in caregiver support groups; and in places where hospice care is delivered. Furthermore, publicity requires that "expression aims in its form and content to be understandable and acceptable."[43] This requires hard work on the part of all participants. Expert policy practitioners, accustomed to the crisp and concise language of bureaucratic and technocratic colleagues, may have to put forth enormous energy to engage with the narrative told by an old man, much less accept his insights as legitimate knowledge from which to build public policy. Likewise, the preoccupation that often accompanies the hard work of caregiving and care receiving can cause individuals so situated to lose sight of the larger political process.

CONTENT OF THE DELIBERATIONS

What is it that participants committed to developing a long-term care system congruent with a public ethic of care will deliberate?[44] Initially, vision-type questions. What are goals of health and social care for the frail elder? Perhaps we hope to extend life at all costs; perhaps "quality of life" concerns enter at some point. What makes long-term care important to us, and what is it we want such care to provide for us? Perhaps we hope that such care will restore us to an earlier level of health; perhaps we hope it will slow down the decline brought about by illness and disease or help us adjust to it. Perhaps we hope that such care will promote our safety and allow also independence, facilitate a way for us to sustain relationships with loved ones, and avoid boredom and loneliness. What priority should long-term care hold relative to other health and social goods needed by the elderly? If we design an expensive long-term care system within our allocated budget, we may well leave unfunded other important social goods that elders find give their lives meaning.

With some understanding of how deliberators respond to these large questions, further deliberation can occur regarding what counts as a need in long-term care. If we value extending life at all costs, then budgeting $35 billion dollars a year on left ventricular assist devices may well be defined as a need within long-term care. If we value long-term care for its potential to slow down the process of disease and decline and/or help us adjust to diminished functional abilities, then such services as rehabilitation, routine physical examinations, foot and dental care, and assistive devices for sensory impairments might well be defined as needs. If long-term care is valued for its potential to preserve relationships with family members, then services that support family caregivers and prevent their emotional and physical decline may be constructed as needs. If long-term care is valued for its potential to affirm human dignity even in the midst of great vulnerability, then such persons as nurse aides, nurses, and social workers, evaluated by their ability to attentively respond to individuals and compensated with a living wage, are defined as needs.

With some understanding of how needs for long-term care are defined, more technical discussions can occur. How should our emerging system of long-term care be financed? How should services be made available and delivered? What should be the relationship between acute and long-term care in our systems of care delivery and financing? These are not simply technical questions requiring technical fixes but are grounded in certain moral, social, and political assumptions and have the same kinds of implications. From a public ethic of care, for instance, we need to ask which kinds of funding mechanisms are congruent with the assumptions of an ethic of care. What kinds of public, institutional long-term care policies are likely to affirm an ethic of care? What kinds of social structures affirm or preclude the possibility of a public ethic of care? Although these questions have technical dimensions best worked out by system experts, democratic practices must precede system solutions.

The discussion above regarding what might count as a need and how needs might be prioritized is intentionally general. No specifics are offered. To do so here would be premature, given that it would presuppose a certain outcome from public deliberations. A public ethic of care could, however, offer a point of view about needs and their prioritization, how the meeting of needs should be met, and how best to finance and deliver long-term care informed by an ethic of care. To demonstrate the utility of a public ethic of care in informing policy decisions, I conclude by pointing to a few possibilities.

FINANCING MECHANISMS CONGRUENT WITH A PUBLIC ETHIC OF CARE

Financing long-term care in a manner congruent with a public ethic of care assumes human interdependence as a more accurate description of our common humanity than understanding persons as essentially self-sufficient and independent. Subsequently we must ask whether particular funding mechanisms promote care for citizens as citizens, or whether they stigmatize and further divide people by neediness. Also, because we recognize the provision of care as a foundational social value owed to all citizens as citizens, funding mechanisms that limit care to individuals who can pay for it are not acceptable. Caring practices are essential and valuable to a well-functioning society; subsequently, collective responsibility for such is required.

Funding mechanisms then that depend on the tax code, on the market, or on some marriage between the two are limited when assessed through the lens of a public ethic of care. Not all citizens are workers; consequently, some citizens will be overlooked and/or marginalized as needy and dependent, even though they may have spent large portions of their lives caring for others. As well, care remains invisible as a worthy public value. Care continues to be defined as a commodity which one purchases or to which one is entitled via participation in the labor force.[45]

Consequently, if we wish to bring a public ethic of care to bear on long-term care, we must identify responsibilities for funding such care in a way that understands the provision of care to be a societal responsibility. Typically, for costs that are potentially catastrophic and unpredictable, as is the case with our need for long-term care, we rely on insurance to spread risk.[46] Social, rather than private, long-term care insurance affirms our common need for care and our commitment to it. Wiener and Illston suggest that "coverage of long-term care on a nonmeans-tested basis will go a long way toward treating disability as a normal risk of life rather than the failure of the individual deserving of public charity through welfare."

INTEGRATING ACUTE AND LONG-TERM CARE

Integrating services and funding mechanisms is also a recommendation congruent with a public ethic of care. Leutz defines such integration as "the search to connect the health care system (e.g., acute, primary medical, and skilled) with other human service systems (e.g., long-term care, education, and vocational and housing services) in order to improve outcomes."[47] Expanding Medicare to cover more long-term care, and expanding Medicaid by requiring less stringent means-testing for long-term care services are a beginning, argues Leutz. One can imagine that other sources of revenue might be added to Medicare and Medicaid.

Integration will not solve the problem of what needs will be met within an integrated system of acute and long-term care. For that, a deliberative process is required. But surely a discussion occurring among those who will be affected by the policies can be imagined. What kind of care do we value when we are in need of long-term care? What kinds of benefits and trade-offs would we be willing to make? Might we be willing to trade expensive treatment, such as organ transplants, for more extensive home, rehabilitative, or institutional care currently not covered in any substantive way? What, if anything, might we be willing to trade for social support, mental health services, or spiritual care? This is not to suggest that deliberations will result in a package to which all agree. If deliberation is done correctly, however, the voices of all those who are affected by the outcomes are respected, and the process by which decisions are made, including reasons given, are transparent and understandable to all.[48]

Regardless of how integration occurs, integration maps onto an ethic of care in that selves are defined more broadly than being simply physical beings who can be restored to health and independent functioning. Integration recognizes the frailty and dependence many experience as they age, and while valuing health, social and supportive care is also affirmed as a worthy social good. In fact, the latter may well begin to receive the same sort of systematic and careful attention to elders' needs and preferences that is currently given to medical care decisions. This furthers an ethic of care's commitment to care that is contextual. Carpenter et al. found that while the value of documenting preferences for medical care has received substantial attention, "relatively little theoretical or empirical work has been done regarding the assessment and implementation of preferences in the area of psychosocial care."[49] Knowing such preferences is essential to providing informed, respectful, and individualized care.

CONCLUSION

The challenge of grounding long-term care in meeting the needs of frail elders, the starting point for a public ethic of care, and finding ways to responsibly care for frail elders at the level of public policy, require the resources of deliberative democracy to do its work well. This process, usually connected to various conceptions of justice, is not at odds with what an ethic of care requires; in fact, it provides a framework in which the need for and practice of care can have a more central location in making political judgments. As well, it furthers the possibilities that the policies and judgments that arise in the public sphere are firmly grounded in a liberal, democratic, and pluralist society.

NOTES

1. S. Sevenhuijsen, *Citizenship and the Ethics of Care* (New York: Routledge, 1998), 82.

2. B. Fisher and J. Tronto, "Toward a Feminist Ethic of Care," in *Circles of Care: Work and Identity in Women's Lives*, ed. E. Abel and M. Nelson (Albany, New York: State University of New York Press, 1990).

3. J. Tronto, *Moral Boundaries: A Political Argument for an Ethic of Care* (New York: Routledge, 1994), 106. Note: Subsequent reference to Tronto in this chapter is in regard to *Moral Boundaries*.

4. Tronto, *Moral Boundaries*, 135.

5. Sevenhuijsen, *Citizenship and the Ethics of Care*.

6. N. Hooyman and J. Gonyea, *Feminist Perspectives on Family Care: Policies for Gender Justice* (Thousand Oaks, Calif.: Sage Publications, Inc., 1995), 188.

7. J. Wolpert, "Fragmentation in America's Nonprofit Sector," in *Care, Community, and Modern Society: Passing the Tradition of Service to Future Generations*, ed. P. Schervish, V. A. Hodgkinson, M. A. Gates, and Associates (San Francisco: Jossey-Bass, 1995).

8. C. Harrington, "The Nursing Home Industry: The Failure of Reform Efforts," in *Critical Gerontology: Perspectives from Political and Moral Economy*, ed. M. Minkler and C. L. Estes (Amityville, N.Y.: Baywood Publishing Company, Inc., 1999), 44, 48.

9. Tronto, *Moral Boundaries*, 180.

10. Tronto, *Moral Boundaries*, 168

11. See Benjamin, in particular, for a helpful and thorough discussion of the history of home care: A. E. Benjamin, "An Historical Perspective on Home Care Policy," *The Millbank Quarterly* 71 (1993): 129–66.

12. M. Holstein and T. R. Cole, "The Evolution of Long-Term Care in America," in *The Future of Long-Term Care: Social and Policy Issues*, ed. R. H. Binstock, L. E. Cluff, and O. Von Mering (Baltimore, Md.: John Hopkins University, 1996), 42.

13. B. Vladeck, *Unloving Care: The Nursing Home Tragedy* (New York: Basic Books, 1980), 31.

14. C. L. Estes, J. Swan, and associates, *The Long-Term Care Crisis: Elders Trapped in the No-Care Zone* (Newbury Park, Calif.: Sage Publications, 1993).

15. J. E. Gladieux, "Medicare + Choice Appeal Procedures: Reconciling Due Process Rights and Cost Containment," *American Journal of Law and Medicine* 25 (1999): 61–116.

16. W. Trattner argues that those who benefited most from Medicaid and Medicare were doctors, pharmacists, nursing home operators, and other health professionals: *From Poor Law to Welfare State, 6th ed.* (New York: The Free Press, 1999).

17. H. L. Nelson, "Pictures of Persons and the Good of Hospice Care," *The Hastings Center Report* 32, no. 2 supp (2003).

18. M. U. Walker, *Moral Understandings: A Feminist Study in Ethics* (New York: Routledge, 1998). M. U. Walker, "Getting Out of Line: Alternatives to Life as a Career," in *Mother Time: Women, Aging, and Ethics*, ed. M. U. Walker (Lanham, Md.: Rowman and Littlefield, 1999).

19. Here I follow an argument made by H. L. Nelson with respect to end-of-life care.

20. Following Nelson (2003) and Young (2000), I have in mind here such things as decision-making procedures and structures (perhaps leaving out of the deliberations those most affected by the outcome), division of labor (who does the work of care, who sets the agenda, and who evaluates it), and culture: I. M. Young, *Inclusion and Democracy* (New York: Oxford University Press, 2000).

21. J. F. Follman, *Medical Care and Health Insurance: A Study in Social Progress* (Homewood, Ill.: Richard D. Irwin, 1963).

22. See Kane, Kane, and Ladd for an extended discussion of the history of the market in providing long-term care: R. A. Kane, R. L. Kane, and R. C. Ladd, *The Heart of Long-Term Care* (New York: The Oxford University Press, 1998).

23. T. Marmor and J. Oberlander, "Rethinking Medicare Reform," *Health Affairs* 17 (1998): 58.

24. See Wiener for an extended discussion of the limitations of the tax incentives and deductions with respect to long-term care: J. Wiener, *Pitfalls of Tax Incentives for Long-Term Care* (Washington, D.C.: The Urban Institute, 2000).

25. J. Tronto, *Moral Boundaries*, 111.

26. Tronto describes this way of "taking care of" as privileged irresponsibility.

27. R. W. Besdine, "Improving Health Care Quality by Reimbursement Policy," *Journal of the American Geriatrics Society* 97 (1998): 78.

28. And third, policies that flow from the discussion of the first two points will establish and deliver opportunities in concrete situations of caregiving and care receiving that respond to individual needs, are contextual, and affirm a social conception of the self. Addressing this, however, is beyond the scope of this chapter.

29. See, for example, the work of Callahan and Cicirelli: D. Callahan, *False Hopes: Why America's Quest for Perfect Health Is a Recipe for Failure* (New York: Simon and Schuster, 1998). V. Cicirelli, "Views of Elderly People Concerning End-of-Life Decisions," *The Journal of Applied Gerontology* 17 (1998): 186–203.

30. T. R. Fried, C. van Doorn, J. R. O'Leary, M. E. Tinetti, and M. A. Drickamer, "Older Persons' Preferences for Site of Terminal Care," *Annals of Internal Medicine* 131 (1999): 109–12.

31. Callahan, *False Hopes*.

32. V. Fuchs, "Health Care for the Elderly: How Much? Who Will Pay for It?" *Health Affairs*, 18 (1999): 11–21.

33. M. Walzer, *Spheres of Justice* (New York: Basic Books, 1983), 87.

34. Walker, *Moral Understandings*.

35. Young, *Inclusion and Democracy*, 17.

36. Young, *Justice and the Politics of Difference*, 23.

37. Young, *Justice and the Politics of Difference*, 23.

38. Young, *Justice and the Politics of Difference*, 34.

39. Young, *Justice and the Politics of Difference*, 55.

40. Young, *Inclusion and Democracy*, 63.

41. Young recognizes that there are dangers of manipulation, deception, and overgeneralization when political communication is broadened. To her critics, Young replies that people can also be manipulated by argument. Furthermore, such practices need not replace argument but accompany argument. Finally, just as strong or weak arguments can be critiqued, so too can better or worse expressions of communication be critiqued. Effective expressions should be thought of as virtues, says Young, not as litmus tests that decide whether one can participate in the deliberations.

42. An important connection to make that cannot be developed here, is that deliberative democracy is congruent with an ethic of care. In short, deliberative democracy is congruent with an ethic of care because 1) the process of democratic deliberation builds from and is reflective of a socially constructed and relational self; 2) it creates a public space in which we can attentively meet the needs of concrete, individual, embodied persons; and 3) it provides a context in which private concerns can become public issues.

43. Young, *Inclusion and Democracy*, 25.

44. This question, of course, already narrows the field of possible discussion topics. Deliberators could, for instance, begin with larger questions about social and health care justice, and about the kind of welfare system that would allow people a fair share of opportunities throughout life. Such questions, however, are beyond the scope of this chapter. One might argue that these larger questions require resolution before focusing more narrowly on long-term care, and in a perfect world, this would be preferred. Yet because Medicare and Social Security are almost universal in their coverage for older adults, these policies carve out a section of political, social, and economic life that approximate a decision sphere where solving problems and effecting change, while nevertheless difficult, is imaginable.

45. J. M. Wiener and L. H. Illston, "Health Care Reform in the 1990s: Where Does Long-Term Care Fit In?" *The Gerontologist* 34 (1994): 407.

46. See Merlis for an extended and useful discussion of the unpredictability and catastrophic nature of long-term care: M. Merlis, *Financing Long-Term Care in the Twenty-First Century: The Public and Private Roles* (Georgetown: Georgetown University Institute for Health Care Policy Solutions: The Commonwealth Fund, 1999), www.cmwf.org/programselders/merlis_longtermcare21st_343.asp (5 Jan. 2004).

47. W. N. Leutz, "Five Laws for Integrating Medical and Social Services: Lessons from the United States and the United Kingdom," *The Millbank Quarterly* 77 (1999): 77–110.

48. Nor is the final package necessarily one package. It may be possible, for instance, to conceive of several options of integrated services. The MediCaring option, while of lesser appeal to elders aged 65 to 80, has potential appeal to those aged 80 and older: J. Lynn, M. A. S. O'Connor, J. D. Dulack, M. J. Roach, C. S. Ross, and J. H. Wasson, "MediCaring: Development and Test-Marketing of a Supportive Care Benefit for Older People," *Journal of the American Geriatrics Society* 47 (1999): 1058–64.

49. B. D. Carpenter, K. Van Haitsma, K. Ruckdeschel, and M. P. Lawton, "The Psychosocial Preferences of Older Adults: A Pilot Examination of Content and Structure," *The Gerontologist* 40 (2000): 335.

Index

About the Editors and Contributors

Vivienne Bozalek is senior lecturer in the Social Work Department and the Women's and Gender Studies Post Graduate Programme, at the University of the Western Cape, South Africa, and head of the Social Work Department at this university. Her research deals with women and social policy, child and family studies, curriculum issues in social work, and feminist epistemologies.

Cheryl Brandsen earned a MSW from the University of Michigan, and a Ph.D. from Michigan State University. Presently she is professor of sociology and social work at Calvin College, and chair of the department. Her research and practice interests are in gerontology, specifically end-of-life care in institutional settings.

Eloise A. Buker is the director of Women's Studies and professor of political science at Saint Louis University. Her work focuses on feminist political theory and postmodern analyses. Her most recent book is *Talking Feminist Politics: Conversations on the Law, Science, and the Postmodern*. Currently, she is working on a coauthored book about a Roman Catholic Maryknoll sister, who was a peace activist in Hawaii from 1930 to 1995.

Amanda Gouws is professor in political science and one of the coordinators of the Gender Studies Program at the University of Stellenbosch, South Africa. Her research deals with feminist perspectives of citizenship. She is editor of *(Un) Thinking Citizenship: Feminist Debates in Contemporary South Africa* (2005).

Maurice Hamington is assistant professor of philosophy at the University of Southern Indiana, where he teaches feminist philosophy and gender studies.

231

He is the author of *Hail Mary? The Struggle for Ultimate Womanhood in Catholicism* (1995) and *Embodied Care: Jane Addams, Maurice Merleau-Ponty, and Feminist Ethics* (2004), as well as coeditor of *Revealing Male Bodies* (2002).

Deborah L. Little is an assistant professor in the Department of Anthropology and Sociology at Adelphi University. Her research is in the areas of welfare reform, care work, and disability.

Dorothy C. Miller is clinical associate professor at the Mandel School of Applied Social Sciences at Case Western Reserve University. She is also director of the Flora Stone Mather Center for Women at Case University. Miller is the author of *Women and Social Welfare: A Feminist Analysis* (1991), as well as other articles on social welfare policy and feminism. Miller is an active leader in the national Women's Studies Association.

Marie Minnaar-Mcdonald is lecturer in the Social Work Department and the Women and Gender Studies Post Graduate Programme at the University of Western Cape, South Africa. She also participated in provincial and national social welfare policy formulation processes (e.g., the Green Paper on Social Welfare). Her research deals with work, gender, and social policy implementation.

Nel Noddings is Lee Jacks Professor of Education Emerita, Stanford University. She is the author or editor of fourteen books and more than two hundred articles and chapters. Her latest books are *Starting at Home: Caring and Social Policy* (2002), *Educating Moral People* (2002), *Happiness and Education* (2003), and *Educating Citizens for Global Awareness* (2005).

Fiona Robinson is associate professor of Political Science at Carleton University, Ottawa. Her research focuses on the ethics of care and care work in global politics and the global economy. She is the author of *Globalizing Care: Ethics, Feminist Theory and International Relations* (1999) and numerous articles and book chapters on ethics, gender, and international relations.

Selma Sevenhuijsen is professor in the Ethics and Politics of Care at Utrecht University, the Netherlands, and has been visiting professor at the University of Leeds, UK, and the University of the Western Cape, South Africa. She also works as an independent consultant. Her research deals with the philosophical foundations and the practical implications of the ethic of care.

Judith Stadtman Tucker is a writer, activist, and founder and editor of *The Mothers Movement Online*, an electronic journal providing resources and reporting on motherhood as a social issue.

Joan Tronto is a professor of women's studies and political science at Hunter College and the Graduate Center, City University of New York. She is the author of *Moral Boundaries: A Political Argument for an Ethic of Care* (1993) and of numerous articles about the nature of care. An expert on women in American politics and feminist political theory, she is currently completing a book on democratizing care.

Margaret Urban Walker is professor of Philosophy and Lincoln Professor of Ethics at Arizona State University. Author of *Moral Understandings* and *Moral Contexts*, she is completing a book on moral repair, the task of restoring trust and hope in the wake of serious wrongdoing and violence. Her research interests include ethical theory, restorative and transitional justice, and moral psychology.